The War-Peace Establishment

The
War-Peace
Establishment

by Arthur Herzog

HARPER & ROW, PUBLISHERS

New York, Evanston, and London

FIRST EDITION

LIBRARY OF CONGRESS CATALOG CARD NUMBER: 64–18055

M-O

Contents

v

Acknowledgment

Portions of this book have appeared, in a different form, in the *New York Times Magazine* and *Think Magazine*.

I should like to thank the hundred or so government officials and private citizens who have generously given of their time to this book in personal interviews; Earl D. Osborn of the Institute for International Order for his encouragement and support; and those who, while in no way responsible for the conclusions reached here, have read and very helpfully commented on the manuscript: Rev. John C. Bennett, Dean of the Union Theological Seminary; Norman Cousins, Editor of the *Saturday Review*; Roger Hagan, Editor of *The Correspondent*; Brownlee Haydon, of the RAND Corporation; Richard Hudson, Editor, *War-Peace Report*; Dr. Robert A. Levine, also of RAND; Robert McKelvey, of Columbia University; Lawrence C. McQuade, formerly of the Department of Defense and now of the Department of Commerce; Dr. Jeremy J. Stone, of the Harvard Center for International Affairs; Dr. A. Nicholas Wahl, of Princeton University.

Introduction: The Search Begins

I SUFFER, I HASTEN TO SAY, FROM NUCLEOMITOPHOBIA, THE FEAR of atomic attack, and my quest for a cure has led me to grapple with the great debate on war and peace as it is being carried on in the United States. James R. Newman, the noted science writer, has said, "The duty to press forward in the search for peace binds everyone. This is the dictate of common sense and morality."

I agreed with that directive, but at the same time I shared the confusion of Reinhold Niebuhr, the eminent theologian, who asked, "We have come into the tragic position of developing a form of destruction which, if used by our enemies against us, would mean our physical annihilation, and if used by us against our enemies would mean our moral annihilation. What shall we do?"

I was perfectly agreeable to writing my Congressman or carrying a placard, but whose, and what would my letter recommend? It is clear that there are important divisions of viewpoint in the United States, especially among those who have concerned themselves most with it, on the question of what to do about the threat of thermonuclear war. To some, risks must not be run; to others, great risks must be taken; and to still others, we have reached the point of absurdity either way. "We are of course all guessing here," says Hans J. Morgenthau, the political scientist, "but I would have to make the guess that Western civilization would not survive such a catastrophe. If this estimate is correct, then obviously an all-out nuclear war in defense of Western civilization is a contradiction in terms, an absurdity. I must say that this absurdity may occur, but if it should occur I would still say that it was an absurdity."

But I wasn't content to have my placard, if I was to carry one, merely say "DOWN WITH THE ABSURD." Edmund Wilson, who is not only a leading literary critic but an informed student of political affairs, offers more specific advice. "To one who was born in the nineteenth century, and so still retains some remnants of the belief in human progress of a moral as well as a mechanical kind," Wilson writes, "it is especially repugnant to be forced to accept preparations for the demise of our society or of a damage to it so appalling that it is not possible to see beyond it." Wilson's search for peace concludes that one should consider paying no more taxes to support the defense effort, an action which our ungrateful government would reward by putting the tax resister in jail. Well, sacrifices for peace may be necessary.

Then I turned to the philosopher Sidney Hook, who asks, "Is it true that our system of nuclear defense is a greater threat to the survival of free institutions in the world today than the Communist movement in all its manifestations—a movement whose aggressive acts brought the present system of defense of the free world into being?"

Who is right in such debates? It's evidently important to make up one's mind. According to Jeremy J. Stone, a military policy analyst, "In areas where we lack understanding or confidence, we prefer inertia or arms race, or both, to arms control and disarmament. It is important for the Soviet Union to understand this fact about us, as it is for us to do so." According to P. M. S. Blackett, the English scientist, "In order to study possible ways in which each country might alter its military posture so as to facilitate a multilateral agreement, it is necessary for individuals to subject their government's defense and disarmament policies to a critical examination." That is a worthy goal, but how is the ordinary citizen to go about it?

The American citizen in the mid-twentieth century has an enormous difficulty on his hands if he wants to understand contemporary foreign and military policy. The military strategies are often complicated and couched in a new and forbidding vocabulary: "first strike," "second strike," "damage-limiting capability," and even "spasm war." Foreign policy, it seems, is no longer straight and simple foreign policy—if it ever was—but must be considered in relation to technology and military strategy. And then even informed opinion seems all split up, into armers and disarmers, cold warriors and arms controllers, realists and idealists, and making a choice between them is hard indeed.

I did not find, unfortunately, that the newspapers throw any considerable light on the complexities of the nuclear age, an observation I was to hear confirmed again and again by those who have specialized in the problems of the cold war. Some publishers, no doubt, emphasize some aspects of the situation instead of presenting the whole, but, even more important, the reporters appear little better informed than the rest of us.

The papers, moreover, make little effort to integrate the news. On the same front page, for instance, you read that the U.S. and Britain are willing to discuss a 10 percent reduction in military budgets with the Soviet Union, the Department of Defense announces that European armies must raise their combat strength, and President Johnson says that the cold war must end "once and for all." On the one hand, the United States wants disarmament, but, on the other, it espouses a multilateral nuclear naval force and is prepared to expand its military commitments to underdeveloped countries. There is, I felt sure, a key to such seeming inconsistencies, but the newspapers fail to offer it. Most disturbing to one who is prepared to exercise his civic obligations and decide among available policies, the newspapers give little indication of the alternatives. Perhaps there aren't any good ones, but at least one likes to decide for oneself.

To be sure, there is no shortage of literature on the subject of the atomic age—if anything, there is too much. More, it seems, has been written on war and peace in our times than in all previous decades combined. A peace research institute reports that no less than 100,000 pieces of literature—articles, reports, books and so on—have been written on the topic since World War II, most of it in the United States and most of it, significantly, in the last few years. This figure, moreover, is exclusive of what must be an Everest-size collection of classified material in government files. One independent study group, the RAND Corporation, for instance, turned out reports for the government at the rate of one a day for ten years. Nothing but a computer could assort all this material, and nobody, I'm afraid, but a mechanical man (with a security clearance) could read it, written as most of it is in the most unapproachable style. Considering the many difficulties, I could see why so many people have turned their backs on the subject of peace.

My feeling was one of bewilderment, and I despaired at ever being able to subject my government's policies to a "critical examination," as Professor Blackett recommends. At this point, I decided to tackle the problem head on: to ferret out and talk to the nation's leading theoreticians on war and peace of varying opinions, to see who they are, what they want and why, and to ask them what hopes for permanent peace they foresee. I determined to conduct this intellectual mission with an open mind, to listen to the arguments of all sides with as much objectivity as I could, though bearing in mind the arguments others had made against this or that position. In this way I hoped to be able to lay out the whole range of choices presently available to the U.S., and, in the end, to reach some logical decisions myself, as befits my obligations as a citizen.

One conclusion can be stated in advance. Debates similar to the one under way in the United States are without doubt occurring in the Soviet Union, China, France, the United Kingdom, Germany and elsewhere, though with different perspectives and vocabularies, and, in some places, with less freedom. (And with less sophistication, too, for nowhere is war-peace theory as advanced as it is here.) It may be useful to foreigners to know what American specialists are thinking, and, in no small sense, on the outcome of these world-wide debates depends the future. "Man has taken his life in his hands," says Gerard Piel, editor of *Scientific American*, and life will never get back to normal. "However long this age may last, even if it should last forever," says Günther Anders, the Austrian philosopher, "it is the Last Age, for there is no possibility that its *differentia specifica*, the possibility of our self-extermination, can ever end—but by the end itself." What gives urgency to the debates, then, is not only the seriousness of the present situation, but also the question of how to avoid the cold war's recurrence. It may be that a cold warless world will require that we reshape a host of notions. Such, at any rate, were some of my thoughts as I set out on the journey I've come to think of as a search for peace.

PART ONE

The Deterrers

I

The Forward Strategists

THERE HAS COME TO EXIST IN THE UNITED STATES UNDER THE COLD
war a body of specialists accustomed to dealing with issues of war
and peace which may be described as a war-peace establishment.
It is not an establishment in the usual sense of a power or institution, but rather one of ideas and theory, of scientists, seers and
strategists, as they've been called, who have worked out the form
and rationale of present American defense and foreign policies, as
well as the doctrines that constitute their chief opposition. Here,
if anywhere, one can get at the inner logic of the nuclear age, at
least from the American vantage.

In the war-peace establishment may be placed many of the
scientists who developed the nuclear weapons and have since been
extremely concerned about their disposition. One can properly put
in the war-peace establishment, as well, those who have been
called such names as defense intellectuals and military analysts;
and it is no exaggeration to say that these men have transformed
American military doctrine. Rooted in the establishment are literally
dozens of institutions of one kind or another whose principal
preoccupation is the cold war. The establishment also contains the
Sovietologists and Kremlinologists who peer over the Iron Curtain
in search of answers, the grand designers of American policy, and
even those who have been called Realists and whose concern with
the *animus dominandi,* the lust for power, has had such a marked
effect on contemporary American thought.

On this Noah's Ark of war-peace theory can be placed those engaged in what they hope is a new kind of scientific investigation, peace research, who have been studying such things as the role of conflict in human affairs and how an economy, conceived in the cold war and dedicated to the intercontinental ballistic missile, can endure. Since this is an American establishment, there is bound to be space for the psychiatrists, and the architects of world government as well as the pacifists who would take up no arms against a sea of international troubles and thereby try to end them. (Military officers, foreign service personnel, members of the aero-space industry, legislators, high government officials and so on are properly part of a war-peace establishment too; if they receive less attention here, it is because the emphasis is on cold war theory, not practice.)

It might even be said that the war-peace establishment makes up what anthropologists call a subculture, that is, a sort of ingroup on war and peace. One thing that clearly marks this establishment is the time it puts in on war-peace questions, sometimes as gainful employment, sometimes as virtually a full-time avocation. Indeed, the price of admission to the war-peace establishment is dedication plus expertise slowly and painfully acquired, and the ability to come up with new proposals and arguments. Members of the war-peace establishment are well acquainted with each other, if not personally through frequent encounters on television round tables and debate platforms, then at least in print, the common forums being such publications as *Foreign Affairs* (speaking for what Richard Rovere calls the American establishment), *Orbis, War/Peace Report, Bulletin of the Atomic Scientists, The Correspondent* and so on. The establishment has even developed its own vocabulary, not just the technical jargon of nuclear war, but such words and phrases as "options," "age of nuclear plenty," "countervailing" and "viable," a word that no paper of the war-peace establishment can be without.

At issue in the war-peace establishment are not only appraisals of the Communist nations and the proper U.S. strategy for dealing with them, but also deep arguments about the uses of actual or potential violence, the future of the United States and even estimates of that primordial substance, human nature. At first glance, the war-peace establishment appears a jumble of strategic and philosophical disputes, but, nonetheless, it is possible to make a taxonomy. To be sure, the lines are not hard and fast—it's possible, for instance, for a person to have his head in one camp, his heart in another and perhaps his job in a third—but the lines do exist, and a sorting such as is offered here is important if only to bring some clarity to an otherwise very diffuse debate.

"What makes the study of ideas on arms policy interesting . . . is that policy recommendations do not come singly, but in rather closely correlated groups," says Robert A. Levine in his book *The Arms Debate*. (James Burnham, in the *National Review*, divides opinion up, like toothbrushes, into "hard" and "soft"—Burnham wants a purge of the softs.) There seem to be three general schools of American cold war thought. The first I've called the "deterrers," the second the "experimentalists," and the third the "peace movement," although the peace movement is in no strict sense a movement and the deterrers are frequently irked by the peace movement's assumption that it has a corner on wanting peace. In search of answers to the issues of war and peace, I turned first to the deterrers, leaving till later to hear what the experimentalists and the peace movement have to say.

Deterrers, whose ideas are accepted by majority opinion in the U.S., are those who have acquiesced in the necessity for the United States to maintain a high level of nuclear strength, on the grounds that this is the best way that war can be prevented. Deterrence, in its military sense, is not a new word, having appeared as early as the 1820 edition of the Oxford English Dictionary, but in the hands of the deterrers it has largely replaced the concept of defense. Deterrence means, literally, "through fear," and deterrers believe that a potential enemy can be induced to forgo certain courses of action through fear of the consequences in much the same sense that parents deter children with threats of punishment and the death penalty deters murder (or so it is often thought). Since threats of force do operate with some success throughout society, deterrers hold that they will serve the positive function of inducing the enemy, indeed all mankind, to accept a less dangerous world order.

This doesn't mean, though, that all deterrers are in agreement.

Some accept the idea of rough equality of arms forces between the U.S. and the Soviet Union in the interests of stability. Some favor a high and markedly superior level of nuclear arms, including a "full first-strike capability." And some, behind the deterrence shield, favor carrying the cold war to the heart of the Communist bloc, under the doctrine known as forward strategy. (Another and different kind of forward strategy means the NATO defense of Western Europe at its eastern frontiers.)

THE FORWARD STRATEGISTS

The chieftain of the forward strategists is Dr. Robert Strausz-Hupé of the Foreign Policy Research Institute at the University of Pennsylvania. His name is pronounced "Strausz-HooPAY," and his supporters are to be found among the more bristling military officers and defense intellectuals. A Strausz-Hupé devotee, so it seems, is Barry Morris Goldwater of Arizona, who solicited from Strausz-Hupé foreign policy advice in his campaign for President in 1964; Goldwater's foreign policy bears a close resemblance to forward strategy.

Strausz-Hupé has contributed a number of books to the ever-growing library of war-peace studies being written in the United States, among them *Protracted Conflict*, *A Forward Strategy for America* and *Building the Atlantic World*, each in collaboration with scholars attached to the Institute. (Whether this platoon authorship is to be accounted for by the urgency of execution, the difficulties of the material or other demands on the writers is unknown.)

"Protracted conflict," says the first of these volumes, "was given classic formulation by Mao Tse-tung." Mao's doctrine was that a war against a technologically superior enemy has to be fought with a more profound understanding of the conflict than the enemy has. The international conflict, as Strausz-Hupé sees it, is really based on "systemic revolutions," rich vs. poor, East vs. West, which the Communists have not created but are taking advantage of better than ourselves. *"The Communists are likely to win World*

War III because they know they are in it," the authors say, emphasizing the point with italics. "Even if the present parties to the conflict would seek, by mutual consent, to compose it now, the liquidation of the most contested issues would not be completed within the life span of this generation. Hence we must reckon with the extension—the protraction—of the world conflict into the next century." The West, in this situation, must not worry "neurotically" about survival, as Communist psychological warfare attempts to make us do. We must accept "the risk of total conflict" in trying to unhinge the Soviet alliances and bring the downfall of the Soviet state. We must be wary of the sirens of stability and seek breakthroughs in new arms. Strausz-Hupé testified against the partial nuclear test-ban treaty.

A "detailed prescription," as Dr. Strausz-Hupé puts it, of what the United States has to do against Communist-sponsored protracted conflict is presented in *A Forward Strategy for America* and *Building the Atlantic World*. The forward strategist doctrine is to fight fire with fire. Militarily, we need everything we can lay hands on, including nuclear-powered aircraft, massive civil defense, space weapons and a biological and chemical warfare arsenal, "particularly the uniquely 'humane' non-lethal agents." Politically, our decision-makers should be on guard against any softening of public opinion. *"The cult of public opinion has gone beyond the bounds of reason,"* the authors underscore, suggesting that it might be a tool of Communist psychological warfare. "Our political system is basically sound, but it must be stripped for action and, in part, reorganized so that it is equal to its dangerous task in a dangerous environment," and "We should kiss goodby . . . the hope that our security difficulties will yield themselves to the magic formula of disarmament."

We should strengthen our alliances, building, in effect, a North Atlantic state as a bulwark against Communism. We should make certain that the underdeveloped nations be anti-Communist. Communism can be pushed by steady pressure out of Eastern Europe and ultimately out of Russia. "Shorn of all ideological connotations, our policy must be based on the premise that we cannot tolerate the survival of a political system which has both the growing capability and the ruthless will to destroy us. We have no choice but to adopt a Catonic strategy." Cato, of course, was the Roman senator who argued that Carthage had to be destroyed. His reason, says the Oxford Classical Dictionary, probably lay "in distrust of Carthaginian resurgence and moral indignation at its character."

Although a loose reading of the forward strategists might convince one that they mean to go to war, it turns out that as brinksmen they stop short of the edge.

A clear distinction should be made between the terms "preventive war" and "pre-emptive war." The first signifies that war is sooner or later inevitable and that the enemy should be taken by surprise after all preparations have been made. The second assumes that the enemy will be prevented from launching an attack at the moment he is about to strike.

Whether or not the United States will decide against waging preemptive war will depend only *in part* on a decision made many years in advance. It will *also* depend on whether or not the pressure of events forces a deliberate or, more likely, an improvised revision of this decision. It is extremely doubtful that a government, once it deems war inevitable, will stick stolidly to a decision made in more secure periods to desist from preventive war. It is even more unlikely that public opinion, aroused to the inevitability of war, will insist that for the sake of consistency, the enemy should be allowed to strike first.

Under certain conditions, the forward strategists advise, the U.S. must be prepared to wage pre-emptive war, and must advise the Communists so. The present strategy, of only striking second, after having absorbed the first blow, they say, is "sound morally," but to make it sound militarily requires a greatly strengthened defense organization, including the antiballistic missile. The forward strategists doubt that we will ever be strong enough to renounce pre-emptive war.

Such in brief is the position of Strausz-Hupé *et al.* A number of questions had reared in my mind, among them how a small-government man like Barry Goldwater could square himself with the Strausz-Hupéan view that demands even larger military expenditures. I wondered, too, why the Soviet Union, if the U.S. adopted a Catonic strategy, would not itself feel compelled to strike first, in self-defense. Indeed, because the forward strategists did not believe in peaceful coexistence, they had drawn the fire of the Soviet Union. Valerian Zorin, a high Soviet official, wrote in 1964:

The fact that the imperialist ideologue, Strausz-Hupé, considers disarmament to be an "unrealizable chimera" is not surprising, but that the Communist Party of China should express similar views and still declare themselves to be Leninist-Marxists is incredible. There is almost no difference between Strausz-Hupé and the Chinese document.

The Foreign Policy Research Institute occupies the better part of two floors near the Penn campus in Philadelphia, and here Dr. Strausz-Hupé has been the director since the organization's inception in 1955. The Institute, in form, resembles a surprisingly large number of study groups which have grown up at universities all over the country in response to the varied problems of the cold war. It receives support from private foundations as well as the university. It conducts contract studies for such government groups as the Department of Defense and the Senate Foreign Relations Committee, studies which, though nonpartisan, are likely to have the forward strategist point of view.

From the tone of his books, I had formed a mental cameo of Dr. Strausz-Hupé, expecting him to be bluff, stern and militant, prepared to cast me from his office at the slightest sign of softness, and I was surprised to find a slim, graceful man of medium height in his early sixties, with wavy gray hair, elegant continental gestures and a tan. He was rather rakishly dressed, in a blue pinstripe suit, suspenders, green socks, a striped shirt and a blue tie with large red dots, one dot embellished by a small but detectable cigarette burn. I'd forgotten, I think, that Strausz-Hupé is a colorful thinker, a dramatist in international relations whose scripts contain heroes, villains and a far-reaching plot, gradually unfolding.

"To a good many people I am an abstraction," Strausz-Hupé said in an agreeable accent, "because I came to academic life late and

I don't move around much." He was born, he went on, in Vienna, in 1903. He had always been interested in international relations, but after arriving here in the 1920's had gone to work on Wall Street, where he had served as the manager of a foreign investments department of a large firm. He wrote his first book, on geopolitics, in 1941. During the war he served the government as an intelligence man, and he is now a lieutenant colonel, USA (Ret.). After the war, Strausz-Hupé had gone back to school, earning, at Penn, his advanced degree and eventually the Institute, which was his own idea.

"I was a warmonger against Hitler," Strausz-Hupé said, "and people still consider me a warmonger, quite unfairly. Just because I believe in more bombs doesn't mean I'm a militarist. Some unilateral disarmers are my best friends. In fact, we are attacked by the far right because of our emphasis on the Atlantic community. I'm perfectly willing to give up U.S. rights; sovereignty, to us, is a legal fiction. Our basic concept is a merger along the lines of the federal structure of the U.S. The willingness to accept the Atlantic Union is where I separate the men from the boys in international relations. We are not necessarily conservative in terms of domestic politics, either, and I'd say the place is about evenly divided between Democrats and Republicans. Ah, but here are the others."

The two men who entered the room introduced themselves. Colonel William A. Kintner, USA (Ret.), was former chief of long-range planning, Office of the Chief of Staff, USA. Dr. James E. Dougherty is a professor of political science at Penn, as is Kintner, and also teaches at a Jesuit college nearby. Both are members of the Institute, Kintner being deputy director, and they are co-authors, with Strausz-Hupé, of some of the aforementioned books. Kintner, a follower, as he later said, of the teachings of the nineteenth-century religious philosopher Swedenborg, is a man in his mid-forties with close-cropped hair and a bold expression, and this, along with the olive-drab suit he wore that day, gave him a strongly military air. Dougherty, though younger than the others, has snow-white hair. In his black suit, he reminded me of a priest. "Shall we go to lunch?" Strausz-Hupé said.

Over cocktails at the Pennsylvania faculty club, Kintner told me that, in his opinion, there were no more than fifteen hundred people in the U.S. who were qualified as military analysts. "I'm talking about a community of specialists who deal with the problem of war and who form almost a separate group. They are generalists conversant on a range of questions, from the anti-ICBM to the Common Market, and who can relate such things into a meaningful pattern, who know, for instance, what happened in the Soviet 1961 test series and who have, of course, top security clearances, as do we three. The group has almost a guild feeling. It's difficult to acquire expertise in this business." Having by now done battle with some of the complex strategies of the nuclear age, I quite agreed.

I asked Kintner to describe his position and he said, "I don't want a thermonuclear war, nor do I think it's inevitable. I'm not a determinist. But I am concerned with preserving the value systems of the West. With all our flaws, such as our racial problem, we've built a fairly decent life in the United States. The Communists are not happy about our system. I think it's a mistake to accommodate ourselves to them, and I would put great stress on maintaining our technological superiority to induce them eventually to accommodate themselves to Western ideas. I think we must take Soviet ambitions seriously. Many powerful societies have gone down the drain," he said ominously.

We gave our orders to the waitress, and Dr. Strausz-Hupé said, "If the Soviets had a decisive margin of power, they would be sorely tempted to go to war. I argue that we must have more weapons because they can launch a preventive war."

"But will the Soviets accept our nuclear superiority?" I said doubtfully, wondering what Carthage would have done with H-bombs.

"They will accept what they have to accept."

But Strausz-Hupé seemed to pull back, because he went on to say that he favored such unilateral American measures as moving our short-range missiles out of reach of Soviet territory, to positions where they could be used only for front-line defense. Thermonuclear war, I decided, was as hard for Strausz-Hupé to swallow as it was for everyone else.

I asked Kintner if he felt that human nature was at the bottom of the cold war. "Yes," he said, "the individual has a lot to do with it. People can be arrogant and power-mad. Human power to do evil exists as well as the power to do good. Wars reflect the perverseness of man."

The mention of man brought Dougherty into the conversation. "There is the *animus dominandi* Augustine talks about—the urge to dominate. The Communists have a messianic dream and the will to power."

"Not necessarily Marx, however," Strausz-Hupé put in. "Marx had his faults—he was an intolerable sponge, always after money and abominable to his associates—but he was really an old-fashioned justice type, coming as he did from an old Sephardic family. It was in Lenin, not Marx, that you find the tremendous interest in and liking for power."

Lunch was served, and after a few mouthfuls Dougherty put down his fork and said, in response to a question, "I feel the League of Nations and the United Nations were both historically premature, in a sense, because they marked an attempt to go all the way from a state system to a universal organization in one leap. Probably the nations must pass through an intermediate phase in which they can gradually divest themselves of their sovereign prerogatives in favor of regional organizations, based upon common cultural values. This is why we stress the Atlantic community. We see it as one grouping of which there may be six or eight over the world. But in any case I don't see real progress toward a world order without changes in the Leninist system."

In Dougherty's view, Communism stands in the way of the development of effective international institutions. He pointed out that the Soviets have long been opposed to strengthening the United Nations, which they regard as a product of Western bourgeois liberal ideas. I recalled that he had once said, in a speech, "Halfway around the world, a huge juggernaut is on the move. It aims to take over the earth. . . . This juggernaut is moving in our direction. It is closer than you think. It is later than you think. The final battle is now being fought in the battleground of the mind." I asked him if his religion had anything to do with this appraisal. He nodded and said, "Most Catholics, and probably most Christians, think that if the Communists achieve world hegemony there will be little room in the new society either for religious freedom or for a spiritual conception of man."

I asked him then how he proposed to combat the juggernaut. This, he said, would require the application of a broad strategic intelligence combining political, economic, psychological and military policies. "During the Hungarian crisis," I said, "did you favor U.S. military intervention?" "I did not think that overt military intervention was required," Dougherty said, "but I was in favor of running in an underground pipeline to supply the Hungarian freedom fighters with antitank weapons. It wouldn't have set off a war, but it would have compelled the Soviets to work out a different solution to their dilemma." Among other things, he advocated stronger propaganda than the USIA supplied and economic measures that would cause difficulty for Soviet "central planners," such as aiding the Common Market to make strong economic overtures to the Soviet satellites. "I would do certain dramatic things to irritate them, such as eroding the Berlin wall with water."

That struck me as extreme. How did he square his religious beliefs with the use of force? I wondered, and Dougherty said, "I see man as a combination of beast and angel, reason and base designs, and I think one of his noblest drives is to rise above his proclivity to use force." In a regretful tone he added, "I'm in the Thomistic tradition, which pursues a *via media*, between idealism and realism, and under certain conditions force is necessary." He went on to say that he subscribed to the Catholic doctrine of the "just war," meaning that in some circumstances a war—including nuclear war—can be justly fought. "But I agree that most wars aren't just, and I also think that even in a world in which conflict is going on, both sides can decide to eschew certain forms of violence, among them thermonuclear war."

It was a pleasant and chatty lunch, despite a few twinges in my stomach that I attributed to nucleomitophobia, and it had given me a flavor of what one group of men with whom the government consults on defense matters were thinking about. On the way out, I asked Dougherty if recent developments, such as the Soviet-Chinese rift and the test ban, hadn't altered his view of Communist-sponsored protracted conflict. "The protracted conflict is still going on under altered forms. The Communist revolution, which has been institutionalized for a half-century, cannot be expected to change course suddenly. The U.S. would be unwise to modify rashly its approach to the Soviets. They still pose a military threat to the Western world," Dougherty assured me.

One way to see the forward strategists in perspective is to contrast them with what have been called "conservative neo-isolationists," like the John Birch Society.

If and when the United States, as the last bastion of freedom, is taken over by the Communists, the terror they will use to enforce, consolidate, and maintain their rule will be both more cruel and more extensive than anything the human race has ever before known or imagined. And our children who survive will one day certainly ask: "What did my parents do to prevent this slavery for America, which they had already seen imposed on so much of their whole world?"

asks John Birch's Robert Welch. But the John Birch Society, aside from opposing any concession to the Russians or the Chinese, wanting to get rid of Castro by force, and believing that squeamishness about the extermination of the human race is virtually subversive, does not really offer a policy, and Welch and company are in no sense war-peace theorists. The Birchers' attention is to what they see as a disguised *internal* threat to Communize the United States. One can only assume that what the Birchers really mean in terms of foreign policy is that a convulsive international test will cause the Communists to wilt overnight, permitting the U.S. to return to a small government unentangled by foreign alliance. The aim, for the Birchers, is "less government, more responsibility, and a better world."

Goldwater does not appear to have reconciled the two views. He sometimes sounds much like the forward strategists.

We must stop negotiating about things that are nonnegotiable, such as the rights of our allies, compromises of our security, treaties like the test ban which can neither be controlled nor enforced. We must not deceive ourselves and our friends into believing that nuclear weapons and modern technology can be negotiated out of existence.

We must stop helping communism, whether by trade, political concessions, technical disclosures, soft talk in the United Nations, recognition of Outer Mongolia, pilgrimages to Moscow, or support for revolutionaries of the Castro type.

He does not sound like them when he mentions, as a potential danger to the United States, "disarmament, or arms control, as the 87th Congress so cutely termed it." The forward strategists favor some kinds of arms control, like getting rid of obsolete bombers, provided they are truly obsolete. Most important, Goldwater, like the Birchers, is for small government, while the forward strategists accept a large, externally oriented government; unlike the neo-isolationists, the forward strategists see a real and long-range international conflict, but they do not believe the Communist military threat is wildly overrated, as the Birchers do. Indeed, some conservative neo-isolationists believe that the forward strategists themselves are fellow travelers. William Kintner, for instance, wrote an article in the *Reader's Digest* in which he denounced "wrongheaded 'extremist' cults" and said that anti-Communism ought to be left to "experts" like himself. An extremist pamphlet struck back, saying that Kintner was a member of the "semi-secret" Council on Foreign Relations, which, it declared, was "Communist-accommodating," a fact, I felt sure, that Moscow would be surprised to hear, the Council on Foreign Relations being staunchly anti-Communist.

Strausz-Hupé himself has been both congratulated and criticized for his ideas. Among those who liked *Protracted Conflict*, for instance, were Dean Acheson, Henry A. Kissinger, Admiral Arleigh Burke and C. L. Sulzberger of the *New York Times,* who said, "This is a remarkable and penetrating book, a brilliant, coldblooded and skeptical analysis of the diplomatic techniques and aspirations of Communism, as developed at its central base, the Soviet

Union. It is profound and its conclusions are direct, logical and terrifying."

Others, though, wondered if Strausz-Hupé hadn't emphasized the conspiratorial aspects of Communism too heavily. Indeed, he seemed to conjure up a Communist Commissar of Conflict in almost complete control of the world situation. "The image of the Russians as incredibly subtle and clever tacticians who have been winning the cold war in a walk is sheer paranoia," writes Roger Hagen, editor of *The Correspondent*. And Strausz-Hupé's acceptance of a high risk of nuclear war is bound to be controversial with the American public, especially as he envisions a cold war that drags on for fifty years.

"In the long run," said Senator J. W. Fulbright, who was clearly worried about the influence of the forward strategists, "it is quite possible that the principal problem of leadership will be, if it is not already, to restrain the desire of the people to hit the Communists with everything we've got, particularly if there are more Cubas and Laos'. Pride in victory, and frustration in defeat, during the Korean War led to MacArthur's revolt and McCarthyism." And, said an article in the *Bulletin of the Atomic Scientists* about forward strategy:

[They fail] to consider whether the provocative nature of the policies they openly advocate can be restricted to the non-military spheres for very long. Indeed, they seem to assume that the Communists will back down under pressure—a highly dangerous assumption . . . they appear more concerned with virility than freedom, as if strength and courage were goals in themselves.

Strausz-Hupé did not strike me as being tough, and back at his office I wondered if there was an inconsistency between himself and his views. He laughed, widening his light, bright-blue eyes. "Basically I'm a moderate man," he said. "I live moderately, eat moderately, and I love leisure. I would have been happy in Victorian England; I'm probably a Tory. I just don't happen to think that war can be abolished, and I accept the role of the state during this emergency. But underneath I'm a modern communalist—not so far from Paul Goodman, the writer—in that I believe in a decentralized society, and I think the penultimate state of man is anarchy. It is for these reasons that the Soviet Union is the very antithesis of what I believe in."

Strausz-Hupé, then, was a utopian of sorts, and I recalled that those who have the most perfectionistic ideals are likely to turn out to be pessimists when those ideals are far from being practiced. His policy can be summed up as follows. There is no *détente* between the United States and the Soviet Union, for the Soviets have not abandoned protracted conflict. The Soviet-Chinese rift is important, but it is premature to suppose that the division is permanent or that it lessens the danger. Nuclear war must be avoided if possible, but it cannot be ruled out as an instrument of national policy. Anti-Communism, not antiwar, must be the substance of that policy. We are in constant danger of softening our militancy. (For this reason, Dr. Strausz-Hupé deplored the film *Dr. Strangelove,* of which he said in a letter to the *New York Times,* "Although, throughout the last few years, it has become fashionable to depict, upon stage and screen, military leaders as pompous fools or dangerous maniacs, Mr. [Stanley] Kubrick's creation represents the most vicious attack to date launched by way of one of our mass media against the American military profession.")

Ultimately, what we have to seek is the downfall of the Communist Government in the Soviet Union, for only then will the world be able to pursue its development in freedom. For Strausz-Hupé, the ultimate is a romantic utopia of small communities unfettered by a strong central state. A key to Strausz-Hupé's view is that Western civilization is clearly superior to Soviet Communism, which itself is highly dangerous. "Menace equals military capability plus intent," Lawrence C. McQuade suggests. For Strausz-Hupé, the Soviet intent toward the U.S. is baleful indeed, and only a tough policy, he feels, can influence it.

"If there is war, I would rather win than lose," Strausz-Hupé said. "Communism is the obstacle to peace. I'm reduced to an analysis of their system and what they've said about themselves. It's all I've got, and I haven't got any more."

THE VISION OF DR. TELLER

My next call was to the house of Dr. Edward Teller, in Berkeley, where he is professor of physics at large at the University of California. Teller is, of course, the scientist identified in the public mind with thermonuclear weapons—the father of the H-bomb, the newspapers never tire of calling him—because of his persistent efforts to get the bomb developed. In the debates of the war-peace establishment Teller is the scientific counterpart to Dr. Robert Strausz-Hupé's forward strategy, only for Teller the emphasis is on forward technology.

Edward Teller was born in Hungary, in 1908, the son of a respected Budapest lawyer. Jews were generally excluded from higher education, and Teller appears to have known early that in order to succeed he would have to excel. After the short-lived Communist regime that came to power in Hungary following World War I, and which left an indelibly unpleasant impression on Teller, he emigrated to Germany, where, in Munich, he was knocked down by a trolley car, losing his right foot. He moved to Leipzig, where he studied theoretical physics, obtaining his doctorate. But there was not much luck in Germany or in all Europe, for that matter, and after Hitler came to power Teller emigrated to Copenhagen to work with the physicist Niels Bohr, under whom other scientists had gathered. As Robert Jungk has written, in *Brighter Than a Thousand Suns,*

. . . this life of dependence pleased no one. It could not go on forever, and posts were sought for the expelled physicists throughout the world. This proved less easy than it had appeared, for the number of vacant chairs in European universities and the space available for work in the laboratories was limited. Hardly any country yet understood that the admission of refugees who brought with them no material possessions but invaluable knowledge would be profitable rather than a burden.

Several of the Copenhagen scientists, caught in this situation, emigrated to the Soviet Union, where, Jungk says, "a terrible fate overtook them": prison, torture and death.

"Only the United States," Jungk goes on, "with its hundreds of universities and institutes, could provide enough appointments for the intellectual refugees." Teller arrived here in 1935 and was soon immersed in the discussions then under way of a possible nuclear chain reaction—another Hungarian, the late Leo Szilard, carried his own store of radium around with him—and Teller was present when Szilard asked Albert Einstein to write his famous letter to President Roosevelt urging that intensive work on the chain reaction begin. Teller has said that he was reluctant for a time to work on the Manhattan Project, on humanistic grounds. But it was the possibility of a German atomic weapon, and the need to forestall it with our own, that induced many scientists to work on the bomb. Few of them appear to have conceived of its use on the Japanese, and whatever the other differences that divide the community of atomic scientists today, there is virtual unanimity among them that the weapon should never have been employed without warning, a view that Teller has expressed repeatedly. "It was necessary and right to develop the atomic bomb. It was wrong to bomb Hiroshima without specific warning."

Teller's work during the war was largely in theoretical research on thermonuclear devices. He was enraged at the lack of enthusiasm for hydrogen weapon research shown by J. Robert Oppenheimer and others. Oppenheimer opposed Teller's model of the H-bomb on the grounds that it wouldn't work, and indeed the bomb that was finally exploded was not the one proposed by Teller. While taking a wait-and-see attitude on H-bombs, Oppenheimer favored a number of innovations, such as the Distant Early Warning System, to give advance notice of enemy attack, and the development of "supermarket" atomic weapons, in all shapes and sizes, including battlefield or tactical ones, suggestions that were subsequently adopted. But Teller pushed the H-bomb, and it was the key development. It made missile warfare possible because its explosive force compensated for the missile's inaccuracy. Everything that has come since in cold war strategy flows inevitably from it: "hardening" of missiles in "silos," or concrete shelters, the downgrading of bombers, the antiballistic missile which is still an important question in the American strategic debate.

Teller, since World War II, has argued consistently that new weapons development is inevitable. One of the reasons he favored H-bomb development was that it represented a new technological principle with great and unknown possible scientific as well as military consequences, and Teller's restless mind opposed restrictions on scientific progress. Others, more fearful, or less fatalistic, about the arms race, have urged restraint in new weapons in hopes that the weapons spiral might be halted. There were those, for instance, who urged that the H-bomb be brought to the point of fruition and then an attempt be made to get the Soviet Union to join in its nondevelopment (that the Soviet Union, as it turned out, exploded an H-bomb less than a year after the United States gave the Teller position a boost). This division among scientists has been severe, and caused ruptures even among old friends.

One of those who has consistently opposed Teller is Dr. Hans A. Bethe, professor of physics at Cornell and former chief of the theoretical physics section at Los Alamos. Bethe heads a group of scientists which has been called the Hansians, who have fought the "hard" solutions of the Edwardians, or Tellerites. "Edward likes to conceive dozens of problems and to stir everybody up about them," Bethe has said. "The problems never get solved and they create conflicts. I believe his mental attitude has been greatly changed by the atomic bomb. Like most of us at Los Alamos, he got a feeling of power when the bomb actually worked, a feeling of the power of science to create such a thing. Most of us got over this feeling; Edward didn't. Besides, he seems to have lost the ability to tell the difference between what might possibly happen and what is likely to happen." On the other hand, says Dr. Luis Alvarez, a physicist who has worked closely with Teller, "I think Edward's position on the H-bomb—to build it—made war less likely. On at least two occasions Edward has played a key role in the making of decisions that insured the survival of the United States in a hostile environment."

The debate over whether or not to produce new weapons still goes on, though in a less intense form than it did over the H-bomb, partly because international tensions have eased and partly because no scientific jump comparable to the H-bomb is in sight. I had begun to wonder what sort of surprises were in store in the laboratories, and as the opportunity came up from time to time I began to ask scientists engaged in weapons research what ideas were under consideration. I have compiled a partial list which may convey the flavor of modern military research. What is secret about this list is the stage of development (or nondevelopment) some of the weapons are in. Many, if not almost all, of them in all probability will never be deployed unless international tensions rise once more, and those in the "far-out" section are little more than glints in scientists' eyes. Nonetheless, six and one-half billion dollars is spent annually by the Department of Defense on research, and the money goes into advanced weapons projects like these.

WEAPONS OF HIGH TO MODERATE FEASIBILITY

Many novel ideas in chemical-bacteriological warfare, some already in existence. Biological: considered strategic because cover broad areas of enemy territory and take time to work. Three types: those that break down artificial immunity (as from immunization), natural immunity, and those which cause diseases, such as anthrax, cholera, plague. Chemical: considered tactical because cover smaller area, work at once. Chemical agents might kill enemy's crops or livestock or human beings. Some used by U.S. as defoliating agents in Vietnam. Gases or other forms of chemicals. Lysergic acid (LSD) considered promising. Will-destroying weapons. Cat so treated cowered from a mouse in a cage. Odorless pacifying gases that cause, for instance, instant diarrhea. Such gases considered good possibility for counterinsurgency.

Antiballistic missile. Cost estimated at between one-half and one billion dollars per city. Also requires blast shelter program.

Much larger missile and warhead to counter ABM.

Orca, or sleeping missile. To deploy in rivers or remote areas or in the ocean, as mines, left unattended.

Turtle. Proposed by Lockheed, a submerged manned missile complex "capable of long-range mobility at very low speed."

Hydra. Being tested by the Navy. Concept of launching rockets from "free-floating vertically positioned platforms at sea."

Bombs: "Gigaton," or 1,000-megaton bomb, exploded 250 miles up, would ignite a city.

Enhanced radiation bombs—the neutron or, on a different principle, the cobalt bomb—would kill people with less property destruction. (One difficulty with such weapons is that they would leave some people with, say, twenty-four hours to live but in full possession of their strength. These would be perfect kamikaze squads.)

Cheap bombs and missiles at (say) $50,000 each. High on the list of likely possibilities. Would make nuclear weapons easily available to underdeveloped countries. Already, the U.S. Cubic Corporation is selling do-it-yourself space kits permitting buyer to put 100-pound payload in orbit at $700,000 a shot.

Small or "suitcase" bombs.

Long-endurance aircraft, either nuclearly or conventionally powered. Could stay aloft days at a time, like air-borne Polaris fleet. Such proposals as Dyna-Soar or Dromedary.

Satellite interception systems, manned or unmanned.

Low-altitude bombardment satellites. Could deliver nuclear weapons to target in three minutes.

Much faster bombers to attack either from space or very low altitudes.

Submarine aircraft carriers.

Directed-energy electromagnetic beam weapons. The "death ray." Might be used as ABM or against personnel.

Advanced antisubmarine warfare devices. Cover the oceans with underwater detection stations.

The green laser, or underwater death ray.

Nuclear-powered autonomous army.

Military bases on the moon.

WEAPONS OF LOW TO ZERO PRESENT FEASIBILITY

Creation of controlled tidal waves or earthquakes.

Weather control—for instance, causing a perpetual fog over enemy territory, or a drought, or freezing harbors.

Doomsday Machine. Thermonuclear weapon of one million megatons which would eliminate the human race through radioactivity.
Plasma bomb. Aim plasma stream, like ray, or bolt of lightning. Make it roll across ground leaving destructive wake.
Antimatter bomb. Vastly more powerful explosions.

Some scientists, aghast at the array of possible weapons for mass destruction, have followed the lead of Leonardo da Vinci and refused to engage in military research at all. Some, too, believe that advanced military research itself should be ended, even if some avenues for new knowledge are temporarily sealed off as a result, on the grounds that ignorance is preferable to ever new and destabilizing tools of destruction. "Accurate prediction of the future course of science is impossible. Twenty-five years from now we may be confronted with a weapon no one has thought of today, but we will be better able to keep it from running rampant if we have by then brought our present weapons under control," says Dr. David R. Inglis, a physicist with the Argonne National Laboratories. "What is likely to happen depends on what opportunities there are for research, which is one of the reasons I'm in favor of disarmament."

What might be called the pure deterrence attitude toward research is expressed at the Department of Defense by Dr. Charles Herzfeld, deputy director of the Advanced Research Projects Agency, for whom new weapons are daily fare. Herzfeld believes that basic research is almost the last item that should be pruned from a military budget. "There is safety in the research race," Herzfeld says. "The arms race is a dynamic thing and I'd rather see it work out in qualitative terms—in research—than in quantitative. Huge quantities of missiles don't appeal to me. By maintaining our research we can make sure that asymmetries do not occur." In this view, advanced military research makes sure that the other side does not achieve a technological advantage that would open the way to a pre-emptive strike. The research is seen as defensive. And, these scientists say, if the other side began developing new weapons made possible by its research, and we had the means to ascertain this, there would be time for the United States then to develop and deploy its own, which was the position taken by the United States in deciding to favor the test ban.

Teller occupies still a third position, one that says the United States should proceed to develop various kinds of new weapons and defensive systems without worrying about stimulating an arms race. Teller says he considers the majority of these projected weapons unfeasible or improper for the purpose of insuring peace. Over the years, however, Teller has recommended a number of innovations, among them that new buildings in the U.S. ought to be dispersed, that we devote 10 percent of the military budget to civil defense, that we have a draft for civil defense, that we build the antiballistic missile and continue testing to do so, that we reorganize the United States armies into autonomous units for fighting tactical nuclear wars, that we deploy space weapons and surveillance systems.

"He considers many weapons likely and desirable to have," said a high-ranking Defense official, "most of which I would consider gimmicks and not useful." Said Senator J. W. Fulbright, at the time of the test-ban hearings, in 1963, "He seems fascinated with the problems of weapons as such. The so-called weapons effects in the antiballistic missiles are what he was particularly concerned about. He is very emotional and very positive about that. He seemed to take it as a personal offense that anybody would suggest that we restrict the unlimited development in this field."

Teller, for his part, has argued two points consistently: that the Soviet Union cannot be trusted and that large-scale weapons development must continue. (During the early 1960's he favored a test ban briefly, but changed his mind when he decided the ABM could be built.) Except for suggesting, perhaps as a palliative, that the U.S. and the Soviet Union be restricted to atmospheric tests of a total of one metagon a year, he has shown virtually no interest in arms control measures that might be agreed upon by both sides, and this disinterest is consistent with his often stated fear that no matter what is agreed to, the Soviet Union will find a way to violate it—for instance, by testing nuclear weapons in deep space or in underground caverns where they might not be detectable. (Other scientists say that muffled explosions are indeed detectable.) His picture of the Russians resembles a nation not unlike Nazi Germany. "The Russians—we are all aware of this fact—are bent on world domination. If the present course is not changed, there is no doubt in my mind that the world before the end of this century will be modeled after Russian ideas and not after ideals of our own."

To many others in the war-peace establishment, this is an exceptionally gloomy view. So, too, is Teller's conclusion that scientific uncertainty necessarily means deep trouble for the United States. "This time has been a time of extremely rapid development, and it has been a time of surprises. At no turn did we know what the next step will bring. . . . Yet what we are trying to do is predict the future," he said in his antitest-ban testimony, "and when some of the best and most outstanding people contradict each other, they do so because the future is necessarily uncertain." This uncertainty, to Teller, means that the Soviet Union, under the guise of peace, will create a technological breakthrough, and this will be "a step away from safety, possibly a step toward war."

To be sure, Teller is a deterrer and not for preventive war. Peace, for him, depends on a high level of deterrence and continuing technological progress. He says, "You cannot be satisfied with what you have because the enemy's power to cancel your capability also continues apace," but, in addition, that the test-ban treaty will stimulate the arms race because the Soviets will work in secret. In other words, American development of weaponry is not an arms race whereas comparable Soviet efforts are. In effect, Teller says that the war camp is the Soviet Union, and peace can only be kept by the peaceful side by deterring the warriors. And for the peaceful side to do its job, it must not be paralyzed by fear of nuclear war.

Again and again Teller has argued that neither civilization nor the earth will be destroyed by such a war. "There is no danger that any atomic bomb of present or future design will ever blow up the earth, the sea, or the atmosphere. This can be stated with all the assurance of which science and common sense are capable." "We must rid ourselves of the unreasonable fear of nuclear weapons.

These weapons were first used against cities. If military reasons (and considerations of common humanity) prevail, they need never again be used in this fashion. Instead, they can be used to neutralize aggression and to provide us with the time in which real solutions can be found to the problems of the modern world." "I am convinced that nuclear bombs can be used for defense in the strictest sense of the word. They can be used in a way which will do minimal damage to the civilian population, and which will be concentrated on the armed forces of an opponent." "My estimate is that if we would spend for civilian defense 10 percent of our military budget, this would put us in a decent state of preparedness. . . . We could survive as a nation and the great majority of our citizens can actually survive an atomic attack." "Danger has always been the natural companion of man." "We have always lived in a dangerous world. We know that life has been on this planet for at least 500 million years, and over those years every single living being has died. . . . Therefore danger, even terrible danger, is not new. Something else is new. Consciousness is new. Realization of the danger is new. And courage and imagination with which such dangers can be combated—these are new."

The only political concern displayed by Teller is his recommendation that the U.S. form a close nuclear bond with its European allies. There is no evident concern with world (or domestic) longings for peace, including those of our allies, or any suggestion that peace might be kept through other means than high-level deterrence. Teller's thinking, right or wrong, is extremely singletrack.

He does, though, lay down a condition whereby the cold war might be ended, that is, the abandonment of secrecy by the Soviet Union. (He has also suggested that the United States, unilaterally, abandon its elaborate secrecy programs, on the grounds that the Soviets already know our secrets and only the Europeans, who should have them, are hurt.) "It is obvious that if freedom of information were fully established throughout the world all the arms control problems would at once become more manageable. . . . Of course, this proposal could not become a reality except by a very thorough change of the world as we know it today. It would effectively mean that Russia would have to cease to be a police state."

Teller hopes to see the Soviet Union change short of war, and to preserve the civilization of the United States, which, to him, is "the only true democracy the world has ever known." It would be false, he thinks, to deny science, to frustrate what Thorstein Veblen called the Instinct of Workmanship, "the disposition to do the next thing and do it as well as may be." Nuclear energy can be of great benefit to mankind, digging canals and harbors, uncovering deposits of minerals and oils, and ushering in a brave new future. Teller hopes, too, for law and order and world government. He is, in short, an idealist, and even, when it comes to his vision of what science can do for the world, a utopian.

As my meeting with Teller approached, I began to wonder about the terms "optimism" and "pessimism" in the nuclear age. Teller clearly considers himself an optimist for, as he says, "The pessimist of the nuclear age is deeply concerned about the arms build-up between nations. He is convinced that man during the next few decades will destroy either his liberty or himself. The optimist of the nuclear age, on the other hand, believes that military preparedness is the price we must pay for something we desperately need, time."

Hans J. Morgenthau, the political scientist, also considers Teller an optimist, but in an entirely different sense. "Herman Kahn and Edward Teller," he says, "are the two most articulate and knowledgeable proponents of the thesis that nuclear violence is a mere quantitative extension of conventional violence and does not differ qualitatively from the latter. It follows from this thesis that . . . nothing has happened in the last two decades which would confront mankind with an unmanageable threat and put in jeopardy its very survival." This view, Morgenthau said, is "simple and optimistic," and "Professor Teller's reliance on the arms race is . . . untenable in its own terms." Citing studies of the Joint Congressional Committee on Atomic Energy, Morgenthau said that Teller's notion that American casualties in a nuclear war could be limited to 10 percent of the population is absurd. But even if a nuclear war had to be fought, and Teller was right about the 10 percent, I wondered how a casualty figure of nineteen million could be discussed in terms of optimism.

Others argue that Teller is wrong to suppose the Russians will exert every opportunity to try to swing the strategic balance against us. They say, too, that more weapons yield no greater relative security to either side and that American deterrence today is secure no matter what the Russians will do. Teller, for his part, appears to be filled with mission and charged with moral urgency. He resigned his job as director of the Livermore Laboratories, a weapons research center near San Francisco, to sound the alarm. "Please," he tells a group of doctors, "stay alive" after an attack. He advises audiences to think of postwar construction rather than attempting to protect property and installations. He congratulates Pomona, California, for having completed the nation's first self-contained civil defense shelter, called the "Unseen City." Teller is optimistic in his appraisals of destruction: "We can, after a number of austere but not necessarily terrible years, rebuild our country to its old, and to a better strength." Wake up! he warns.

The job of trying to wake up the United States cannot have been easy. Close friends of his told me that Teller, who suffers from colitis, has been endangering his health. His differences with many other scientists have been sharp. One of them, Harrison Brown, accused Teller of "willfully distorting the facts." (Teller is one of the very few scientists involved in defense matters to be so challenged.) And he has been subjected to public ridicule. While I was in San Francisco a nightclub skit was portraying Edward Teller in a strait jacket.

No doubt because of some rough public handling, Teller, I'd heard, could be touchy and suspicious with the press.

I had made my way through a dark, hillside garden, and Teller came to the door, limping slightly. He greeted me, rather guardedly, and stared at me quizzically for a moment. I returned the gaze. He has, I thought, an appealing face, with dark, somber eyes, impressive lines and tragicomic, bushy eyebrows. He led me into a large living room, barrenly furnished, Victorian in its dark woodwork, in which a grand piano stood conspicuous, and I recalled reading that he loved music, would play for hours on end and had said that the piano was the only possession he really likes. Teller introduced me to his wife Mici, drinks were served and we sat down.

Teller said at once that he had to know where I stood on the spectrum of war-peace issues, such as the test-ban treaty. He seemed to fear, above all, a subtle distortion of his views into a club against him, and I reflected that such an attitude in itself was rather revealing of the depth of the disagreements in the United States. I replied that I hoped to be objective, but Teller said, "There's no such thing as objectivity on these questions. Feelings run strong. They are questions of individual judgment, and all one's experience goes into one's appraisals." He referred to the attacks on him, and I asked him then if he had resented them. "Not me personally," he said, "but my wife, oddly enough, has." He glanced at Mici Teller, who sat impassive.

I said, after some minutes of prodding by Teller, that, like many people, I hoped that the Soviet Union would observe the limited test-ban treaty and that it might be the first step toward peace on what President Johnson called a journey of a thousand miles.

The Tellers laughed, a little derisively, I thought. "Excuse me," Teller said. "What proof do you have?" I mentioned the events usually cited to show that relations between the U.S. and the U.S.S.R. have improved—the absence of Soviet jamming, the "hot line" between Washington and Moscow, the limited test ban, the UN resolution against weapons in outer space, the Sino-Soviet split. None of these, Teller said, had changed his mind.

"The Russians are not bad," he said. "They merely want to conquer the world. There is little doubt in my mind that Khrushchev was more agreeable than Stalin. Stalin was an obnoxious person who wanted to conquer the world. Khrushchev was less obnoxious. He was so kind that if we were willing to surrender he would accept it without attacking us. He too believed in world conquest. His successors will consider it their duty to conquer us."

Many people in the war-peace establishment do **not** believe the

Soviets are out to conquer the world; others, though quite suspicious of the Russians, believe that if disarmament is out of the question at least we should search for stability through limited agreements. I asked Teller about stability.

"If you could change the world into a world in which no weapons could be made, that would be stabilizing," he said. "But agreements we can expect with the Soviets would be destabilizing. The almost certain consequence of disarmament agreements is that the Soviets would violate them."

The American government's position has been that the U.S. could detect important violations in ample time to take countermeasures.

"Excuse me," Teller said. "We haven't penetrated their secrets. When they resumed testing in 1961, Washington was unprepared for it. When missiles began arriving in Cuba we were unprepared for them. What we are inhibiting is our own development."

He went on to say that a hallmark of science was the unforeseen. In the case of the H-bomb, for instance, some of the consequences had shown up later—the development of bombs that were both economical and "clean," that is, low in fallout. "I won't say I foresaw those things, but I did know that one can't always foresee. Scientific development is necessary. I do not want to give up the technological benefits that will accrue from many new techniques, especially as weapons development is necessary anyway."

Many would forgo the scientific benefits for a while if they could forgo the weapons of mass destruction, too, I said.

"Ah. But you imply weapons in our hands are as dangerous as they are in the hands of the Russians. I can't see the U.S. in the position of an aggressor. Nor do I believe that Soviet actions are a reaction to steps we make ourselves. The question is, do we put agreements with the Russians first, or do we conciliate with people who agree with us, our allies? I'm in favor of sharing our nuclear secrets with our allies—that is a risk I will take. I want to strengthen NATO, to join the Common Market and to create eventually an Atlantic Union."

Some scientists have accused Teller of being in love with weaponry, I ventured to say. Throughout our conversation I had sensed that he was struggling to control his temper; he flushed then. "When I did those things it was because others didn't want to. I begged others to take over. Since no one was willing, I had to do what I could do. Do I love weapons? I haven't noticed it.

"Listen. Many people disagree with me, and for this reason perhaps I have no influence today. I have never had very much. Once I had a little influence because I realized that two plus two makes four." He was referring, of course, to the hydrogen bomb.

"I believe that the debate has been overcomplicated. The beginning of wisdom is simplicity. I will take no risks with the benevolence of the Soviet Union. Our only guarantee of peace is strength in the hands of those who want peace. The difference between me and the others is simple—peace by strength or peace by conciliation. I choose strength.

"I don't think the Soviet state can be overthrown short of war, and I don't think war is inevitable. We must change them slowly. If for a decade or two they make no further progress, then they will change their ideas, away from world conquest. In the meantime, the Soviets are winning the cold war, and our object must be to stop them. My motives? They are exceedingly simple and straightforward. I want to survive and I want my children to survive. Forgive me. I perhaps am tired tonight." He looked suddenly done in.

Mrs. Teller led me to the door. As I left, I glanced back. Teller remained motionless in his chair, his head bent, his face fatigued and shadowed.

"Nevertheless," Teller has said, "our search for peace must continue." I continued on my way.

II

The Analysts

EVERY HOUR ON THE HOUR DURING THE DAY AND FAR INTO THE evening on business days the planes of the air-shuttle service fly between Boston, New York and Washington, and the shuttle has become the Via Appia for those who come to offer advice and counsel to the government of the United States. In the Cambridge area alone, it has been estimated, five thousand people are government consultants, a good many of those being college professors and a good deal of the consultation being on matters pertaining directly or indirectly to the conduct and prosecution of the cold war. There is no doubt that the use of so much specialized assistance directly reflects the complexities of our era. Frequently making the run to Washington are those whose expertise lies in matters military, and who have been called such names as military analysts, military intellectuals, academic strategists, defense intellectuals, war thinkers and even New Civilian Militarists.

"One of the most remarkable changes in the intellectual landscape over the past dozen years, especially in the field of public affairs," writes Bernard Brodie, himself a recognized civilian strategist,

is the appearance of specialists in military strategy who are (a) mostly civilians and (b) trained in and accustomed to using scientific method in dealing with the problems of their chosen field. . . . Their special abilities have been recognized and utilized, often with enthusiasm, by the military services, and the relations between these "scientific strategists" and members of the military profession is on the whole quite close. Although their numbers are still small compared to numbers in the ranks of other scientific disciplines, they have been collectively of enormous influence. Most of the distinctively modern concepts of military strategy that have been embraced by the military services themselves have evolved out of their ranks.

The predecessors of today's military analysts are such figures as the American admiral, Alfred T. Mahan, the famous German general, Karl von Clausewitz, and Giulio Douhet, an Italian general who recommended the saturation bombing of civilian populations as a means to break an enemy's will to fight. The earlier strategists have been criticized because they evolved strategic principles which they held to as though they were natural law, like the pre-1914 German emphasis on mobilization planning, and their modern counterparts are supposed to have learned by their mistakes and put their trust in flexibility. But there are other differences, too, for the modern military intellectual is most likely a college professor, not a member of the armed forces, and he attempts to combine three kinds of expertise, military, foreign policy and science, for such are the interlocking requirements of strategy that the three are ultimately indivisible.

Eclectic thinkers, the analysts are adepts in modern technology, unlike Dr. Strausz-Hupé, and, unlike Edward Teller, they often have skills as foreign policy experts. "Except for extreme groups," says Leonard Sloss, of the Stanford Research Institute, "you will obtain a large consensus among strategic thinkers that we must maintain effective deterrence and at the same time continue to work on ways of reducing world tensions and the risk of nuclear war." On the other hand, writes Jeremy J. Stone, "Unfortunately, relatively few people in the U.S. community of strategic analysts feel deeply the importance of reducing the Soviet threat through disarmament."

To listen to what others say about them, it is singularly hard to get a picture of the military analysts. Contrary to Brodie, for instance, their relations have been far from easy with the old-line military officers, who have often seen them as brash upstarts. "In common with many other military men, active and retired, I am profoundly apprehensive of the pipe-smoking, tree-full-of-owls type of so-called defense intellectuals who have been brought into this nation's capital," says General Thomas D. White. "I don't believe a lot of these often overconfident, sometimes arrogant young professors, mathematicians and other theorists have sufficient worldliness or motivation to stand up to the enemy we face." I wasn't quite clear about pipe-smoking tree owls, but it was plain that General White resented the fact that the analysts were in prominent positions at the Department of Defense.

If the tree owls have sometimes been too dovelike for the generals, they are too hawklike for the peace people. The late sociologist C. Wright Mills, for instance, accused the analysts of engaging in the "crackpot metaphysics of militarism," and Professor Irving L. Horowitz claims that "These are the men who believe in the balance of terror, who feel that we must proceed with reason and think about the unthinkable." H. Stuart Hughes, Harvard professor of history, writes, though, that "The new stategists of deterrence are one of the best reservoirs of brains in the country," Hughes' reservation being that he is dead-set against deterrence. The civilian militarists, says a leading professor of law, David F. Cavers of Harvard, "trust only the weapons. They view the resolution of international disputes as determined primarily by the relative military strengths of the disputants and regard wars as inevitable." I wondered if that was so. The unkindest cut of all comes from Marcus Raskin in the *New York Review of Books:*

A majority of those who have drifted into the field of defense strategy were trained in more traditional disciplines—economics, applied physics, mathematics, engineering, and to a lesser extent the behavioral sciences. It is understandable that the specialists in violence should want to be taken seriously by their old colleagues and to prove that there is some intellectual and moral basis for the way they spend their lives. If this could be proved, the defense specialist could become more than a huckster selling "counterforce" or "minimum deterrence," and rationalizing the weapons his employer has decided to develop. He would be eligible to share once again in the image many academic men have of themselves as balanced, independent, disinterested, and good.

If opinion about the analysts is sharply divided, the analysts themselves add to the confusion by being split into sects, like Hindus. Some favor nuclear sharing with our allies, some favor a more aggressive policy toward the Soviet Union, and some disagree with both propositions. Some recommend the multilateral force, or MLF, and some see it as an impediment to better relations with the Soviet Union. The analysts differ about the quality and scope of Soviet ambitions, the importance of NATO, about whether wars are bound to become thermonuclear, about whether the United States should maintain a nuclear force so strong as to permit us to disarm an enemy and so on. To get the full range of their thought, it is necessary to talk with several. I decided to begin with Henry A. Kissinger of Harvard, who, if not the first of the new breed, was at least the first to come to public attention, and I found myself on the air shuttle to Boston.

Keep Your Nukes Up

Kissinger, like the other civilian strategists, is constantly away at conferences in Germany, England, Washington or wherever, but at last I sat down with him at his office at the Harvard Center for International Affairs. He proved to be a short, round-faced man in his early forties with horn-rimmed eyeglasses and a cautious manner. Kissinger had been identified with the "pro-German" school of policy people, and since his accent identified him as German-born himself I wondered out loud if there was any connection. Kissinger told me at once that he was Jewish. He had lost, he said, three aunts, eight or ten cousins and two-thirds of his friends in Nazi concentration camps. His attitude toward Germany, I decided, was not likely to be a sentimental one.

Kissinger came to this country at fifteen—I recalled hearing that fifteen was supposed to be the dividing line between those who lose their accents and those who don't—had worked his way through high school and, after a period of military service, graduated from Harvard with a degree in political science, *summa cum laude*. An article of his had appeared in the magazine *Foreign*

Affairs—"It was my first work on military policy and I never dreamed I'd become an authority on the subject"—and he soon found himself appointed to work with a study group of the Council on Foreign Relations, a private but highly influential circle that comes close to being the foreign policy establishment of the U.S. From this research emerged Kissinger's first book, *Nuclear Weapons and Foreign Policy,* published in 1957, which established him overnight as an expert, for it was the first time that the two subjects had been analyzed in relation to each other for a large audience. It may be a measure of deepening public sophistication that there have been dozens, if not hundreds, of such books since.

Kissinger's first book marked him as a believer that force is one of the inescapable elements in international affairs, a view that is held by all deterrers:

In a society of "sovereign" states, a power can in the last resort vindicate its interpretation of justice or defend its "vital interests" only by the willingness to employ force. . . . The motive force behind international settlements has always been a combination of the belief in the advantages of harmony and the fear of the consequences of proving obdurate. A renunciation of force, by eliminating the penalty for intransigence, will therefore place the international order at the mercy of its most ruthless or irresponsible member.

The analytic group of deterrers, such as Kissinger, Thomas Schelling, Albert Wohlstetter and Herman Kahn, hold certain ideas in common, whatever the differences that separate them. Robert Levine, in a perceptive discussion, identifies them as "middle marginalists," by which he means that their dread of thermonuclear war and their fear of Communist long-range ambitions exist in about equal amounts. Weapons are meant primarily to deter, but they may have to be used. Rationality can be used to exert control over irrationality, and escalation of war can be controlled, as, perhaps, can the arms race. Europe is the ultimate prize the Communists seek, and hence the Alliance, in one form or another, is crucial in this view to American interests. We ought not to taunt the Communists with our military strength, but neither should we be passive, and we must find policies that both force a very gradual transition to a peaceful world and do not present us with the choice between holocaust and surrender.

The analysts, on the whole, are cautious about accepting what some believe to be a genuine *détente* between the Soviet Union and the United States. Though tensions seem to have eased, the missiles are in place and therefore none of their nuclear strategies have been invalidated. All the major trouble spots still exist, unsettled, and the Communists have in no way forsworn what, to the analysts, is their long-range objective of assisting in the birth of global socialism. And if the Soviet Union is undergoing considerable mellowing, the analysts believe that this is the fruit of American nerve and resolve, and therefore, if the process is to continue, the Americans would make a mistake to take the pressure off.

To those who say that the present situation, though less risky, is still far from genuine peace, the analysts reply that "peace" has never really interested them. It is a concept too abstract, too long-range, too intellectually hollow, because all through history today's peace is tomorrow's war. The analytic goal is not peace but stability. "Our concern with the transformation of Soviet society," Kissinger said a few years ago,

causes us to be either too rigid or too accommodating. It makes us overlook that we have to deal in the first instance with Soviet foreign and not with its domestic policy. From the notion that a settlement depends on a change in Soviet society, it is not a big step to the view that a liberalization of Soviet society is equivalent to a settlement. In such an atmosphere, it is not surprising that a controversy should have raged about the desirability of relaxing tensions but not about the conditions which would make such a relaxation meaningful, about the need for peace but not about the elements of stability.

War, he says, could be fought with Piper Cubs. "The implications of total disarmament are far too little understood for us to announce it as an immediate end."

Kissinger describes the policy of the Soviets as "protracted limited conflict," the "limited" being a shading that marks him as some-

what less anxious about them than Strausz-Hupé. Kissinger has
been extremely concerned, though, about Soviet territorial designs
in Europe and elsewhere, and especially about Soviet "nuclear
blackmail," a term that appears in one form or another thirty-one
times in just twenty-six pages of *The Necessity for Choice*. Kissinger's search for stability within these limitations of reality led
him, first, to criticize the doctrine of "massive retaliation," which
he described as "the strategy of a satisfied power content with its
place in the world, eager to enjoy its benefits undisturbed." But
massive retaliation, Kissinger said, was no longer credible except to
deter surprise attacks on ourselves in view of the disastrous consequences of all-out war. The real problem was to deter attacks
on the ground, and Kissinger's answer was tactical nuclear war to
be fought in a carefully controlled manner so that cities would be
spared.

Although tac nukes, as they're sometimes called, have the military advantage of making it difficult for an enemy to mass his
troops and may, under some circumstances, provide an alternative
to a larger nuclear war, Kissinger's doctrine was challenged because
military counselors felt that if both sides were equal in tac nukes,
the advantage would still go to the side with the superior over-all
forces. Tac nukes include weapons as large as, or larger than, the
one which destroyed Hiroshima, and the ravages to Europe from
their use would dwarf those of World War II. And what looks
tactical to one side would look awfully strategic to another, raising
the possibility of an escalation into an all-out nuclear war. For
these reasons, many Defense Department analysts prefer to preserve the "firebreak" between nuclear and conventional weapons
until absolutely forced to cross the line. To them, the appearance of
the familiar mushroom cloud on a battlefield might be the beginning of the end.

Kissinger later modified his stand in various ways. At first, for
instance, he was convinced that "War between nuclear powers has
to be planned on the assumption that it is likely to be a nuclear
war," but he changed his mind to the extent that "No war in the
nuclear age can ever be completely free of the specter of nuclear

weapons." He was certain about the missile gap: "It is generally admitted that from 1961 at least until the end of 1964 the Soviet Union will possess more missiles than the United States." At the end of 1964 the score reads something over 1,000 deployed U.S. ICBMs and Polaris missiles, to something over 200 by the Soviet Union. Kissinger, of course, shared the common error of all experts about the missile gap, but it does prove that even the military experts can be wrong. He admitted that he was wrong, to some extent, at least, on his suggestion that the U.S. use tac nukes first in a battle, for he decided that "The conventional capability of the free world should be sufficiently powerful so that a nuclear defense becomes the *last* and not the *only* defense." These changes in position led some to ask, unkindly, "I wonder who's Kissinger now?"

Kissinger's consistent interest, however, has always been Europe and the proper foreign policy to take toward it. One of the syllogisms of the war-peace establishment is that those who are most concerned with the Soviet Union want the strongest kind of Europe as a counterweight, one that will eventually succeed in drawing the countries of Eastern Europe into its orbit. Such a view is Strausz-Hupé's, who advocates a Europe armed with thermonuclear weapons and federated with the United States. Kissinger is not a forward strategist, but he does want a united Europe in close partnership with the U.S. and he believes that Europe, not just France and England, will inevitably be armed with its own nuclear weapons.

Early in the Kennedy administration Kissinger was a leading foreign policy adviser to the National Security Council with an office in the White House and access to President Kennedy. Such were the differences between the White House and Kissinger on the questions of the MLF and U.S. Berlin policy, which he thought would antagonize the West Germans, that he resigned. This doesn't mean, though, that the fight is over. Many of Kissinger's views are still represented by important people, among them Governor Nelson A. Rockefeller of New York, to whom Kissinger has given foreign and military policy advice.

Facing Kissinger across his narrow desk, I asked him first if he felt his earlier analyses still held. "I like to think some of my theoretical concepts were correct," Kissinger said, "though I can't say I invented them. But I did contribute to such notions as flexible response and the uses of tactical nuclear weapons. I said missiles would be hardened underground and was told it was impossible. I still believe there has been an overemphasis on strategic nuclear war, and I tend to put a higher value on some political factors than many others do. I'm only a kind of strategic analyst, you know. I'm also a foreign policy analyst, and my interest is in the development of societies."

That brought us at once to Europe, and I asked Kissinger to elaborate on some of his differences with Washington. "I disagree with our European policy," Kissinger said, picking his words carefully. "I think it is too doctrinaire and too theoretical. It will end by dividing Europe even further. There are two specific issues. One is the control of nuclear weapons, which Washington says we must hold on to as a brake on the British and French. The other issue is Germany."

With great opposition, not only from those of Kissinger's persuasion, but also from people who see the scheme as worsening relations between the U.S. and the Soviet Union, Washington's plan has been centered around the proposal for the MLF, a multilateral naval force manned by seamen and officers from all the participating NATO countries and equipped with nuclear weapons, the control of the nuclear trigger to be retained by the U.S., at least until some satisfactory shared control can be worked out. It's indicative of the division on the question that one of the originators of the MLF idea is Robert Bowie, whose office is next door to Kissinger's.

Kissinger's objection, as he explained it, stemmed from his feelings on Germany. "I believe the German problem to be the key to European stability. I believe that Germany should be an important ally. I do not think it can be the bellwether of our European policy. I'm afraid of a divided country with *that* history being exposed to too many temptations. The way to control her is *not* to make her into the leading European power."

How was this happening? I asked.

"The proposed multilateral force will make the Germans a nuclear power," Kissinger said. "Germany will have paid several billion dollars for this force by the time she's through, and we won't be able to hold the line. Inevitably there will be debates henceforth about the control of these weapons which might strain allied relations even further."

Under the arrangements contemplated, the mixed-nation crews of the MLF would be able to handle nuclear weapons, but the warheads would be "locked," presumably with what is called a PAL, or Permissive Action Link, a device installed on such weapons so that the warheads become operational only on command by remote control. I asked Kissinger, then, how simple handling of nuclear weapons would provide the Germans with the knowledge of how to manufacture them, but Kissinger declined to answer, on the grounds of national security. Was he opposed, then, to the Germans having nuclear weapons?

"I'm not against it," Kissinger said, "but I want other European countries to have a hand in it. I want Germany integrated into something larger than itself. Germany is the most fluid society in Europe, and the country which is exposed to the most foreign pressures. Therefore, I'm worried by the tendency to make her the arbiter of Europe politically. At one time, I was without doubt the most pro-German of the foreign policy advisers, but we've gone too far in the other direction in the sense of isolating France and putting Britain on the sidelines."

Both Kissinger and the supporters of MLF believe that the European drive toward nuclear arms is more or less inexorable, but the MLF people hope to forestall the creation of separate *national* nuclear forces, especially as far as Germany is concerned, by giving the Germans and other participants at least a vote on the deployment and control of such weapons through the NATO navy. Otherwise, they fear, the Germans will work with France to develop their own nuclear arms, particularly if de Gaulle convinces them that no nation can be sovereign without its own national nuclear force.

Kissinger proposes something else. "I say we ought to accept the fact that both Britain and France have nuclear arms already. We should try to help consolidate this force. Then, with the British and French, with American help, having established their force, the Germans and the other Europeans can join in if they wish. There would be an all-European deterrent, without Germany being the senior partner. I'm not saying it will work, but I am saying we should try."

I asked Kissinger what hopes he had for better relations between the United States and the Communist bloc. "I would hope that a dynamic Europe will have a powerful attraction on the satellites," he said, "but the Soviet Union must be made to see that a change in status in Eastern Europe doesn't represent an attack on Soviet territory. I have hopes that newer generations of Russians might want to make Russia a more modern and therefore less doctrinaire society. It is not inconceivable that the Soviet Union will move toward becoming a Western type herself, though keeping the liturgy of Communism."

Kissinger presents a picture of both optimism and pessimism. When he says that the United States ought to assist in the birth of a European nuclear force, he is saying other things as well. One of them is that disarmament is complicated and, because of this, some spread of nuclear arms in one fashion or another is likely. The top priority of U.S. foreign policy, to Kissinger, should be a strong, resolute Europe. To Kissinger, the world is a dangerous place and will be so, whether we like it or not, for years to come. But it need not mean thermonuclear war.

"TOSCA" AND THE COLD WAR

"We're trying to grapple with unfamiliar problems," Robert R. Bowie, the director of the Harvard Center for International Affairs, said to me. "In the past, war was seen as a periodic eruption and military force as significant only in those periods. Our image now is that of a world in change, and military force becomes significant at all times because you are trying to shape opposing forces. You are trying to create the proper conditions and, at the same time, limit the choices open to your opponent. Much of the thinking today is abstract theory, even when it appears to be concrete, which is why the academics have been able to enter the field. After all, we have no experience with thermonuclear war, and the expertise of the military is less of a unique quality than it has ever been in history. The influence of the academic community is a new factor, no more than ten years old, and already it has had a substantial effect in helping to clarify the country's thinking. We are using many new methods of analysis."

Among those new methods one in particular has gained renown, a form of applied mathematics known as game theory, of which a leading practitioner is a Harvard economist named Thomas C. Schelling. It has seemed to some that game theorists occupy another world, of "cool and ultraprofessional assessment of risk-taking," as H. Stuart Hughes put it, and in order to talk intelligently with Schelling I felt I had to do some boning up.

Game theory, I learned, was the invention in 1927 of the late Hungarian mathematician John von Neumann, among whose other contributions to cold war theory and practice were the computations that permitted H-bombs to be fitted to missiles. Originally, game theory was thought to be a research tool useful to the study of economics, which itself may be classified as a conflict science since it is concerned, at least partially, with competitive behavior. In the category of games, as the theorists define them, falls any formalized conflict in which there is a range of choices specified by rules, an outcome, and an assignment of what are called "payoffs." Not surprisingly, the game theorists came to see that their technique might apply to the study of war.

Game theory, it seems, is different from gaming, the latter being simulation games played with computers, live people, or both, to test possible outcomes in specified situations. Game theory, on the other hand, is a totally abstract mathematical device for clarifying choices, although its logic is sometimes cast in the form of riddles or parables. Probably the best known of the game theory riddles is called the Prisoner's Dilemma. Two accomplices are picked up on charges of murder and put in separate cells. The D.A. pays a call on each, with the same proposition. If he will say the other did the deed, he will get off with a light sentence. The D.A., it is evident, does not have sufficient proof to go to trial, and the rational course for each prisoner to follow is to cooperate and say nothing, for, if each does this, both will go free. But neither can depend on the other. If one remains silent and the other accuses him, he will get the chair. Therefore the logic of the situation points to the conclusion that each prisoner must accuse the other.

Game theory, according to Anatol Rapoport, a mathematical biologist from the University of Michigan, "is concerned with the logic of conflict, that is, with the theory of strategy. In this lies both the strength and limitation of the technique. Its strength derives from the powerful and intricate mathematical apparatus that it can bring to bear on the strategic analysis of certain conflict situations. The limitations are those inherent in the range of conflicts to which this analysis can be successfully applied." Rapoport worried that game theory was being used to stimulate or prolong the cold war. "It may happen," he said, "that if we acquire the necessary wisdom, many of the conflicts that the strategy experts in their professional zeal insist on formulating as battles of wits (or, worse, as battles of wills) will be resolved of their own accord." Rapoport, I knew, is a nuclear pacifist, one who thinks a nuclear war would not be justifiable under any circumstances.

In a game, as the theorists define it, the object is to win, but game theory is not concerned with sloppy mortals who make the wrong move but with perfect players, that is, with the inner workings of a conflict situation in which the outcome is not known in advance. It is a way, then, of computing uncertainty. There are various kinds of games, like the "zero sum" game in which a loss to one side is a gain to the other, and the "non-zero-sum" game in which the loss to one does not necessarily mean an advantage to the other, and which puts stress on the advantages of cooperation. "In Puccini's opera Tosca," Rapoport points out, "the chief of police Scarpia has condemned Tosca's lover Cavaradossi to death but offers to save him in exchange for Tosca's favors. Tosca consents, the agreement being that Cavaradossi will go through a pretended execution. Scarpia and Tosca double-cross each other. She stabs him as he is about to embrace her, and he has not given the order to the firing squad to use the blank cartridges. The problem is to decide whether or not it was to the best advantage of each party to double-cross the other."

I'd always assumed that it was not to the best advantage of Tosca and Scarpia to perform the double cross, considering the outcome, and that the essence of tragedy was that people made the wrong choices, often out of bad motives. I was surprised and rather dismayed, therefore, to find out that, according to game theory at least, Tosca and Scarpia had done the logical thing. From Tosca's point of view, if Scarpia has kept the bargain, she can now kill him to avoid his embraces and Cavaradossi will nonetheless go free. If he has not kept the bargain, she is *still* better off killing him, to avoid having slept with him for no advantage at all. Scarpia reasons in the same way. Even with the double cross he can have Tosca, and if she double-crosses him he has the satisfaction, presumably from Hell, of knowing his rival is dead.

To the game theorists, there are four choices for each protagonist in this sort of drama—the best-best, the best-worse, the worse-best and the worse-worse—and logic invariably points, as it did in the Prisoner's Dilemma, to choosing the worse of the best in order to protect oneself. The worse of the worst gives no satisfaction, and the better outcomes hold too great a possibility of the worse of the worst for either player in the event of a double cross.

The implications of this analysis are, of course, infinitely depressing in terms of thermonuclear war, but game theorists believe the obvious solution to such impasses is to recognize a common interest which calls for communication. And then, as Rapoport says, "Whether game theory leads to clear-cut solutions, to vague solutions, or to impasses, it does achieve one thing. In bringing techniques of logical and mathematical analysis to bear on problems involving conflict of interest, game theory gives men an opportunity to bring conflicts up from the level of fights, where the intellect is beclouded by passions, to the level of games, where the intellect has a chance to operate." To Rapoport, at that point wisdom must take over.

From my reading of Schelling, I was sure that he was more pessimistic about the possibilities of wisdom taking over than Rapoport was. "Among diverse theories of conflict," Schelling says in his book, *The Strategy of Conflict*, "a main dividing line is between those that treat conflict as a pathological state and those that take conflict for granted and study the behavior associated with it." His own idea was "to focus on the more rational, conscious, artful kind of behavior . . . a contest in which the participants are trying to 'win.' . . . We can call this field of study the *strategy* of conflict."

Game theory figures heavily in this strategy because, even though abstract and theoretical, it is a treatment of decision-making under uncertainty, where the decisions of one side depend on the decisions of the other. Schelling says:

Whenever we speak of deterrence, atomic blackmail, the balance of terror, an open-skies arrangement to reduce the fear of surprise attack; when we characterize American troops in Europe as a trip-wire or a plate-glass window or propose that a threatened enemy be provided with a face-saving exit; when we advert to the importance of a threat that is so enormous that the threatener would obviously shrink from carrying it out or observe that taxi drivers are given a wide berth because they are known to be indifferent to dents and scratches, we are evidently deep in game theory.

Its application is not so much specific as general. As Bernard Brodie writes,

Actually, many strategic analysts do exceedingly good work in their field without having any great understanding of game theory, though they would unquestionably use some of its concepts. What does matter is the *spirit* of game theory, the constant reminder that we will be dealing with an opponent who will react to our moves and to whom we must in turn react. It is amazing how little this simple conception has characterized war plans in the past.

Its principal function, then, is not to provide formulas for action but to strengthen the imagination to operate in unfamiliar situations, and Schelling and other game theorists are fully aware that it has no direct relationship with real life. Schelling has said that none of his ideas on military and foreign policy depend ultimately on esoteric theory.

Schelling's particular contribution to game theory has been to draw analogies between "non-zero-sum" conflict situations—say, the jockeying for position of two cars in a traffic jam and the conflict of the Allies and the Soviet Union over Berlin. The principles behind game theory seemed, to Schelling, admirably suited to an analysis of deterrence, of which he may be said to be one of the nation's leading philosophers. "On strategic matters of which deterrence is an example," he writes, "those who have tried to devise policies to meet urgent problems have had little or no help from an existing body of theory, but have had to create their own as they went along." The military profession is concerned with the use of force, which is why, he says, it has produced no deterrence theory, for deterrence is a psychological process consisting of the *non*use of force, of the skillful threat to use it only when necessary. For this reason, deterrence must be made credible to an opponent, and anything that subtracts from that credibility makes for a weaker deterrent.

To Schelling, deterrence is not something new or unique but is, in fact, an active principle of life, and he sees it used everywhere, in gang warfare, criminal law, marriage and even child-raising. As he says,

Some aspects of deterrence stand out clearly in child discipline: the importance of rationality and self-discipline on the part of the person to be deterred, of his ability to comprehend the threat if he hears it and to hear it through the din and the noise, of the threatener's determina- threatened party's conviction that the threat will be carried out. Clearer perhaps in child discipline than in criminal deterrence is the important possibility that the threatened punishment will hurt the threatener as much as it will the one threatened, perhaps more.

To Schelling, the trick is to get one's way without actually resorting to violence, which may involve a number of techniques,

among them the rational uses of irrationality, such as one side deny-
ing, even if it lies, that it has any freedom of action or control in a
given situation, or threatening to go to the brink. Within the game-
theoristic situation of deterrence, Schelling proposes, on the one
hand, a continual manipulation of the adversary as a means of
keeping the peace, and, on the other, keeping communication open
so that one side can indicate the advantages of cooperation to the
other and avoid a thermonuclear, *Tosca*-like finale. "Perhaps as we
become less confident of brute force and more attentive to the role
of threats, we can become more subtle, more careful, more civilized
about them. If there was no 'balance of terror' in prenuclear 1914,
it was partly because people didn't know enough to be terrified."

I had wondered what sort of person Schelling would turn out
to be. Far from carrying boxing gloves, I'd heard, he is a kind man,
a doting father to his children, an excellent teacher and one well
liked by his students. He is a top-flight Pentagon consultant, dealing with strategic deterrence and spending two-fifths of his time on
national security affairs.

"I'm Schelling," said a medium-sized, youthful-looking man in
his early forties with a close-cropped, Harvardian haircut and a
brisk though affable manner, and we sat down in his office at the
Harvard Center for International Affairs. I asked Schelling first
how he had started in military analysis, and he told me that he had
been trained in standard economics, that is, such things as price
structure and national income.

"I worked with the Marshall Plan in Europe in the late 1940's
and early 1950's," Schelling said, "and I became fascinated with
negotiations and what went into them, like threats and inducements. When I went to Yale in 1953 I thought I'd like to work in
the area of bargaining, and I realized there ought to be a relationship to game theory, so I went and looked it up. It enabled me to
recast my ideas in new terms. I worked at the RAND Corporation
for a year, in 1958, and, in looking over the field, I found a great
vacuum in military strategy. There was no theory of limiting wars,
for instance, and no basic theory of deterrence itself, which is the

use of latent power to constrain the other fellow. That is what strategy is—to influence and control what the other side will do."

Schelling went on to say that it was too bad the term "game theory" was coined, because it suggested parlor games, which it obviously wasn't, but since von Neumann had called it that the name had been retained. The specific uses of game theory were tactical, in helping to fool an opponent, or getting maximum results from, say, a bombing run by showing what pattern of distribution would produce the most destruction. Game theory proved mathematically that, in some cases, one could best mislead one's antagonist, not by trying to outsmart him, but by relying on chance. If you wanted to set an office safe or pick one out of six planes a President should ride in, you were better off to roll dice or take the numbers out of a hat than to attempt to work it out logically, for there was always the chance that the opposition (or the burglar) would discover your thought patterns. The same principle of randomizing could be used, Schelling said, for disarmament inspection. To foil a country trying to hide or concentrate its military equipment, Schelling thought the inspectors might well use a roulette wheel to decide what sites to visit.

"What I got out of game theory was more of a conceptual framework, a way of organizing problems," Schelling said. "It helps one to see, in game theory terms, whether some outcomes are better than others for both parties. In parlor strategy games, like bridge, the loss of one side is always equaled by the gains of another, but that isn't true of strategic games in the real world, where cooperation may give the best advantage to both sides."

Part of that cooperation lay, Schelling said, in keeping choices open, and he went on to speculate that wars occur not so much as the result of a specific decision to start fighting, but because all the other choices have long since been eliminated. At the beginning, side A may have had a number of options, even ones that did not appear relevant, but as it cut them off one by one war became increasingly inevitable until the actual decision to fight was more or less perfunctory. "World War I," Schelling said, "had a lot to do with the railroad systems. They were such, once mobilization had been ordered, that the equipment simply wasn't good enough to let the armies disband without terrible confusion, so that if remobilization had had to be ordered quickly it would have been impossible. Therefore the mobilizations had to continue. We don't know what determines war and peace, but freedom of action and versatility are important parts of the problem."

Deterrence, in Schelling's mind, was clearly a device to prevent the other side from foreclosing its own options—in other words, to prevent *it* from reaching the point of having to make the decision to go to war. "Insofar as we are dealing with military policy," Schelling said, in his clipped, lawyerlike way, "we are dealing with both threats and reassurance." I waited, and he added, "But the proper management of threats is more important than anything else."

This brought us to a question I had been longing to ask. Schelling appeared to imply a continuously high degree of potential or actual antagonism between both human beings and states. On the other hand, nations like the U.S. and Canada had managed to coexist, without threats, and didn't that put a few holes in Schelling's theory? He smiled and said, "Is it that a friendly nation is a friend or not a threat? I doubt if Canada would be as friendly a nation if it were the same size as the United States. We would be competitors, and it is harder for competitors to get along."

It is in this high-hostility world that deterrence plays a vital part, according to Schelling. He is fond of illustrating what deterrence is with examples from traffic. A pedestrian, simply by not looking, can deter vehicular traffic down the street when he is crossing against the light, even though he would get hurt more than the driver of the car that hit him—he *knows* the driver will stop. (If he doesn't, of course, it's curtains for the pedestrian, but Schelling has never pretended deterrence isn't a dangerous game.) He'd observed in Copenhagen that bicyclists never turned to see if a car was behind them; by doing so, they would give the automobile more latitude, since the driver would know the cyclist was alerted. These and similar techniques, Schelling said, are practiced, often unconsciously, by nations in the attempt to control the behavior of other nations.

I asked Schelling how he felt about some of the ways that have been suggested to end the arms race. "Reducing missiles won't do any good because what counts isn't the number of missiles but the intention behind them. Fewer missiles might increase the incentive to attack." Well, I said hopefully, how about general and complete disarmament?

"GCD," Schelling said, "is a fraud, for nations can always rearm if needed, and whether the weapons be light planes with atomic weapons aboard or clubs, nations will find themselves an armory. If the United States had been wrong to associate itself with 'general and complete disarmament,' it is equally wrong to have identified itself with aspirations toward world government. The same people who want one government would shudder at the idea of one political party. The notion that world government eliminates strife and guarantees international peace is simple-minded. Civil war and revolution are not only a possibility, but they are likely, and with one world government the chances of war would be raised, not lowered. My personal philosophy is that many governments are better than one, and I think the world is safer with several governing nations working with each other through diplomacy."

Competition, though, is only one half of Schelling's cosmology. The other is cooperation. Deterrence, to Schelling, *is* cooperation, not necessarily through international agreements but cooperation of various kinds, not only formalized through international agreements, but steps made unilaterally though in step with the other side. Cooperation, for Schelling, emerges in the doctrine of arms control, a term he chose to use in one of the best books on the subject, *Strategy and Arms Control* after many hours of discussion with his collaborator, Morton Halperin, and which the authors defined as

all the forms of military cooperation between potential enemies in the interests of reducing the likelihood of war, its scope and violence if it occurs and the political and economic costs of being prepared for it. The essential feature of arms control is the recognition of the common interest, of the possibility of reciprocation and cooperation even among potential enemies with respect to their military establishments. . . . What we call "arms control" is really an effort to take a long overdue step towards recognizing the role of military force in the modern world. The military and diplomatic worlds have been kept unnaturally apart for so long that their separation came to seem natural. Arms control is a recognition that nearly all serious diplomacy involves sanctions, coercions and assurances involving some kind of power or force, and that a main function of military force is to influence the behavior of other countries, not simply to spend itself on their destruction.

Although some use the term "arms control" interchangeably with disarmament, in Schelling's hands "arms control" is the subsuming word, and disarmament is merely a form of it. It happens to be a form in which Schelling has little interest; indeed, just as to Schelling disarmament and peace are incompatible, so arms control and disarmament are incompatible. "I was almost expelled from a Pugwash Conference because of the belief by the Soviets and some Americans that anyone who thought about arms control wasn't interested in disarmament. And it is true that people who want drastic disarmament should be impatient with arms controllers," Schelling said.

Among the measures listed by Schelling as worthy arms control devices were slowing down the technological race, reducing the danger of surprise attack through open skies, making both sides invulnerable to surprise attack, preventing local wars which could escalate, and decreasing uncertainty through the exchange of information. Schelling made the first public proposal for a "hot line" between Washington and Moscow, and he was one of a handful of men who drove the idea to reality. Although some of Schelling's arms control ideas required international agreements, many did not (such as the recent declaration to cut back on the production of fissionable material), and it is the unilateral steps that now appeal to him.

"I find the situation much improved from what it was five years ago because the danger of surprise attack and accidental war have gone down. The world is much safer than I thought it would be, and for this reason my interest in joint action has diminished. I pay little attention to the Geneva negotiations. The most promising course is to get the Soviets to agree to a fairly expensive inferiority and taper off ourselves. Otherwise, we need an understanding on what to do if deterrence fails and a war gets started. We need an understanding on controlled war."

To some, there have appeared to be two Thomas Schellings, the one who postulates a law of the jungle and the other who says that cooperation and arms control are possible even in the jungle. In his ideas about cooperation, Schelling separates clearly from forward strategists like Strausz-Hupé, for whom most forms of cooperation are either useless or self-defeating if the real end is the overthrow of the government of the Soviet Union. Schelling's notions of cooperation lead him to hope that the Soviet Union will not build an anti-ballistic missile so that the United States will not feel compelled to follow suit, and he is opposed to Kissinger's ideas about nuclear sharing with our Allies, on the grounds that it weakens the deterrent and makes cooperation between the basic antagonists less easy. Nor does Schelling display any overriding fear or dislike of the Soviet Union, and in this he is characteristic of the analysts as a whole.

According to Robert Levine, "The analysts will always opt for short-run stability, for next year's goal of keeping the peace." Schelling's goals are almost entirely short-run, for none of the proposed blueprints for peace seem real to him. To the peace movement, convinced that only blueprints for disarmament will ensure peace, Schelling is a pessimist, and perhaps he is in saying that national power, rivalry, territorial disputes and so on are a more or less permanent part of the landscape. His advice is to make the best of the realities:

We may wish to solicit advice from the underworld or from ancient despotisms. The ancients exchanged hostages, drank wine from the same glass to demonstrate the absence of poison, met in public places to inhibit the massacre of one by the other, and even deliberately exchanged spies to facilitate transmittal of authentic information.

The Real RAND

I was eager to visit the RAND Corporation, about which so much has been written and said. It was the GHQ of military analysis, and, more than that, RAND was supposed to have originated many of the strategies that ultimately affect every man, woman and child of us if they succeed but more noticeably if they fail. RAND's reputation, like the missiles themselves, is intercontinental. "The American Academy of Death and Destruction," a Soviet periodical called it, a view shared by some at home who appeared to believe that RAND was building a Doomsday Machine in a subbasement with which to destroy the entire world. RAND is something new under the sun, and for this reason it is not well understood.

There is no Mr. RAND (who some doubtless imagine as a Daddy Warbucks sort of figure, doubly mysterious because he spells his name with capitals), and like many of the ideas held about the organization, the name RAND is a little exaggerated. Though RAND stands for Research and Development, it does only research, and no development, not even of a Doomsday Machine. RAND is what is popularly known as a "think factory," and the progenitor of a host of similar places such as the Stanford Research Institute at Palo Alto, California, and the Institute of Defense Analysis in Washington, which cerebrate for various government military groups. One of the most noticeable features about American intellectual life since World War II is what might be called its institutionalization into thought centers of one kind and another, and nowhere is this more clearly true than in the kind of thinking that has been applied to the cold war. No less than three hundred study centers of all sorts now consult for the Department of Defense. The amount of brain-power such places can agglomerate is impressive. RAND, for instance, has a staff of 1,100, of whom 600 are professionals, and 280 of them Ph.D.s, enough to staff a university.

In a report covering the first fifteen years of its existence, RAND explains that it is "dedicated to the task of contributing to the public welfare." Founded in 1945 to "assist in the formulation and implementation of Air Force plans, policies and programs," to quote from its original Air Force directive, RAND at first was a division of the Douglas Aircraft Company. The umbilical cord was severed in 1948 when RAND became an independent entity, assisted by a million-dollar loan from the Ford Foundation which later became an outright grant. Since then, RAND's budget has grown every year, until in 1964 it topped the twenty-million-dollar mark, of which 70 percent is called Project RAND and represents RAND's Air Force contract. The terms of this contract are, to say the least, unusual, the envy of those whose contractual chains bind them to this or that specific job, for, on paper at least, RAND chooses its own projects and the Air Force generals can request but not command. The rest of RAND's work is for either government or non-profit agencies, for RAND takes no jobs from private business, one of its functions being to appraise for the government cost estimates of defense contractors. RAND remains the cream of advisory groups, and, almost alone among them, RAND's contracts omit the travel-by-coach-only clause in government contracts so that its experts, who fly by night to Washington, may go in the comfort of first-class.

Perhaps because the organization has a very considerable reputation in the government, the morale at RAND, I was told, is high. One reason why RAND was created as an independent, instead of a government, agency was to free it from red tape, and also to permit higher pay, longer vacations, better retirement plans and so forth, than would have been possible in civil service. A top RAND analyst may earn $25,000 a year or more, and RAND tries, not always successfully, to keep its pay level on a par with what its specialists would earn in private industry. (Some RAND specialists, I was told, could double or triple their pay in business.) The publications policy is liberal, for RAND fights a running battle to free its reports from the Babylonian captivity of secrecy classifications, there are no time clocks, and the offices are open all night. RAND, then, is a kind of military-intellectual's sanctuary, near the beach. "RAND," says Thomas Schelling, "is more than a collection of people. It is a social organism characterized by intellect, imagination and good humor."

RAND's base of operations consists of a fair-sized, modern, sprawling, unobtrusively but heavily guarded building in downtown Santa Monica, California. The visitor acquires a badge from a guard, and mine, at least, bore the warning, in red, that I must be escorted at all times, a directive faithfully followed by my RAND Vergil up to the door of, but not inside, the rest room. I'd expected, I suppose, a Dr. Strangelovian world and a few things do stand out: banks of computers, a special room where war simulation games are played by earnest men with thick books of statistics, and rooms used during the lunch hour for a form of blind chess called *Kriegsspiel*, once enjoyed by the Prussian general staff. Mostly, though, RAND consists of small, very plain offices and, scenically at least, it offers little. More fascinating are the RANDsters, as they are sometimes called, and the work they do.

Roughly speaking, two sorts of enterprises are conducted at RAND. By far the largest component, and the one usually overlooked by critics of what goes on there, is the technical staff, engineers, mathematicians, computer experts and so forth, who account for 85 to 90 percent of RAND's activity. The technicians were among the first to suggest what were called, after the war, "earth-circling spaceships," and they have since designed such military gear as low-altitude radar. The first air defense nuclear rocket was a RAND idea, and the feasibility of fitting H-bombs to missiles and then hardening the missiles was, in part, proved at RAND. The technicians study such problems as swept-wing design and the development of a supersonic transport, and one of RAND's proudest accomplishments is what is called "deferred procurement of spares," the idea of buying spare parts only when they are needed, which sounds obvious enough but which has evidently saved the taxpayers a great deal of money. It is, in short, the sort of slide-rule and desk-computer drudgery that would have to be done by any country maintaining an enormous military establishment.

The controversial side of RAND is represented by those who have, in John J. McCloy's slightly alarming phrase, drunk "the heady wine of military strategy, methods of destruction and power politics," the civilian strategists. RAND strategists have often come from what is called in the defense intellectual business the "software" side, meaning the social sciences, as opposed to the engineers and physicists who produce "hardware," or weapons, and RAND counts on its staff some eighty-seven economists, twenty-one political scientists, eight psychologists, three logicians, two linguists and one geographer. RAND analysts advise NATO on weaponry, or consult on the strategic hamlet program in Vietnam. Almost all the well-known military intellectuals have served RAND in one capacity or another (and so, for that matter, have some prominent American nondefense intellectuals, such as Margaret Mead, who was a RAND consultant). At RAND, modern military analysis first took hold, and just as the weapons have become increasingly bizarre and unsettling, so have the strategies to guide them.

"The rudiments of strategies that have come to be identified with RAND showed themselves as early as 1948," a cheerful RAND strategist named James Digby told me. "The idea of counterforce and issues of air power crept up then. One of our early jobs had to do with the air defense of the United States, and though we realized some planes might get through, the general feeling was that science would make air defense perfect. That umbrella feeling began to disappear around 1948, and we began to think about a world in which air defense couldn't be counted on. We saw that strategic offense might be useful as deterrence—that word began to be heard at cocktail parties then—or for the destruction of the enemy's offensive ability."

In 1951 RAND acquired a mathematical logician named Albert Wohlstetter, who before the war had been a self-styled "fellowship bum," studying mathematics and logic and law and English literature on the side. Wohlstetter had worked as a quality control man in the aircraft industry during the war, and afterward he had served as a government housing expert. He had headed, for a short time, a small housing company with advanced ideas, and it was about this time that RAND asked him to take on a project that he almost rejected because, he said, it looked dull.

But the perfectionist in Wohlstetter stirred as he examined the problem. He was supposed to do a systematic study of American air bases overseas and, as a matter of course, he re-examined American strategy. The battle plan, at this time, was that American planes would react massively to a Soviet attack. In time of peace, all medium and some heavy bombers were based in the U.S. and moved to Europe in time of war; others used overseas bases only for staging and refueling. Wohlstetter studied this plan in almost unbelievable detail, down to such fine points as the pumping rates of fuel hydrants, and under a different set of assumptions from those of the Strategic Air Command. Wohlstetter assumed, for purposes of his study, that the Soviet Union struck first, and not on the group in Europe but on SAC itself. The results, Wohlstetter said, prevented him from sleeping.

Wohlstetter's findings were received with consternation as well by others. For it turned out that the difference in the performance of a damaged and an undamaged Strategic Air Command was fantastic. It came as a big shock, and it was almost unbelievable. Here was the most powerful force in the history of the world, and it was completely vulnerable. The bombers took hours to get ready, on unprotected bases. Bombs in general were not in the same places as the planes, but were concentrated in a few storage sites. Most of the bombers had to be matched with tankers in order to reach the overseas bases from which they were expected to operate during the war. But the tankers made only half the speed of the bombers, and so in case bombers and tankers had to be scrambled while under attack, it was difficult for them to make the rendezvous for the transfer of fuel. Finally, the overseas bases which might be reached in this fashion were even more vulnerable to attack than the bases at home in the United States. Wohlstetter's findings stabbed at the very root of strategic deterrence, for if the deterrent could be destroyed, then it could not properly be said to exist.

Wohlstetter began giving briefings on his findings, in all holding some ninety such sessions in the United States and at bases overseas. As a result, though slowly, the SAC battle plans were changed for better coordination, the use of overseas bases for touchdown refueling only and so forth. I was curious to know how the military men could have made such a blunder, and Wohlstetter said, "It wasn't just the military. Analysts missed too. And it wasn't stupidity. The trouble was of a familiar kind in the history of ideas, big and little. They all looked for new, sensible answers to the old questions. For decades both advocates and critics of strategic bombing had defined the problem as one of penetrating enemy defenses and then destroying the industrial support for making war. Jets and surface-to-air missiles clearly had made it harder for bombers to penetrate defenses, but once through with nuclear weapons they could more easily destroy targets. Disagreement centered on the net effect of these two sorts of technical changes. But the crucial questions turned out to be outside the old framework. They concerned how to protect bombers on the ground so that they could live to face the other obstacles active and passive defense threw up against them. It's harder always to find the question than the answer."

I could imagine that something of the same rigidity had affected the French in their Maginot Line, and I could readily see the advantages of having civilian specialists who see old problems afresh. Wohlstetter had gone on to take the Air Force problem one step farther by identifying clearly the difference between what he identified as a first and second strike, the latter being the capacity to retaliate after having been hit first. This distinction would not have been critical in times past, but for World War III it well might be. Once Wohlstetter had clearly stated the difficulty, the conclusions were more or less inevitable. The American striking force had to be made invulnerable to a first strike in order to be available for the second. Safety, in other words, consisted in being able to survive the first blow because the enemy, knowing this, would not be tempted to strike you. Further, your safety, presumably, would be reassuring to an enemy because he would know that you knew you were invulnerable and would not be tempted to strike him first, out of desperation.

If surprise attack, one-half of the problem, was at least partly taken care of by invulnerability, the other half was the possibility of war by accident, and Wohlstetter originated at least three safety devices now in use: the Bomb Alarm System, which is supposed to tell, in the absence of other information, that a nuclear weapon has not been used; the PAL, or Permissive Action Link; and the famous "fail-safe" procedure. (All these ideas come under the rubric of arms control, to which RAND has contributed many ideas.)

Since then, RAND strategists have probed ever deeper into what one of them called "the fine, internal structure of war." Malcolm Hoag, a RAND analyst, sketched the strategic evolution in broad strokes. First, he said, deterrence was aimed at cities. "It is the policy of those with a small number of weapons, when you don't argue about targets, and it is the idea of the French today." Then, as the U.S. acquired a larger arsenal, the strategy changed with the avowed purpose of making it safer for civilian populations, the idea being to strike military installations first in the hope that cities of both sides could be spared. This is called "counterforce," as opposed to "countervalue," or striking cities, and it, too, has been partly superseded by what RAND people call "neo-counterforce," meaning that what before had been seen as a "penalty," to fail to destroy a military installation, might now be considered a "bonus" if it meant avoiding damage to the cities nearby. In short, neo-counterforce called for the greatest possible precautions to spare cities, in the hopes that the enemy would observe the rules of the game and spare our own.

Such, in simplified form, is the sort of *Kriegsspiel* behind the strategy of deterrence, as worked out by analysts on blackboards and in war simulation games. The RAND analysts, I noticed, were concerned at every point to reduce the damage if war should occur, and not just to ourselves but to the Soviet Union as well, and the effort had led them into an almost metaphysical maze. By limiting the damage, does deterrence become less credible and war more likely? If war should occur, is one justified in not destroying all the enemy's offensive potential when he, in turn, could then proceed to use this potential on you? Can limited wars be prevented from escalating? Does the deterrent ultimately depend on the threat of escalation? These and similar intricacies, far from being conversation pieces, are the stuff and substance of modern strategic arguments, and on the answers to them depend what kinds of military forces one chooses, with serious implications for disarmament as well.

RAND strategists, with some exceptions, appear to agree: (a) that we should attempt to control wars; (b) that we should not "buy" all the strategic weapons available, on the grounds that the amount of destruction purchased begins to have diminishing returns, and, also, that it stimulates an arms race; and (c) that we should rely more upon a second strike than on the threat of a first.

These notions are in conflict with the doctrine of massive retaliation once openly espoused by the Air Force and still believed in by large wings of it. Massive retaliation depends not only on a first strike but on one that would utterly devastate the enemy's military capacity, and when Air Force men today agitate for a larger military budget, what they want to purchase is enough planes and rocketry to accomplish this. RAND's notions of the "fine, internal structure" of war met Air Force displeasure, and the schism deepened with the advent of the Kennedy administration, for RAND analysts suddenly appeared in leading civilian roles in the Department of Defense, such as Charles J. Hitch, an Oxford don before he came to RAND, as the Controller, Alain C. Enthoven, Assistant Controller, and Henry Rowen, Deputy Assistant Secretary of Defense.

These men brought with them still another RAND tool, the notion of defense cost accounting, which a RANDster described in these terms: "The only known way to compare objectively claims for competing weapons systems is to examine what they cost to achieve a given objective and to compare that cost with other systems." Cost-accounting techniques led to the cancellation of such billion-dollar projects as Dyna-Soar, a manned satellite interceptor, Skybolt, an air-to-ground missile, and the RB-70, a reconnaissance bomber, and it may yet lead to the elimination of the heavy bomber itself, all on the grounds that the objectives of such weapons can be handled as well by something else, regardless of the loss of this or that peripheral military capability.

All these well-publicized decisions were at the expense of the Air Force. RAND was by no means alone in promulgating the new strategy of flexible instead of massive response—General Maxwell D. Taylor, for instance, arrived at similar conclusions—but RAND was an Air Force creation and the Air Force struck back. It refused to renew RAND's contract, paying it, instead, on a monthly basis, and such were the strains when a RANDster visited his civilian friends at the Department of Defense that he was instructed by the home office to make certain there would be no hint of a conspiracy.

RAND has other opponents, as well, from all sorts of people in all sorts of places, including people connected with it. One RAND consultant thinks that "RAND's subtleties are likely to have a paralyzing effect on those who must deal with them," and a general connected with RAND thinks it is impossible to attempt to make a science of war, showing his dislike of computers, war gaming and the other logical techniques that contribute to a RAND analysis.

RAND has also run afoul of Congress, and in a manner that led to the sort of legislative *non sequitur* which worries those who are afraid that the Congressional I.Q. is not up to dealing with the complexities of the cold war. The imbroglio began when a Congressman accused RAND of advocating the surrender of the United States, a statement evidently based on a nonreading of a RAND study of four surrenders in World War II. The study's point was that the war may have been prolonged by demands for unconditional surrender, but it led to a Congressional rider on an appropriations bill, passed in 1959, forbidding the study of the surrender of the U.S. with federal funds. (The issue is not that surrender is really considered a possibility, but that Congress should pass a piece of legislation based on a misinterpretation of a study no Congressman had read, and then there is another question— whether the government should willfully ignore a possibility that is always a risk for a nation that goes to war.)

RAND's most vociferous critics, though, are those who believe its strategies are the prime cause of the cold war. "RAND horrifies me. They don't know what the country is for," a leading scientist says. "Largely because of the influence of RAND," wrote a reporter in the *Atlantic Monthly*,

the United States now has a rationale for an interminable Cold War. The thousands of scientists and scholars influenced by RAND have given powerful demonstrations of their ability to create. But do they step back from the fascinating process of creation to see what it is they have wrought? Can these thinkers who have given of their talents seek a way to stop the mechanism and the will of the monster?

RAND, for its part, usually dismisses its critics of both gemlike hardness and tissuelike softness with the same phrase: "They don't like the complexities of the world, which is why they don't like RAND." In this, RAND displays just a touch of condescension about those less well acquainted, it feels, with the inside dope and ultimate realities.

RAND thinkers do disagree among themselves: some favored the test ban, some opposed it; some think the U.S. should acquire space weapons, some don't. "The key question at RAND," says Robert Levine, "is the stability of the arms race versus what happens to the Alliance," that is, the differences between those who oppose the spreading of nuclear technology and those who want to defend Europe by conventional means, and those who believe they can patch up the Alliance with the lure of nuclear arms, no matter how provocative to the Soviet Union it seems. The RANDsters, though, are deterrers, and most agree with Nathan Leites, who says, "I think it is better to treat the Soviet leaders strongly. They respond to strength. The threat of offensive action by us leads to submissiveness and reasonableness on the part of the Soviet Union. I do not think they are devils, however, and as soon as we come to realize this it will be a step toward the reduction of military power."

If RAND shares the prevailing ideas about force and the Soviet Union, if it has no plans for a secret war, and if its people seem intelligent but otherwise normal, the organization does have one extremely important distinction, and that is the power of expertise, gained both by years of working with the problems and by access to the most secret information. "We look at things in the same hard-nosed way that the government does," a RANDster said, "which is why they listen to us, and we've helped the government concentrate on areas that bear scrutiny." It has seemed to some of those who have listened to RAND experts at innumerable symposiums on arms control, disarmament and peace that, almost invariably, their attitude toward new schemes and proposals is negative, and that they exercise a conservative force on change. Those in the war-peace establishment who feel that deep change is needed regret that RAND cannot be pressured into service.

As a high priest of deterrence, Albert Wohlstetter has been instructive on the difficulties of the doctrine. In "The Delicate Balance of Terror," which Thomas Schelling has called "one of the three or four articles in this field in the past dozen years that have really counted," Wohlstetter elaborated a theme that I took to be his germinal notion: "Deterrence in the 1960s," he said, "is neither assured nor impossible but will be the product of sustained intelligent effort and hard choices responsibly made." Correct decisions, he went on, "entail a new image of ourselves in a world of persistent danger. It is by no means *certain* that we will meet the test."

Wohlstetter, I knew, was one who had vigorously fought the sharing of nuclear arms, the deployment of tactical weapons, a large first-strike force and other measures he felt were destabilizing and dangerous. Before leaving California, I stopped in on Wohlstetter in San Francisco, where, having resigned from RAND, he was teaching a course on international security at the University of California. Wohlstetter, a handsome, red-haired, articulate man who sometimes wears a beard, is very much on the side of the angels of culture: fastidious, a gourmet and an expert on music and art. His wife, Roberta, is a prize-winning historian in her own right. Wohlstetter had a cold on the day I called and talked to me from his bed, taking swigs from a cup of tea laced with brandy. I asked him about deterrence.

"There are good and bad, that is, adequate and inadequate, or stable and unstable, deterrents," he said. "The stability of a deterrent is measured by the shocks it can sustain. A good deterrent is one that works in *crises* when the risks an adversary might feel in not striking would be very large. We want a deterrent that will make striking with nuclear arms the worst of all possible alternatives available to an adversary, even when the alternatives may look bad. A poor deterrent might make striking the best of a bad lot of alternatives. We know from the actual history of our deterrent force that an adequate deterrent doesn't just happen without effort. It has to be carefully constructed at any given state of the technological art, and is always subject to technical upset. The object of a deterrent is to reduce the chances of war.

"There are some people who think that deterrence is easy, if not automatic. But they seem to me to miss the main point, which is that the problems of accidental war and surprise attack are inseparable. For example, if accidental war were inevitable, as these people think, this would supply one motive for preventive war. If you only had to worry about accident or misunderstanding, it would be very easy to make the nuclear response so insensitive to warning or actual delivery or attack that it would be extremely unlikely that you would respond to a false alarm. But then it would be fairly easy for an adversary safely to plan for an actual attack. On the other hand, if one simply wanted to be completely certain—" he paused to drink from his cup—"of responding in case of an actual attack, you could set up an automatic, trigger-sensitive response to even very ambiguous signals that some hostile force was being prepared. Then, of course, the chances of accident would rise enormously.

"Significantly, some of the chief proponents of the view that deterrence is easy try to prove this by assuming a retaliation system that is automatic. But the United States, quite correctly, I think, doesn't have an automatic response system to radar systems or even to the impact of nuclear explosion. The problem is to reduce simultaneously the dangers of both surprise attack and accidental war. You can't reduce those risks to zero, but they have been drastically lowered in the last few years by the exercise of intelligence and care. Some of the extreme solutions which have been suggested would have raised the risks."

Wohlstetter had on his bed table an old review of the novel Fail-Safe, and he handed it to me, saying that both the book and the review illustrated some of the confusions about accidental war. The review, I saw, was by I. I. Rabi, a well-known physicist and a leading scientific consultant on military matters, and it said, in part: "The book packs a tremendous wallop. I read it in one sitting because I simply could not put it down. And afterward, night after night, I travelled with Bomber Group 6 as they fought their way to Moscow. This book should have the impact of *Uncle Tom's Cabin*. P.S. There should be a Russian edition as soon as possible."

I had a feeling Wohlstetter and Rabi were speaking different languages. Many scientists are convinced that deterrence theory was largely an empty rationale because nobody would fight a thermonuclear war. To them we had developed nuclear weapons largely because we liked them, and in this fashion pushed the arms race along. There was the likelihood that we would have been able to maneuver the Soviets out of an arms race, had we been clever enough, they thought, and the job was still to get the country thinking in terms of a lowered reliance on nuclear arms.

Wohlstetter lay back on his pillow and said, "You get the impression that the fail-safe procedure is the problem, not one attempt at a partial solution. I'm obviously concerned about accidents, and I think they are possible, but this one is not. In the book, a condenser blows out and activates a machine which displays a code with three letters and three numbers, and that means war. But there is no such machine with even a much larger number of windows, and the commands are given by voice. The sort of accidents that are most easily insured against are precisely the mechanical errors.

"But most important, what's implied here is the notion that accidental war is inevitable according to the laws of probability. This idea, which is endorsed by the authors and subscribed to by some eminent scientists, is based on an elementary logical fallacy. I regard the fatalism fostered by this argument of inevitability as extremely dangerous. It encourages the belief that the holocaust will be on us unless by some desperate act we achieve some improbable immediate drastic change in the world order. It leads to utopian and extremist solutions."

Those Wohlstetter feels have extreme and utopian views include both "hards" and "softs," and he criticizes them for their "enormous sense of urgency," for wanting simple solutions to durable problems. This applies, he says, to Barry Goldwater as well as Bertrand Russell, and Wohlstetter has quoted Russell as saying, in 1948:

Atomic weapons, if used, will at first have to be dropped on West Europe, since Russia will be out of reach. The Russians, even without atomic bombs, will be able to destroy all the big towns in Europe, as the Germans would have done if the war had lasted a few months longer. I have no doubt that America would win in the end, but unless West Europe can be preserved from invasion, it will be lost to civilization for centuries. Even at such a price I think war would be worthwhile. Communism must be wiped out, and world government must be established.

Russell today, of course, leads peace movement actions in England and appears to regard immediate nuclear disarmament as the only sane course.

"I regard Russell as a very great man," Wohlstetter said. "I spent much of my teens reading his logical writings and I have a great affection for him. For this reason his extremism affects me the most. But both preventive war and unilateral disarmament amount to a surrender of the intelligence. The sense of urgency accounts for both. I believe it has contributed to the inflamed character of the debate. I'm not eager to promote emotion. I'm temperamentally as well as intellectually opposed to it. Our government functions best when thought is being exercised, and when leadership is temperate, not hysterical. I agree that military men and politicians have also done poorly on these complex issues. It's just that those who claim to have the final solutions have done no better."

And the American peace movement? I asked. "If the peace movement includes anyone who has worked seriously at the job of reducing the chances of war, as I have over a dozen years, then I'm part of it. But if you mean anyone signing petitions or waving banners with the slogan 'peace,' then I'd say it's a mixed bag. I disagree with someone like A. J. Muste, the anarcho-pacifist, but I have great respect for him, and I'm perfectly willing to grant men like Linus Pauling or members of the SANE Nuclear Policy Committee the sincere desire to avoid war. I happen to believe that some of the things they advocate would make war more likely, but at least that's subject for debate. What I think is intellectually disreputable is that in styling themselves 'the peace movement' many of these men suggest—indeed, they come right out and say it—that those who disagree with them on how to avoid war are prowar." Wohlstetter's voice, I observed, increased a notch in intensity.

"Many people tend to be hostile to the fact of hostility itself," he went on. "I don't by any means exclude the possibility of large changes in the Soviet Union and the opening up of their society, but I don't believe it will happen soon. But even if you had, say, world Communism, you would not have eliminated war. The world with its nationalism and slow nation-building moves completely away from the one world idea. The world, as I've said, is a dangerous place, and I find the idea that war can be eliminated implausible. I don't believe that peace is anything that gets achieved once and for all with certainty, and I clearly haven't got 'the word.' But I do think that with intelligence we can and will avoid a nuclear holocaust, and that we can, slowly and piecemeal, build a more orderly and safer world. I suggest the importance of having less absolute goals than perfect peace if you want any peace at all."

"GENGHIS" KAHN

Of all the military intellectuals—the new hybrid of scholar who has flourished in the cold war environment and who lays claim to represent the first attempt in history to deal with war in a systematic, even objective manner—the man who has come virtually to embody the profession is a forty-two-year-old scholar named Herman Kahn who shot into view in 1960 with the publication of *On Thermonuclear War*, a massive tome on the subject which surprised its publishers by selling thirty thousand copies, though nobody could be certain how many people had actually read it. The book had grown out of massive, three-day briefings Kahn had first given to high government officials, which had been received with both shock and admiration. If anyone can be said to be in on the subject of thermonuclear war, it is Herman Kahn, whose pages exude the aura of a top-level conference room, and he has a way of making almost anyone else who has written on the subject of modern war appear naïve.

I marked Kahn as an important stopping place on the pilgrimage I was making into the difficult, uphill country of war and peace, but before visiting him I sat down with *OTW* and a subsequent, more popularized volume called *Thinking About the Unthinkable*. Kahn's argument, I thought, could be reduced to three major points. The first is that thermonuclear war is "thinkable," by which Kahn merely means that it could happen if any nuclear weapons exist at all. In part he also means that it is important to understand how nuclear forces may actually be used, and he has worked out a number of "options." For instance, he feels it is important to understand that nuclear war may not be simply a "spasm" in which every button in the house is pressed. The current U.S. strategy of "no cities except in reprisal" derives in part from Kahn's study of how a thermonuclear war may be controlled. Although the temptation is to look away, it is far better, in fact it is a requisite for survival, to stare the devil in the face. Second, the nation needs a vastly sophisticated military apparatus to attempt the deterrence of any conflict, large or small. Finally, to say that deterrence was a policy meant that one had to be prepared to *use* the weapons that constituted the deterrent, or else deterrence might be fatally weakened. It was not that Kahn failed to understand that mere uncertainty might deter the Soviets. He felt, rather, that such a deterrent was of a low quality and that something more reliable both was needed and could be obtained. Finally, in spite of our best efforts, deterrence might still fail. If that was the case, one had to try to protect one's society as best one could, and this had led Kahn to some strong recommendations for civil defense and for having proper tactics available if a war had to be fought, including the ability to implement a cease-fire of some kind as soon as possible. The country, in Kahn's opinion, could be rebuilt faster than most people think. "The survivors," he said in a famous phrase, "would not envy the dead." Splitting away at his infinitives, Kahn said, "All in all, it seems valuable to at least keep open the option of fighting and surviving."

I found Kahn's book, written in an elaborate, bolero-like style, each theme repeating itself over and over, almost impossible not to put down, and during one of the many days my copy lay gathering strontium 90 I picked up a review of *OTW* that appeared in the magazine *Scientific American,* by the noted science writer James R. Newman. "Is there really a Herman Kahn?" Newman asked. "Doubts cross one's mind almost from the first page of this deplorable book: no one could write like this; no one could think like this. Perhaps the whole thing is a staff hoax in bad taste."

To Newman, anyone who supported a policy that stood for the possible use of nuclear arms was being guilty of "bloodthirsty irrationality," and he had once told an audience, referring to Kahn as "Mr. Genghis . . . I mean Herman Kahn," "I shall not go so far as to say that we are today being misled by a serpent, but you will not misunderstand me if I say that among contemporary seducers and deceivers there are not a few who make the Devil seem, by comparison, a good-natured and simple-minded woolly bear." Newman compared deterrence to a vulgar error on a par with all other superstitions and misbeliefs that have always deterred men from wisdom, finding a modern example in the Scopes trial, and which "work their mischief today and make men hold fast to beliefs which keep enticing them into a morass which obscures the path to peace, and which threatens a catastrophe that will erase civilization."

It was easy to see why Newman would have detested Kahn. The latter's writing was bearish, untidy, sprawling, the former's meticulous, pointed, refined. Kahn was a specialist in military analysis, trained to consider war with the detached logic of a scientist, while Newman was a passionate spokesman of culture and humanism. No doubt, Kahn's jargon must have brought Newman to a white heat—his ironic metaphors like "spasm war," his coined phrases like "not incredible first strike" or even "unthinkable." ("He means 'unspeakable,'" Newman has said contemptuously. "'Unthinkable' would refer to something like a four-dimensional cube.") In his review, Newman had singled out a passage from *OTW* which, to him, exemplified the archenemy's spirit:

Under these conditions of post-atomic attack, some high percentage of the population is going to be nauseated, and nausea is very catching.

If one man vomits, everybody vomits. It would not be surprising if almost everybody vomits. Almost everyone is likely to think he has received too much radiation. Morale may be so affected that many survivors may refuse to participate in constructive activities, but would content themselves with sitting down and waiting to die—some may even become violent and destructive.

However, the situation would be quite different if radiation meters were distributed. Assume now that a man gets sick from a cause other than radiation. Not believing this, his morale begins to drop. You look at his meter and say, "You have received only ten roentgens, why are you vomiting? Pull yourself together and get to work."

I had no doubt that Newman must have been revolted by this bleak vision of human ineptitude, but, on the other hand, Newman himself did not say what he proposed to do about preventing such a war. Kahn, for his part, was evidently annoyed at Newman, for he wrote to Dennis Flanagan, the editor of *Scientific American*: "I have just read Mr. Newman's review of my book and can only say that it should not have appeared in a magazine called *Scientific American*." The review, Kahn thought, was neither scientific nor American, and he felt Newman's position was basically an objection to thinking about thermonuclear catastrophe. Kahn offered to write an article to be entitled "Thinking About the Unthinkable" (which he later wrote, as a book), and Flanagan replied: "I do not think there is much profit in thinking about the unthinkable; surely it is more profitable to think about the thinkable. . . . I would prefer to devote my thoughts to how nuclear war can be prevented. It is for this reason that we must decline your offer to give us your article."

I found this unpublished correspondence revealing, for it showed clearly the differences between those whose opposition to thermonuclear deterrence is on moral grounds and those who accept it because, like the mountain for the climber, it's there. And if Kahn had his critics, he also had his supporters, even one like H. Stuart Hughes, of the peace movement. "I think one can say without qualification," Hughes said, about *OTW*, "that Kahn has written one of the great works of our time . . . what Kahn tries to do—and what, so far as I know, no one else has tried to do in so thoroughgoing a fashion—is to look thermonuclear war in the eye and to treat it as a reality rather than a bad dream."

One accomplishment cannot be denied to Herman Kahn, for more than anyone else he has opened up national debate on thermonuclear war, even in making a legion of enemies. "It takes an iron will or an unpleasant degree of detachment or callousness to go about the task of distinguishing between the possible degrees of awfulness," Kahn wrote, and I was anxious to meet a man with the iron will and/or the detachment. I doubted if there would be much difficulty. Kahn was known to express himself freely, whether to reporters or peace groups.

When I telephoned Kahn at his home at Chappaqua, New York, at 9:30 A.M., he thanked me for having wakened him. He had had only an hour's sleep, having worked all night, but it was time to be up and about. "I'll be glad to talk with you, as long as your interest is serious," Kahn said. "Up to ten hours, if you like." I feared, I said, that ten hours of thermonuclear war was more than I could handle.

Kahn had left the RAND Corporation in 1960 after twelve years there, and shortly after he had been among the founders of a new "think factory," the Hudson Institute, some thirty-five miles north of New York City at Harmon-on-Hudson, New York. Peace, I gathered, was good for the study of war, for the Hudson Institute is a cluster of pleasant, two- and three-story buildings set in a grove of trees on a quiet hillside, with the river far below and occasionally visible through the branches. I arrived there several hours early, in order to look around, and I learned that Hudson had been formed because, despite the government's multibillion-dollar commitment to research, relatively little was being done in policy planning—that is, not how weapons would be used but why—and long-range problems of world order. The other "think factories," I gathered, were considered at Hudson to be insufficiently independent of the government and too narrowly technical.

If its selection of advisory members was a clue, Hudson was out to consider many points of view, for its board managed to span Edward Teller, Louis B. Sohn, an advocate of world law, and

A. J. Muste, one of the most radical and outspoken men in the peace movement. ("I was one of the few who could go in there without there being any suspicion I'd be seduced," Muste later said. "I don't think Kahn and the others are devils; they are trying to find a way." Muste, plainly, did not agree with the way.) In spirit, Hudson is probably softer than harder, a blend of both realism and idealism, although it was evidently anxious to avoid either label. As its brochure said, "While the Institute will not seek to be foolishly idealistic, it does believe that the existence of large numbers of readily deliverable H-bombs and an active arms race make it necessary to devote serious, detailed, informed thought to such things as disarmament and world government."

The policy research at Hudson is handled by a staff of twenty-six analysts, about evenly divided between physical and social scientists, with a few additions from the law and journalism, and they are aided by a small number of bright girls, not long out of college, who may earn $7,500 a year. The atmosphere is distinctly informal, the dress casual, and the blackboards are full of arcane symbols and scrawlings. In the lunchroom two young women talk not of men but of war. "If 'N' equals 1 and 'P' equals 2, the ratio of 'hit' to 'kill' . . ." one said. The other interrupted, brandishing a slide rule. "I don't give a *blip* about that. The point is . . ."

The Hudson analysts are attempting to be future historians, and they have created a list of possible worlds of the 1970's and 1980's, from one placidly at peace to one with a dozen countries bristling with nuclear arms and on the verge of mass war. I asked Max Singer, the Institute's counsel, which future he thought most likely and he said, "Experience says that none of the safe worlds we can predict in the year 2000 will work, yet we know that one of them will have to work if there is to be a world. It's only common sense. Unfortunately, although experience is still the best guide, it is no longer adequate. The world has become too complicated."

I saw what is probably Hudson's unofficial motto chalked on a blackboard, a reversal of the Latin adage, "If you want peace, prepare for war," altered to read, "If you want peace, *understand* war." Donald G. Brennan, the Institute's former president and now conducting research there, said, "We're a young and new field, trying to discover ourselves. The parallel I think of is economics. The economists feel that they have come to understand the broad workings of the economy and are able to control depressions. In the same way, we are trying to grasp the inner workings of war in order to control it."

Brennan told me that the Institute itself does not take a position in policy matters but that all the analysts had ideas of their own. (Some fairly sharp differences, for instance, exist between himself and Kahn.) "Let me tell you what I *don't* believe," Brennan said. He took a poster and held it up. It was a photo of the Kremlin overlaid with red, and headed, "A SERIOUS REMINDER FROM SYSTEMS DEVELOPMENT CORPORATION." It said:

War to the hilt between capitalism and communism is inevitable. Today, of course, we are not strong enough to attack. Our time will come in 20 or 30 years. In order to win, we shall need the element of surprise. The bourgeoisie will have to be put to sleep so we shall begin by launching the most spectacular peace movement on record. There will be electrifying overtures and unheard of concessions. The capitalist countries, stupid and decadent, will rejoice to cooperate in their destruction. They will leap at another chance to be friends. As soon as their guard is down, we shall smash them with our clenched fist.

DIMITRI Z. MANUILSKY to the students
of the Lenin School of Political
Warfare, Moscow, U.S.S.R., in 1931

Brennan rapped the poster. "This was put up in several factories with military contracts. It is believed by reputable authorities to be unauthentic—a fraud." Brennan went on to say that, in his opinion, some degree of the current international trouble was founded on misunderstanding.

I had heard a good deal about Kahn at Hudson. "Herman's got an intellectually responsible position," one of the analysts said. "Those who criticize him confuse analysis with advocacy. Herman doesn't *advocate* war. But he typically overstates his case. He was trying to shake things up when he began, and he used a combination of humor and shock to clarify his arguments. I'm afraid it affected his style. And then, Herman doesn't believe in describing thermonuclear war with peace-movement adjectives. You wouldn't expect a surgeon to say, 'Look at that dreadful, shocking appendix,' would you?"

Kahn, I was told, is in favor of an antiballistic missile for a few cities, partly as "insurance" against new countries that might acquire bombs. He is in favor, too, of the MLF, provided it is properly deployed and operated, and is used as an entering wedge for a European Defense Community, and not just as an answer to de Gaulle. He does not wish to share nuclear arms with Kissinger and Europe.

"Does he believe that there is a *détente?*"

"Herman likes to be in the minority, but this time he agrees with the *New York Times* that there is a *détente.*"

"Have any of his essential conclusions changed?"

"No, because the missiles are still in place."

I met Kahn just after lunch. In the anteroom of his office, I saw a valise bulging with papers and among them were several cans of Metrecal, to which my eyes automatically reverted when he entered the room. Corpulent and tall, with a broad, pale face, thick eyeglasses and a not unpleasantly sinister expression, Kahn brings to mind a sort of thermonuclear Zero Mostel.

Kahn invited me to his home in Chappaqua. We picked up his car, and on the drive over I asked Kahn to tell me about himself. He was born, he said, in Bayonne, New Jersey, of Polish immigrant parents, moving to the Bronx, New York, when he was still a young child. By choice, Kahn said, he had abandoned the playground for books, and he had been, I gathered, a child prodigy who could easily outpoint his teachers on such varied subjects as mathematics, physics, economics and even the stock market. Among people who have worked with him, Kahn has the reputation for extraordinary mental prowess and I asked him what his I.Q. was. Kahn said he had been told it was about 200, which, being close to the top mark theoretically possible in an I.Q., put him on a plane with John Stuart Mill.

I asked Kahn if he had any intellectual forebears, and he responded, "I owe a lot to the classical economists. They were often limited in their considerations, but people like Adam Smith taught me that life consists of hard choices. Economics is often called the dismal science, and for a reason. You never know when the good you are trying to do will cause harm instead. Innocence, in my view, is a major sin. Economics teaches you this, as it teaches you to look at problems in a detached way. From fairly early in life I wasn't afraid to face hard questions."

Kahn went on to say that he served in Burma with the Army during the war. He'd been sniped at but had seen no real combat. After the war, he was working for a Ph.D. in physics at the California Institute of Technology, at Los Angeles, when he decided, for financial reasons, to drop out for six months and work. He took a job with RAND, not because he knew RAND was doing high-level studies for the Air Force, but because the place was "close to the beach. But I got caught up in the place. They were doing the kind of thing professionally that I'd always done as an amateur—that is, putting together a broad picture and pontificating on a range of issues, and now I was getting paid for it. The six months kept stretching out. I never got the Ph.D."

Kahn, talking virtually nonstop in a staccato style, turned off on a quiet street, and we emerged in a medium-price real estate development. Children, Kahn's two among them, played on the street. There was the rattle of bicycles and the yelps of dogs. Kahn, slowing down, called to his children and waved to neighbors standing on their lawns. "I'm the disgrace of the neighborhood because I don't keep my garden up," Kahn said familially as we drove into the two-car garage.

Inside, we were greeted cheerfully by Kahn's wife Jane, a warm woman a few years younger than her husband. With an air of wifely determination she took the Metrecal. I gathered that Kahn had been neglecting his office supply and Jane had decided to consolidate the stock. She asked if we would like tea, and Kahn and I entered a sparsely furnished living room and sat before a low, round coffee table. Kahn occupied a sling chair. I then asked

Kahn a question that had intrigued me. I asked him if his studies had influenced his choice of a house.

"I considered the location," Kahn said. "It wasn't the determining factor, but it was a plus factor." The house, he said, was beyond the destruction range of a twenty-megaton weapon dropped on New York. A few windows might be broken, but he would have fallout only with rare wind conditions. "I make such calculations automatically," Kahn said. He said this without a trace of emotion, and I remembered the dreadful appendix. I asked, did he have a bomb shelter? He'd tried to build one but he'd run into rock. He was thinking of trying again, although he was opposed to private shelters, being in favor of a public program. Did he have a radiation counter? Two of them, Kahn said.

There was a somewhat awkward pause. I remembered then that Kahn had once estimated the chance of thermonuclear war at between 10 and 25 percent in the next ten years, and I asked him if he stood by the figures. "We have reduced the chances of war by accident. In some sense such estimates are silly, but if I had to give one I would say that a large nuclear war is as likely as not in the next forty years, especially because of nuclear proliferation and because of frustration developing among countries that would be then relatively well armed." Why didn't he find a haven if he felt that way? Why did he remain in the U.S.?

"For two reasons," Kahn said. "There is the standard nuclear incredulity, which I have as well as everybody else. In this case, it is particularly difficult to take drastic personal action on the basis of calculations concerning hypothetical events. Then, I think I am doing good and useful work here for both myself and others. However, if I thought the probability of war was very high, I might do something, but where would I go? It's an *Appointment in Samarra* situation—wherever you go it catches up with you. During the last war some people in the Pacific picked an island they thought would be safe—it was Guadalcanal. Australia or New Zealand, I suppose would be best." About seventy-five American nuclear migrants, I knew, had moved to New Zealand.

Mrs. Kahn arrived with tea and cakes. "No, you don't," she said, as Kahn reached for a cake. Kahn took some cake and Mrs. Kahn threw up her hands.

I wanted to know about those briefings, and Kahn told me that in addition to his work at RAND he had served as a consultant in the Department of Defense, the Atomic Energy Commission and the Gaither Committee, as well as a number of corporations. He'd achieved, he thought, something of a global view of American nuclear strategy and began giving briefings to people at RAND. Word of these lectures went out, and Kahn was called to Washington to present them to leading government officials. The briefings lasted three days, and places at them were as eagerly sought after as tickets to a hit Broadway show. *OTW*, Kahn said, consisted of three of those briefings in edited form.

"I'm the only man I know who can be funny on the subject of thermonuclear war in public briefings," Kahn was saying, and I reflected that the grotesque is capable of turning the full circle to humor again. Some of his jokes, though, hadn't conveyed in print, and they had given Kahn a reputation among the insiders for having been overly dramatic and frightening the public. One of Kahn's jokes was the californium bullet, the *reductio ad absurdum* of technical development. A recent book, *The Domesday Dictionary*, defines the californium bullet, in all seriousness, as "A bullet made of californium, a fissionable element of high efficiency useful in very small amounts for the production of pistol or rifle bullets. Presently prohibitive in cost. A reduction in manufacturing expense could provide soldiers, hunters, police and thieves with a side arm capable of exploding its charges with a force estimated at approximately 10 tons of TNT."

Kahn was saying, "I was trying to make people face up to these problems. This generally means saying things starkly and bluntly. I also believe humor helps in creating a detached and professional atmosphere. The briefings had two concerns. They worried about the Russians, but they worried about the arms race in a way that people did not. Now soldiers have their traditional virtues: fidelity, honor, bravery. These are necessary virtues, of course. The man who urges caution at the conference table will often turn out to be a coward on the firing line. The field commander has to be audacious in order to overcome his own natural reluctance in battle. He *must* worry about what he can do to the enemy, not what the enemy can do to him. But it just so happens that those traditional virtues are all wrong for staff officers in preparing for nuclear warfare.

"What I was doing was a kind of psychoanalysis. I was taking a man who had been trained for thirty years that caution was wrong in a soldier and telling him that he must be prudent. I was changing his *character*. I begin by being cozy and reassuring. Not everyone gets bone cancer from fallout, I say, only 2 percent. Casualties in atomic war would be high, but perhaps not intolerable. I tell them the old joke about the man who asks a girl if she will sleep with him for a million dollars. Of course, she says yes. He then offers her two dollars and she slaps his face, saying, 'What do you think I am?' He answers, 'I know what you are. We are just haggling over the price.' 'But observe,' I then say, 'we have now established what the girl is and we have set limits on her price. Nobody knows exactly what the price would be. It depends on the girl, the man, the circumstances, and so on. But nevertheless, we do know that the price is somewhere between two dollars and a million, and we can possibly reduce the uncertainty to some degree by further analysis or investigation.

" 'Let us now take up the subject of thermonuclear war and find out (a) whether the United States has a price and (b) what the price is.'

"I make up a scenario. Let's call the countries 'P' and 'Q' "—Kahn, I felt, was beginning to imitate his lecture style—"so as to make them as far away from reality as possible. (But 'Q' is Russia.) 'Q' invades Europe, which 'P' is committed to defend under the NATO treaty. 'P' says to 'Q,' 'What are you *doing*? Don't you *know* that I've got a thousand missiles aimed at you? Are you *crazy*? If you persist in this mad attack, I'll let you have it. Withdraw at once!' Whereupon 'Q' says, 'Will you stop taking up my time, please? I've got enough to do already attacking Europe. I know you know I know you have a thousand missiles aimed at me. I've been studying you for years. You know that I know that you know that I have a thousand missiles aimed at you, and if you let me have it, I'll let *you* have it. You wouldn't *dream* of shooting at me.' And the attack continues.

"The president of 'P' has twenty-four hours to decide. If he hits, 'Q' will retaliate, which means 180 million casualties for 'P.' 'Gentlemen,' I say to the audience, 'is the price right? Would you hit the button?'

"Occasionally a junior officer will stand up and say that we must honor our treaty commitments, and I say jokingly that he can leave the room—this is a briefing for senior officers, not field commanders. I turn back to the audience. Everybody looks at the senior officer present, who almost invariably says, 'That's a hypothetical question.' I answer, 'Yes, I'm trying to establish what you are.' The senior officer present then has the problem of looking either like a fool or a coward. He invariably prefers looking prudent to looking foolish. He then agrees that 180 million is too high. I then suggest that we haggle over the price. It is practically impossible at this point to argue that more than half the country should be risked, and since senior officers are reluctant to admit that they can be deterred, they would generally compromise at one-third of the population, occasionally less. In other words, even military officers are willing to concede that the United States would not and should not live up to its most solemn obligations, no matter how solemn and binding, if the cost was more than one-third of the population. So I say, 'Gentlemen, you are deterred right now. Sixty million casualties is what you say the Russians can inflict.' At this point the same men who were unwilling to rely on anything but pure massive retaliation in spite of what they knew about Soviet capability and who were unwilling to accept arms controls were ready to change their basic ideas."

Kahn, visibly tired, left the room for a moment, and I turned to Mrs. Kahn, who had been listening. She told me she was a mathematician herself and had met her husband when she worked as a research aide at RAND. I asked her if Kahn, with such worrisome thoughts constantly on his mind, ever seemed anxious. She thought a moment. "Well, there's this bit of Kahniana," she said. "One morning during the Berlin crisis we were having breakfast when the radio went off. It was just on the blink, but Herman thought for a second or two the station was switching to Conelrad, which would mean an alert. He turned white as a sheet."

Kahn returned and sank into the sling chair, reaching for another piece of cake. Jane Kahn said firmly, "No more cake." Kahn withdrew his hand. So far in the conversation he had worried about the arms race instead of the Russians, and I asked him how he felt about them. "On 90 percent of the issues I'm softer than Strausz-Hupé, Schelling and Kissinger, although in a Central War I might be harder than anyone. You might say that I am soft when the Russians are soft and hard when the Russians are hard. People tend to see the Russians in terms of their own personalities; a bureaucratic, rigid type would see them as bureaucratic and rigid and an aggressive person would see them as aggressive. I must have the outlook of a businessman because I see them as businessmen, a different kind of businessman from myself but a businessman all the same. I know I am wrong to some important degree, but at least I know my bias. You might sum it up by saying that the right wing has an enemy, I have an opponent and the peace movement has a misguided friend."

Kahn went on quickly, "The Russians do have a degree of ideological sincerity, and we make a mistake when we don't realize it. They don't have the messianic fervor of the early Christians, but they do have ideological force. I think they like the idea of terror, and they will urge wars of national liberation. For that reason they are a threat to peace, even though the threat is more likely to arise through the escalation of small conflicts than through any immediate large-scale confrontation."

I asked Kahn to tell me more precisely what the issues separating the U.S. and the Soviet Union were. Kahn thought a moment behind his glasses. "With the waning of ideology there are no questions between the U.S. and the S.U. that have to be fought out with nuclear weapons." (I noticed that he always presented the two countries in this mirror-image fashion.) "The U.S. has no basis for conflict with the S.U. We're like a big winner at a poker game, we'd like to go home. The Russians have a lot of self-restraint. Their slogans are filled with it, like 'Don't let the enemy provoke you to self-destruction,' 'Don't throw away Communism in a fit of anger,' and so forth. There's no reason for a to-the-death conflict other than fear.

"In the vertebrate kingdom the ritualistic or agonistic type of combat is quite typical: rattlesnakes wrestle instead of using their fangs, moose butt each other, a defeated wolf bares its throat but the winner doesn't kill it. The U.S.–S.U. struggle would probably degenerate into an agonistic conflict if we had enough time. The 'if,' of course, is an important caveat."

Although Kahn was putting some emphasis on the danger of Soviet ideological expansion it was evident that he would not agree with those who said that the Soviets were waging a protracted conflict against us and would ultimately attack. The thrust of Kahn's argument, to the contrary, seemed to explain the cold war more or less in traditional terms of a power clash between conventional nation-states, and I asked him if that were true. "Yes," he said. "I see nation-states in conflict over spheres of influence. If there is a power vacuum, states clash, as they always have. I take a tragic view of history.

"In this sense nuclear weapons are merely another element to a more or less conventional historical situation. Nuclear conflicts are 'thinkable' in the manner that all wars have been thinkable. Nuclear weapons, once in existence, can't be wished away. You can't destroy them so long as men have the knowledge of how to build them again. And since they do exist, and nations have them, and nations have a tendency to go to war, one must face the fact that they may be used."

I asked Kahn if he thought that war was an inevitable feature of human affairs.

"There has been an interesting change in the conception of war," Kahn said. "Earlier in history wars were fought for adventure, kicks, as antidotes to boredom, for gold, glory and God." He paused to flavor the alliteration, then repeated it: "For gold, glory and God.

Such notions persisted right up to World War I. Observe that the peace groups at the time had to argue against the feeling that war was a good thing. People still believed that war made noble qualities bloom. Such ideas died in the trenches. Except in pre-World War II Germany, Italy and Japan war propaganda didn't take hold, and even in Germany and Italy not very much. The idea of war has become increasingly unthinkable. Now we talk of wars for prudential or defensive reasons or of war by escalation or accident. We talk of pre-emptive war, another defensive concept. But people do get bored and they are neurotic and they do hate. There is a combative instinct and there are dark things in the human soul that do come out. You will always have conflict, but it needn't necessarily result in war. It could take various forms. For example, both death and taxes are inevitable, but in very different forms. So is conflict inevitable, but it need not take the form of war.

"And there could be rules. I can't swear this story is accurate, but I've heard that the Tuareg Arabs will steal each other's cattle, rape women and kill the men, but they won't poison each other's wells."

All this, I thought, implied a necessity for a broad change in social organization, and I said so. "Yes, it would probably require a world government," Kahn said. "Obviously I would prefer a world government. I'm not certain how we would get one or what form it would take. There are terrible problems." And he went on to mention the probability of civil war in a world state, the difficulty of absorbing the Communist Chinese, the possibility that the "status quo states," as he called them, could easily have their economies wrecked by taxes imposed by have-not countries and so on.

He ended up by saying, "I'm much afraid that the only way a world government could come about now would be through a terrible convulsion, and even then the problems would remain. In any case, if we get the time, I believe that the trends of the last three hundred years will be reversed. The two basic ideas in Western civilization have been order and justice. Our emphasis has been on justice; I believe there will be more emphasis on order, and we will see more of the big nations pushing the small ones around in the name of order. Some degree of order will have to be imposed.

We will need enough order so that there can be justice." He went on to say that he favored a strong Atlantic Alliance but doubted its feasibility. The best he could really suggest, when you got right down to it, was the Common Market, NATO and a U.S. defense policy more or less like the one we have now, and I said so. Kahn said, with an affirmative nod of his broad head, "The present policy, while not optimal, is not wildly unsatisfactory. No policy seems better."

"But the high probability of war . . ." I began. We have to die sometime, true, but all at once? I thought. Kahn was saying, "We are all aware that the present course holds many dangers. The job of those who would change it is to show that a different path holds less risk, less danger and less immorality than the one we are on."

Kahn has been accused of creating a mathematics of death, and I asked him about his morality. "I have a morality of consequences," he said in his staccato style. "There are those who have a morality of acts; they judge good and bad in isolation. To me this can be irresponsible. If an act has bad consequences, it's a bad act and that is the way to judge it. Of course one must include all the consequences in adding up the balance sheet. According to my morality the use of nuclear weapons can be justified if the consequences of using them, awful as they are, are better than the consequences of not using them. I agree there are few circumstances that would justify their use.

"The sense of outrage that some people have isn't legitimate. For one thing, they don't want to take any risks, and we must take risks. We really haven't any choice. There's a kind of spoiled-child attitude about some people. When the world isn't perfect, a small child objects. It's like blaming a hospital because people are sick."

Someone had once rushed up to Kahn's wife and said, "How does it feel to be married to a monster?" and I asked Kahn how he felt about the attacks against him. "Many people don't like a person who thinks through a problem in a cool, detached way. We admire passion and commitment, but being willing to face the fact that there are problems isn't a sign of a deranged mentality. I've been accused of playing an Eichmann-like role in supporting an evil policy. My kind of analysis does make war more thinkable, and perhaps I personally overanalyze, but I'd rather err in that direction than the other. I think we must face the possibility that there is no decent way out, but on the other hand maybe there is. The present situation has a kind of hopeful stability. You might say I believe in a policy of planned muddling through."

After dinner, Kahn drove me to the train. I more or less tended to feel, as I pondered on the way, that all the answers weren't in yet. Kahn, like the other analysts, accepted the prevailing American view of history, which, I thought, might be right but then it might be wrong, too. And did he put too much stress on the failures of history rather than its successes? Was he too analytically realistic and not utopian enough? Perhaps idealistic or utopian schemes would be the only true realism after all. Couldn't men and nations change? And if they could change, mightn't deterrence stand in the way? These were matters for further debate. A horn presaged the train as we pulled under the elevated station and, thanking Kahn profusely, I raced up the stairs to the platform, standing for a moment in dismay. Kahn's strategy had left me on the wrong side of the tracks. I could only hope he and the other analysts hadn't left the country in a similar fix.

"What distinguishes the 'analytical' middle marginalist," writes Robert A. Levine, in his book *The Arms Debate,* about analysts of Kahn's persuasion, "is that, whether for reasons of temperament or roles as 'technicians,' their thought tends to *start* with where we are and where we might get rather than with value judgments about where we want to be." And Kahn himself has written: "I tend to feel that analysis can be as important as advocacy and that we have relatively too little of the former. I am more or less committed to being primarily an analyst. Therefore it is unlikely that I will be loyal to any particular set of proposals."

The analysts differ from the forward strategists in trying to work on a year-by-year basis for their twin goals of stability and freedom rather than trying to steer a long-range course toward the elimination of Communism. Analysts, unlike the forward strategists, are willing to accept the existence of the Soviet state because they think it can give up its international ambitions, whereas Strausz-Hupé is convinced that by its very nature it cannot. The analysts, too, make less virtue of the glories of Western culture and American democracy (although this view does underlie, albeit inexplicitly, a good deal of their thought). In one sense, the forward strategists are more optimistic than the analysts, for they feel that the Soviet Union will back down in the face of an aggressive America. Generally, though, the analysts are more optimistic about arms control, the Soviet Union, the possibility of avoiding serious strife and so on, than the forward strategists are. They put more emphasis on the possibilities of cooperation between the United States and the Soviets, and they are greater adherents of nuclear safety. Indeed, their strategies stress stabilized deterrence, with both sides being invulnerable.

The analysts, however, share with the forward strategists several notions that are keys to deterrence. One might be described as the doctrine of the dirty hands, meaning that international relations cannot be conducted by pristine, overly moralistic methods. It may be necessary to kill. Another is that nations—and nationalism—are more or less here to stay for the foreseeable future. Still another and very important, though often overlooked, point is that nations act according to their own laws, which cannot be compared with those governing individuals. What individuals contribute to state behavior is a lust for power, which can only be restrained by force. But here deterrence philosophy borrows from still another group in the war-peace establishment, the realists.

III

The Realists

WHY ARE NATIONS SO WEDDED TO HOSTILITY THAT THEY THREATEN each other with nuclear arms? Why do they resort to force? Why can't they reason things out as sensible individuals might? In search of answers, I turned next to the realists to see what light they could throw into the dark cave of the cold war. Among the deterrers, only the realists offer a theory of motivation in political and international affairs.

Everybody, of course, considers himself a realist, but the word as used by theologians, philosophers and political scientists (sometimes with a capital R) refers to a specific theory of political behavior. Hans J. Morgenthau, a realist, identifies two schools of thought:

One believes that a rational and moral political order, derived from universally valid abstract principles, can be achieved here and now. It assumes the essential goodness and infinite malleability of human nature, and blames the failure of the social order to measure up to the rational standards on lack of knowledge and understanding, obsolescent social institutions, or the depravity of certain isolated individuals and groups. It trusts in education, reform, and the sporadic use of force to remedy these defects. The other school believes that the world, imperfect as it is from a rational point of view, is the result of forces inherent in human nature. To improve the world one must work with these forces not against them. . . . This theoretical concern with human nature as it actually is, and with the historic processes as they actually take place, has earned for the theory presented here the name of realism.

87

Realism is not specifically a cold war philosophy, and it would have no place in a discussion of the war-peace establishment except that it has provided a basic rationale. The realists, though deterrers, disagree with the forward strategists that there is a Communist monolith ready to gobble us up, and they differ from the analysts in putting much less faith in the stabilizing qualities of high levels of nuclear arms. They take issue, too, with what might be called popular idealism, as exemplified by such notions as "World Peace Through World Trade" (IBM), "Peace Through Understanding" (the New York World's Fair slogan), and "Come let us reason together," Isaiah's Biblical directive which President Johnson is fond of quoting, and to which the realists would answer that if reasoning together were possible most of the problems would be already solved. The realists take exception, as well, to the ideas of the experimental scientists, the moralists and the immediate disarmers. In short, realism is set against what it perceives as pious platitudes, empty hopes, planless programs and meaningless hostility. Realism, writes Gordon Harland, is "a clear recognition of the limits of morality and reason in politics; the acceptance of the fact that political realities are power realities and that power must be countered by power; that self-interest is the primary datum in the actions of all groups and nations."

Realism's two seminal thinkers are the Protestant theologian Reinhold Niebuhr, professor of Christian ethics at the Union Theological Seminary in New York, and Hans J. Morgenthau, political scientist at the University of Chicago, Niebuhr representing realism's religious side, Morgenthau its secular. (The literary output of both has been little short of astounding. Niebuhr has written no less than sixteen books and over a thousand articles, while Morgenthau has accounted for nine books, several of elephantine girth, three more as editor and over two hundred articles, in several languages.) George Kennan, former U.S. Ambassador to Russia and Yugoslavia and author of the post-World War II policy of containment, is a realist, along with dozens of eminent scholars. Realism can also be clearly discerned in the speeches of Senator William J. Fulbright, of Arkansas.

Realism's influence, though, is perhaps more subtle than overt, and its spirit, like Shelley's idea of intellectual beauty, floats unseen among us. "I suppose the thing Niebuhr has done for me more than anyone else [has] is to articulate the irony of our condition as a country in the world today," says James Reston, associate editor of the *New York Times*. Arnold Wolfers' statement about Niebuhr can be applied to realism in general: "None of us working in international relations on the outside can ever hope to be able to prove that a decision maker would have acted differently if he had not heard or read what one of us brought to his attention. But at least in the case of Niebuhr, many prominent men agree that they have been deeply influenced by his thought, and therefore probably influenced in their actions."

Realism, essentially, is a theory of human nature and its effect on politics and international relations. One learns from Niebuhr in such books as *Beyond Tragedy, The Children of Light, The Children of Darkness* and *The Structure of Nations and Empires* that man's troubles cannot be accounted for by poor education (as many liberals think), by a faulty economic structure (as the Communists think), by obsolescent social practices (as many scientists think), by a lack of vision (as the peace people think) or by poor communication (as some scientists think). Niebuhr has been a warrior for progress in education, economic development, communication and so on, but he is opposed to explanations of human failure based on a single cause. To him, reform must be accomplished in full knowledge of what it's pitted against: man's stubborn pride, egotism, will to power, "brute inheritance" and, subsuming all, his Original Sin.

For the secular Morgenthau in *Scientific Man versus Power Politics,* "The intellectual and moral history of mankind is the story of inner insecurity, of the anticipation of impending doom, of metaphysical anxieties. These are rooted in the situation of man as a creature which, being conscious of itself, has lost its animal innocence and security in religious, moral and social worlds of its own." Morgenthau, then, reaches Niebuhr's conclusions without the use of Original Sin; to him, man's fundamental power urge is really his pathetic attempt to govern his environment and make it secure. Both agree with Hobbes that man seeks "power after power until death."

To the realists, then, the individual is engaged in a quest for power of which politics is the tangible embodiment. For Niebuhr, politics is the "pursuit of interest defined as power," and "The struggle for political power is merely an example of the rivalry which goes on at every level of human life." Morgenthau says the same: "Power politics, rooted in the lust for power which is common to all men, is for this reason inseparable from the social life itself." Power politics extends to the relations between states and hence leads to wars, which, Niebuhr says, have their origins in "dark, unconscious sources of the human psyche." Military might, to Niebuhr, is a nation's "fists and arms," for war will be with us permanently: "The man in the street, with his lust for power thwarted by his own limitations and the necessities of his social life, projects his ego upon his nation and indulges his anarchic lusts vicariously." "Even where legal relations hide relations of power," Morgenthau says, "politics is to be understood in terms of violence, actual or potential; and potential violence tends here always to turn into actual warfare." As Kennan put it, "Violence is the tribute we pay to original sin."

Niebuhr, Morgenthau and the other realists are concerned with presenting *what is,* not because they like it or defend it, but because, to them, an appreciation of the realities is a surer ground from which to start than a platform grounded in the air. Niebuhr, for example, was out to galvanize the Christian faith, to rescue it from a sort of pietistic perfectionism which resulted in paralysis, not action, and it's a measure of his success that, according to Dean John C. Bennett of the Union Theological Seminary in New York, Christian realism has brought about "the revival of Protestant theology in our time." For Niebuhr, every intended good act contains the seeds of evil, for we cannot foresee the consequences of what we do. Action, he says, *is* dirty at times, and it may be impossible to be both a good politician and a good Christian. Act, Niebuhr says, and hope for redemption on high, or as Luther said,

"Sin bravely." Niebuhr's prayer is that the wise society will skillfully use man's ineradicable self-love creatively, and, though a perfect society is impossible, man can progress as he learns to surmount his limitations. Man, in short, can transcend himself, for "none of us, no matter how selfish we may be, can be *only* selfish." Man is capable of agape or pity, or radical self-giving, as symbolized by Christ on the cross.

If Niebuhr wants to toughen flabby Christianity, Morgenthau wants to put muscle into liberalism. "The invariable hesitations and vacillations of liberal governments, when faced with a decision implying even the remote danger of war, are due to these inherent traits of liberal philosophy," he writes. Liberalism's fault is that it relies on reason and on panaceas like immediate disarmament and world law in defiance of the realities. As Morgenthau says in *Politics Among Nations,* "There is no shirking the conclusion that in no period of modern history was civilization more in need of permanent peace and, hence, of a world state, and that in no period of modern history were the moral, social, and political conditions of the world less favorable for the establishment of a world state." It will not be found through misguided liberal attempts to overlook the national interest. It must be attained working with the national interest, through a peace-preserving and community-building diplomacy carried on with a concern for human nature as it is and historic processes as they are. Senator Fulbright says much the same: "If there is any absolutely reliable lesson that we can derive from the history of nations, it is that there are limitations to policy, profound limitations which reflect the imperfections of human nature and which cannot be overcome by noble designs and grandiose declarations."

Hardened Realism

It is, of course, impossible to trace social influences directly, but the United States, in moving away from the pacifism, isolationism and moral timidity that characterized us before World War II, has accepted many of the precepts of realism. Some realists, in fact, believe that the philosophical pendulum has swung too far and that today's commonplace realism, in the words of Dean Bennett, has "hardened." What is meant by this is that realism's belief in power and pragmatism has been widely accepted, but without realism's teaching of the need for balance, sympathy and vision. "Americans, unfortunately," says Fulbright,

tend to take a single-factor approach to world politics. Prior to World War II, we thought of international relations too much in moral and legal terms. Since 1945 we have increasingly shifted our thoughts to the terms of military strength and balance-of-power alliances. Actually, a successful foreign policy has many facets—military, political, economic, cultural, moral and ideological. All of these must be used, not independently and consecutively, but interdependently and simultaneously. Realism in world politics consists in knowing how and when to shuffle the various factors in the face of changing dangers and opportunities.

If realism set out to cure American thought of excessive moralism, here, too, the realists feel the mark has been overshot and what has emerged is the idea of force as its own justification. As Dean Bennett writes:

We would be the last to renounce Christian realism of this kind in principle, but it is important to look at some of its applications.

Are there not signs that this Christian realism has given rise to the idea that, since all we do is accompanied by guilt, we need not recognize any moral limits because the same forgiveness covers the guilt involved in the most monstrous deeds, provided these deeds seem to be required by a policy that we have chosen with what is called "responsibility"? The policy can then be defended in terms of what it is designed to protect, either our national security or the free world. But as the cost of the policy in terms of violence increases, we are tempted to apply this promise of forgiveness to the increasing evil rather than to weigh afresh the moral significance of that increasing evil.

This is no argument in favor of a return to that perfectionist legalism. It is only a suggestion that there may be forms of violence that go beyond any moral limits and that, whatever we may do about them, we should avoid rationalizing them in terms of Christian realism.

Realism has always said that power is an inexorable factor in international affairs and must be reckoned with squarely, but here too, some say, the tendency has been to neglect other factors.

"I'm a realist myself," said James King, senior research associate at the Institute of Defense Analysis, on whom I called in Washington, "in the sense that I consider *Realpolitik* an inescapable feature of international relations, though not the whole story by any means. At the same time, I feel the power analysis has been overdone. Military analysts, for instance, have taken the realist assumption lock, stock and barrel and used it as the basis for their conclusions, even though, if pressed, they will agree that it is not an adequate explanation of international affairs. Specifically, even though many of them don't believe it themselves, they insist that our strategy should be formed, and our military plans made, *as if* the Russians will attack the moment a set of conditions can destroy 90 percent of the Strategic Air Command. This is to proceed as though the Soviets were bent on world conquest, like an Alexander. Nobody believes that any more, but the analysts treat it as a conservative and therefore necessary operating assumption. But of course the assumptions we make about the adversary determine our own courses of action and these, in turn, influence the adversary's intentions. The realist assumption, unadorned, therefore, hardly seems the way to get agreements, of the kind we need a lot more than we need additional armaments, with the Soviet Union. The realist assumption, as applied by the analysts, in other words, leads to an unjustified preoccupation with military force. More than that is required for security."

With a heightened stress on national power has come its equation with military force. Niebuhr said to me, "Everybody seems to consider himself a realist, even Barry Goldwater. Realism as a philosophy meant that self-interest could be harnessed in the service of an open society. It is concerned with power, authority and prestige but never advocated the use of military force, per se." He also has said, "If the bomb were ever used, I hope it would kill me, because the moral situation would be something I could not contemplate." (But he adds, as realists do, "At the same time you cannot disavow its use prematurely without bowing yourself out of responsibility for the whole generation.")

The idea that hardened realism has become the servant of military policy is also expressed by Morgenthau, whom I found to be a short, white-haired man ensconced in a Gothic, book-lined office at the University of Chicago. Morgenthau waved his hand and said, "Yes, realism helped lay down the basis for deterrence, in making the use of force acceptable to liberals who were squeamish about using it. But there is no doubt that realist ideas have been taken over by the military. My own ideas have been made to look harder than they are in this context. Force is only one element of national power. Since we live in an anarchic age, violence is the last resort of nations to protect their interests, and I don't find those conclusions changed by the bomb. At the same time, nuclear war is absurd because it can't achieve the changes for which you might wage it. To fight a nuclear war for the Western presence in Berlin is absurd; it is equally absurd for the Soviets to go to war over Cuba. Nuclear weapons are a suicidal absurdity."

Fulbright, I noted, has said much the same:

Without becoming militarist in the sense of committing themselves to the military virtues as standards of personal behavior, the American people have nonetheless come to place great—and, in my opinion, excessive—faith in military solutions to political problems. Many Americans have come to regard our defense establishment as the heart and soul of our foreign policy.

Anti-Communism has always been a fulcrum of realist thought, and it was Niebuhr who summed it up in a famous epigram: "Man's capacity for justice makes democracy possible; but man's inclination to injustice makes democracy necessary." Nonetheless, I wondered if realism's anti-Communism hadn't become hardened, too. Dean Bennett told me, "Niebuhr found in the idea of the balance of terror something that explained the human situation in general. The excesses of Stalinism influenced him enormously, but this aspect of this thinking has been toned down. He would now accept the fact that some of the excesses of Communism may have been due to the tremendous difficulties of organizing societies and that, for some parts of the world, Communism may be capable of transformation. Both Niebuhr and I, of course, would like to help other countries avoid the terrible fate that the Soviet Union experienced under Stalin, but at the same time I believe that we agree that there has been a tendency for realists to overplay the military side of our strategy."

Again, I found an echo in Fulbright, who said, "The master myth of the cold war is that the Communist bloc is a monolith composed of governments which are not really governments at all but organized conspiracies, divided among themselves perhaps but all equally resolute and implacable in their determination to destroy the free world."

Realism's critique of hardened realism, then, is that its own precepts have been warped out of proportion, its notions of selflessness, redemption and balance forgotten. Niebuhr puts this succinctly when he says, "A pessimistic view of human nature in general does not lead to a hard view of the adversary in particular. The realists are usually misrepresented by this logic." How, then, do the realists advise that we proceed?

WHAT THE REALISTS WANT

Realism stresses the national interest as an inescapable quality, the organic instead of ideological relations between states, and the existence of irrational factors like national prestige. ("You're dealing with Russian realists, too," King said, "who won't respect you unless *you* have strength.") Nations, in this view, do not follow the ideal logic one might expect of good individuals, for a nation must at all times protect itself, and its relations with other states are likely to be competitive and hostile. It follows that realists, while approving of such measures as international scientific conferences, cultural exchanges, trade and so forth with the Communist nations, do not put excessive faith in them as a means of alleviating the cold war.

The realists, like other deterrers, accept the intractability of national power and with it the fists and arms of military might. For this reason, it might be expected that they have little trust in general and complete disarmament, and, indeed, says Senator Fulbright,

The discussion of "general and complete disarmament" is, in my opinion, an exercise in cold war fantasy, a manifestation of the deception and pretense of the new diplomacy. In a world profoundly divided by ideological conflict and national rivalries—conditions which are almost certain to prevail for the foreseeable future—it is inconceivable that the world's foremost antagonists could suddenly and miraculously dispel their animosities and vest in each other the profound trust and confidence which "general and complete disarmament" would require.

The realists are deterrers, in that they believe that power must be faced with power, that nations, which are naturally aggressive, must have their swords confronted by the shields of others. In particular, it is the Soviet Union that must be deterred, not because it is a Communist state but because of its imperialism. "It is not Communism which is at issue between the Soviet Union and the West but Communist *imperialism*," Fulbright says, "and . . . insofar as it renounces expansionist and subversive ambitions, the Soviet Union can enjoy a safe and honorable national life without threat or danger from the West." The point to be noted here is that Fulbright believes that the Soviet Union is capable of acting as a "normal" state even though a Communist one instead of as an ideological entity in its foreign policy. Strausz-Hupé and Teller would disagree rather violently with this view, saying that a Communist state is by nature an imperialist state. For this reason they demand their Catonic policy.

Believing as they do in normalized hostility between states, the realists would favor normal deterrence—that is, the kind of deterrence states might ordinarily exercise against other states. This view, along with a sort of gutlike dislike for both nuclear weapons and the emphasis on modern military strategy, leads them to favor a decreased reliance on nuclear arms. It is noticeable, for instance, in Fulbright's speeches that while he makes passing references to the need for strong American military force he moves immediately to call for demythification of our foreign policy or a discussion of the adverse effect the cold war has had on American life. Morgenthau says explicitly that he is a minimum deterrer. "By minimum deterrent," says Marshall D. Shulman, professor of international politics at the Fletcher School of Law and Diplomacy and author of *Stalin's Foreign Policy Reappraised,* who may be loosely classified as a realist, "is meant a military policy which would enhance U.S. security, since it would not encourage the other side to add more weapons himself, which would then have the effect of lowering our security. The level of military force required can't be described with precision because of changing military technology and because the deterrent is at best a subjective matter."

The realists, then, postulate both continued hostility in the world and the need for less reliance on purely military force, a capsule that is evidently difficult for many people to swallow. Shulman describes the complexities of this position: "The simple polarities, the simple linear scale usually used to describe U.S.–Soviet relations, is a disservice. The important thing is to encourage a more differentiated view. I believe that the character of our relationship with the Soviet Union is a limited adversary one, involving conflict of a fundamental sort but which, at the same time, is not contradictory with the overlapping of elements of mutual interest. I believe the conflict is likely to continue for the foreseeable future, and if you cannot transform the situation radically, at least you can reduce the hazards of general war." He adds, "The essence of the realist position, I think, is its recognition that power is the essential backdrop of politics, but military power, especially nuclear, has its limitations, although it is essential in some measure. 'Power' must be a broad enough conception to include not only such other attributes as economic capability, but also others less tangible, such as the effectiveness and élan of a society, and the attractiveness and applicability of its dominant ideas."

Hans Morgenthau has been a stout propagandist against nuclear arms and their dangers, but he has bewildered some by appearing to oppose "peace":

The next to the latest euphoric interval occurred in 1959 in the aftermath of Mr. Khrushchev's visit to the United States; its symbol was the "spirit of Camp David." At that time I assumed . . . the thankless task of contrasting the illusory character of that "relaxation of tensions" with the inescapable realities of the cold war. Today [Morgenthau wrote in 1964] we are living in another such interval and the task must be performed again. It is, indeed, even more urgent today than it was in 1959 because then our illusion was primarily intellectual and had no great political consequences, whereas today that same illusion is reflected in policies advantageous to the enemy. Responsible people are even talking about "replacing" the cold war with the war against poverty, as though the cold war had already come to an end.

Morgenthau is not opposed to the "hot line" to Moscow, the limited test-ban treaty and other "peaceful" developments. He does want the U.S. to recognize its national interests and to use what levers we have, such as trade in wheat and other commodities, to obtain Soviet concessions and thus move, even though slowly, through diplomacy toward true peace instead of pretending that we have peace, doing nothing, and perhaps taking a step toward defeat and even war as a consequence.

The realists, then, are opposed to violent flip-flops in American policy, vacillating between threats of nuclear war and wild genuflections to peace when there is nothing of the kind in prospect, they say. The answer, to them, is in diplomacy, diplomacy of a traditional kind, steady, creative, with its sights clearly set. The purpose of foreign policy, Fulbright says,

is the very gradual improvement of human life on earth. Our success is not guaranteed and if our efforts are to be coherent and sustained, we must accept this fact with sobriety and serenity. Besides patient and continuous effort we must bring to the task a little of a sense of mission—and I emphasize little. A consuming messianism will surely lead us to false hopes and frustrations, while action without purpose is action without meaning or hope. But a little of a sense of mission can guide us—unencumbered by either extravagant hopes or unwarranted despair—toward worthy and attainable objectives. These are not easy counsels. But they are, I think, counsels of reality.

Those I have included among the realists are far from monolithic in their attitudes. Morgenthau, for instance, criticizes George Kennan for imagining that what Kennan calls "polycentrism"—the belief that the Communist world is breaking up into many centers of power—means a thaw in the cold war. Niebuhr, whose ideas on military policy are not distinct, appears to accept a higher level of stable deterrence than Morgenthau does. Shulman, whose realism lies more in his desire for a balanced view of U.S.–Soviet relations than in any explicit theories of human nature, sees the Soviet ideological threat as somewhat stronger than Fulbright does, and, as for Fulbright, he is clearly a realist in some contexts but not in others, as, for instance, his faith in trade as a meaningful factor in lessening international tensions.

Nonetheless, the realists do agree on key points: that the U.S. and the Soviet Union can reach some accommodations without a change in the form of government of either; that American policy is immersed in myths, a chief one being overreliance on an enormous military establishment and force; that American policy must not be rigid, as many realists suspect it is in such places as Berlin, Vietnam and Cuba. Though pessimistic about human nature and the nature of states, the realists have their transcendental "escape hatch," their hope that history will defeat their expectations. "In the long run, I'm in favor of a radical change in the structure of international relations," Morgenthau says. "World government is appropriate for the technological conditions under which we live."

IV

The Government Idealists

THE CROSSROADS OF AMERICAN COLD WAR THOUGHT IS THE GOVernment of the United States. The ideas looked at so far are not mutually exclusive, but each has its partisans in Washington: forward strategists who foresee a blistering battle of ideologies and want weapons to go with it, analysts who deal in questions of stability and the balance of military strength, realists whose concern is power and the national interest. Washington, too, feels the influence of those critics of deterrence from the camps of experimentalism and the peace movement. Finally, into this ideological potpourri must be put American hopes, misguided or not, for freedom and even democracy around the world. The mix that emerges in Washington may be called Government Idealism.

It is by no means pure idealism, being thoroughly conditioned by the exigencies of government and the realities of life, and there are those who deny that the results can be called idealism at all. Part of the problem of attempting to assay the thinking of the government is the way it works as viewed by the information-seeker from the outside, and it may be useful here to sketch some of the hazards confronting the earnest citizen who comes to Washington seeking a clear picture of his government's policy on cold war and peace.

One of the myths about Washington is that it's a small-town kind of place, taking its character from the sloe gin and magnolias of the South, and, to judge by mile on mile of ponderous, sleepy government architecture, the wide boulevards on which traffic moves virtually unimpeded except in the worst of the rush hours, or the horrible tie-ups that occur after a light snow for which New York or Chicago would barely break out galoshes, one is inclined to agree. But, like all myths, this one is useful only up to a point. For Washington is an introvert, and lives and suffers in private. One of its doctors has described the "Washington syndrome" as a chronic inflammation of ambition coupled with insecurity, resulting in chest pains, migraine headaches and ulcers, with severe flare-ups occurring at election time. What strikes the visitor as he moves around electrically nervous government corridors is that Washington is an enormously powerful, big-time sort of place.

The reason for this, of course, is the size of the federal budget, nearly $100 billion, but not so obvious to many people is on what the money is spent. Another myth, especially beloved by conservatives, is that the government spends its money on unneeded domestic social services. The truth, according to Congressman Morris K. Udall of Arizona, is that in 1939 forty-four cents of every budget dollar was used for labor, health, education and other welfare programs, while in 1963 the figure came to seven cents. In 1939 government welfare programs came to $30 per capita, but in 1963 the figure was $16. According to Senator George McGovern of North Dakota, the United States military budget in 1963 was higher than the combined cost of *all* social welfare programs from 1933 to 1940 combined.

The big money in Washington goes into foreign affairs. If one puts under this heading not only the work of the State Department, foreign aid, foreign loans and the like, but also the cost of the military establishment, past (interest on the national debt, veterans' payments and so on) and present, then perhaps two-thirds (or even more) of the federal budget goes into foreign relations broadly considered. "Indeed, today," said a Senate Subcommittee on National Policy Machinery in 1961, "almost every department of our government, and some eighteen independent agencies, are involved with national security policy. Four government agencies and six international financial organizations work in the field of foreign economic aid alone." Even the space budget—the twenty billion dollars allotted to put a man on the moon, spread over a ten-year period, amounts to five and one half million dollars a day—comes partly under the rubric of foreign relations, since it is designed to raise American prestige abroad.

With the big federal money, power has come to Washington as never before and with it unparalleled responsibilities. It has often seemed to information-seekers from the outside that high-ranking government officials are running independent duchies, withholding or dispensing their favors as they see fit. While some are doubtless guilty of arrogance, it must also be said that government officials are almost unbelievably busy and harassed. Superiors—and all government officials except the President have superiors—are constantly calling the *ad hoc* committee meetings which are Washington's style of business and which constitute the principal reason why Washington officials continually break appointments. "If you want to see anybody in Defense or State or any other department I know of, they seem to be perpetually off in committee meetings," said Ambassador David Bruce. "In government," said a leading official, "the position you are always in is the 'now' position."

Washington, then, flourishes in an atmosphere of peptic crisis which serves to give off a faintly alarmist quality. It also makes life difficult for the information-seeker from the outside attempting to get a grasp on his government's ideas. The harried government official has little time for explanations. If time is a barrier, so is what might be called bureaucratic secrecy, the desire of officials to protect both themselves and their freedom of action from a press whose search for news is such that even a single ill-chosen word may make a headline. Officials, indeed, must worry about what the public, the political opposition, the Allies and the Communists will say. All this produces, on the part of our public servants, an extraordinary diplomacy and tact conducive to platitudes. It also leads to the practice of talking for "background" only, a "ground rule" requiring that statements not be attributed to their source. This habit, in turn, leads to the unhappy journalistic device of attributing quotes to an anonymous person, with the result not only of making statements suspect (who is to say that the reporter hasn't made them up?), but also of giving government a flavorless cast, as though policies were made by computers and not by specific men.

Another difficulty for the outsider is the secrecy imposed in the name of national security. To look at government files, with their mushroom-shaped cardboard slips inserted in the top drawers and reading "Open" or "Closed," one might think that everything in Washington is classified. Consider, for instance, the following illuminating exchange before a Senate committee between Barry Goldwater and Secretary of Defense Robert S. McNamara on military procurement.

SENATOR GOLDWATER: I am just wondering why we were not told about it. We have to pick things up in the papers. Now, you have all through your testimony yesterday, beginning on page 35 and going to pages 36, 37, down to 38 (deleted).
SECRETARY MCNAMARA: (Deleted.)
SENATOR GOLDWATER: (Deleted.)
SECRETARY MCNAMARA: (Deleted.)
SENATOR GOLDWATER: (Deleted.)
SECRETARY MCNAMARA: (Deleted.)
SENATOR GOLDWATER: (Deleted.)
SECRETARY MCNAMARA: (Deleted.)
SENATOR GOLDWATER: (Deleted.)
SECRETARY MCNAMARA: (Deleted.)
SENATOR GOLDWATER: (Deleted.)
SECRETARY MCNAMARA: (Deleted.)
SENATOR GOLDWATER: I think this is the weakest part of your argument thus far. . . .

"The public record," says Dan Ellsberg of the RAND Corporation, who has made a study of national security, "is far from complete for either the present or the past. There are large systematic areas that are simply not available." The extent of secrecy sometimes amuses government officials themselves. "How does one know," said a former top-ranking White House aide—not for attribution—"if you've got all the clearances, if there isn't still another level that even *you* don't know about?"

But it must be said, too, that the government has devised a

security system of a quite different and even better kind. If much material is classified, there is still so much that is not classified that it is virtually impossible either to go through it or to decide what is important and what is not. In a sense, the United States must kill the Soviet CIA with kindness. Nor are the classification lines hard and fast. One has in Washington the faintly bizarre experience of being flatly told in one office that a subject is entirely classified and can under no circumstances be discussed, only to find, an hour later in a different office, a government official happily telling all. A lot, it seems, depends on the personal judgment of various officials as to what ought to be told.

Some officials, indeed, are bold enough to make their own peremptory declassifications. Judging only from what is revealed in their stories it is apparent that many reporters have been given access to classified material.

One State Department official observes that papers are sometimes marked "Top Secret" with the intent of making people read them. "In our office," he said, "it's happened that people mimeograph an editorial from the *New York Times*, stamp it 'Secret,' leaving off the reference to the *Times*, and circulate it to see the reaction. The others are wildly impressed with the boldness of the new 'policy directive.'"

A reasonable conclusion is that one can learn a great deal in Washington but that one must talk a great deal to a great many people to do so. And the outsider must keep in mind the admonition of Professor Harold K. Jacobson, who says, "When those of us outside the government attempt to appraise current policies, we suffer a number of quite severe limitations. Our information is never as current as those in policy-making positions. Nor do we fully see and understand all of the complexities that plague those who have to make decisions."

THE DEPARTMENT OF DETERRENCE

In no sense, of course, is Washington merely a passive receiver of ideas, for it also generates them and makes them explicit in action, and the government specialists on war and peace are members par excellence of the war-peace establishment. At the Department of Defense, or DOD, as it's called, the specialists are proud of what has been accomplished since 1960 in shaping the enormity of Defense into a coherent whole. "Hell," said a DOD official, "there's fifty-two billion a year in this and it's hard to get a grip on. But there is more of a sense of rationality than there has been in the last ten years."

The rationality DOD officials speak of means, to them, that the strategies they espouse are at least in rough correspondence with the weapons purchased to effect them. These strategies have a bearing not only on the military forces but on other policies, such as the diplomacy permissible in the Cuban missile crisis, the economy of such defense industry centers as Southern California, our relationship with our Allies and the stated long-term American goal of "general and complete disarmament."

Three strategies (with variations) are available. The first has been called Air Force counterforce, which may be summed up as the idea that the best deterrence is a visibly overwhelming offense, including an expanded bomber program and, in all probability, weapons in space. Air Force counterforce rests on the threat of an American first strike, and its concern is to save American lives through the early destruction of enemy offensive power. Strategists of this persuasion often believe that the U.S. ought to have a striking force that would permit us to disarm the Soviet Union, so that their retaliatory striking force would be relatively harmless.

At the opposite extreme of policies that have received active consideration at the DOD is "minimum" or pure deterrence, meaning the ability with a comparatively small number of missiles to cause "unacceptable damage" to an enemy's civilian population in retaliation to an attack. The American missiles would be presumably invulnerable to attack. "I know of no responsible official within the department who would support [a cities-only strategy]," Secretary McNamara has said. "To serve as a maximum deterrent to nuclear war, our Strategic Retaliatory Forces must be visibly capable of fully destroying the Soviet society under all conditions of retaliation."

But there is also a variation of minimum deterrence known as finite deterrence and which can be described as minimum deterrence the way an expert would lay it out, that is, with a certain built-in flexibility of response, and this seems to be the strategy suggested by former Deputy Secretary of Defense Roswell Gilpatric, in the magazine *Foreign Affairs,* as a possibility for American defense in the 1970's. Minimum-finite deterrence implies nuclear parity; that is, neither side would seek an offensive advantage over the other.

The third strategy can be described as an intermediate one. It rejects Air Force counterforce as encouraging a comparable Soviet rise in armaments, with no net gain for the United States. (Air Force counterforce would also be more expensive since it would also require an invulnerable second-strike capability.) This middle strategy calls for a "damage-limiting" capability, meaning that the American defenses would ride out a Soviet attack and then retaliate on enemy offensive capability so as to limit further damage to the United States. "Such a strategy," said McNamara in 1964 about the damage-limiting one, "requires a force considerably larger than would be needed for a limited 'cities only' strategy. While there are some differences of judgment on just how large such a force should be, there is general agreement that it should be large enough to assure the destruction, singly or in combination, of the Soviet Union, Communist China, and the Communist satellites as national societies, under the worst possible circumstances of war outbreak that can reasonably be postulated, and, in addition, destroy their war-making capability so as to limit, to the extent practicable, damage to this country and to our Allies."

Officials at the Department of Deterrence, as it might be called, insist that the outsider cannot make too much sense out of American military strategy without the "numbers," the "numbers" being a DOD euphemism for "facts," about the size, reliability, accuracy, targeting and so forth of both the American and Soviet missile forces. Nonetheless, the DOD itself has contributed to the fuzziness of the debate, for such is the flexibility of the American plan that it can be presented in various guises, as "softer" or "harder," depending on the audience. "We would explain it with a different emphasis to, say, Barry Goldwater than to other people," said a Defense official. Indeed, if the above statement by Secretary McNamara is read closely, it is apparent that it is subject to various interpretations. Although "the destruction, singly or in combination, of the Soviet Union, Communist China and the Communist satellites as national societies" sounds bloody, it could still be the "softer" strategy of the finite deterrent, if the damage-limiting capability was small.

These strategies are usually used in reference to deterring a "Central War" between the Soviet Union and the United States, but they are also available for the defense of Europe under the strategy of escalation. William Kaufmann, in his book, *The McNamara Strategy*, says, "McNamara never subscribed explicitly to the strategy of escalation. Rather he talked around and about it." In the event of a Communist attack with conventional arms, the idea would be to use conventional weapons in return. Should this fail, the United States would escalate the conflict, using battlefield nuclear arms. The most desired result would be for the enemy to be convinced of American purpose and withdraw; the worst result would be for the enemy to go straight to a full-scale strategic attack, even in the face of almost certain self-destruction. If he should retaliate with battlefield nuclear arms, the United States would respond with long-range tactical nuclear arms, striking his centers of supply. If this action precipitated a like response, the United States would begin a nuclear strategic bombardment of Soviet military forces inside the Soviet Union, and, should the Soviet Union retaliate to this too, the destruction of Soviet society would commence. Damage to the United States would be limited because the United States would be able to destroy much of the Soviet missile force.

This thermonuclear minuet is not really expected to occur with such planned precision. It's much closer to a garage mechanic checking off lubrication points on a printed chart, so that all areas of the car are covered. To the DOD, the object is to plan for all contingencies, to attempt to save lives under any possible conditions, and to try to stop a war before it reaches the level of destroying cities. To critics, the trouble with the plan is that, because of the numbers and varieties of weapons required, disarmament becomes extremely difficult if the escalation ladder is to be maintained as the level of weapons goes down.

If the Soviet Union struck first at the United States, damage would also be limited because the Soviet Union might not throw all its strength in the air at the same time. "It's important to realize a lot of targets remain for a second strike," a DOD consultant told me. "For instance, some of the Soviet missiles might not work. They would have to be repaired. Similarly, there may be mechanical problems with his bombers. Also, his bombers might return and reload. Some of his launchers may have a reload capacity, or he may use the same guidance system for several missiles. He may have in mind fighting a controlled nuclear war and may not deliver all his missiles at once. We are dealing with many uncertainties, and we must make a variety of assumptions. We have a pretty respectable damage-limiting capacity under certain conditions. Though losses to the U.S. in a thermonuclear war would be staggeringly large, they would be worse if we didn't have that capacity. Our damage-limiting capability could make the difference between fifty and a hundred million casualties. This is worth looking at."

Still a third set of conditions remains to be satisfied: a first strike upon the Soviet Union by the United States. The U.S. maintains a set of some forty-five intelligence indicators—of troop movements, activity at missile sites and so forth—which are meant to provide a gauge of Soviet intentions. If these indicators showed that the Soviet Union was about to strike, would the United States really ride out the blow? Officially, the United States says yes, but there are many signs—among them the statement by President Kennedy, "In some cases we might have to take the initiative" in thermonuclear war—that under certain conditions the United States would feel compelled to strike first with nuclear arms.

"Deterrence," a DOD official says, "has turned out to be a lot more difficult and complex than people thought."

The difficult debates over deterrence that go on at the Department of Defense are well illustrated by the one over the antiballistic missile on which the U.S. spends one-half billion dollars annually in research and whose fate comes up for review every year. Edward Teller and the forward strategists are ABM proponents. (To Teller, the perfection of the ABM requires atmospheric testing, which is the main reason he gave for opposing the test ban. Many government officials declared it could be adequately researched underground.) Others fear that, though meant for defense, the ABM will cause a new spiral of arms.

An ABM system, it's generally assumed, would consist of large missiles capable of shooting down incoming missiles, having distinguished them from decoys. It has been estimated that an ABM would cost, along with the radar to go with it, between a half and one billion dollars per city protected. It raises the issue of *which* cities would be thus guarded, and the answer is only the largest and most important ones, the theory being that these would be the likely targets for blackmail or attack. (It might be noted that the United States has a more serious problem in urban defense than its opponents, being far more highly urbanized.)

The strategic developments in our age have always come in chains, and this one is no exception. The ABM is designed to protect against Soviet attack and to discourage other nations from becoming nuclear powers (called the "N^{th} country" problem), on the grounds that the U.S. already has its safeguards ready. It might well make possible a far smaller American missile force because, if cities were adequately protected, the demand for a "damage-limiting capability" might be less. But the results might be the opposite, too. The ABM requires an extensive fallout shelter program because, in the complicated chess of the nuclear age, an enemy might choose to destroy by fallout rather than blast, courtesy of the prevailing westerly wind generally found in the United States. He could shoot his missiles beyond a city and count on the wind to bring the fallout back. The ABM, it is considered, has its maximum accuracy at short range, and if an incoming missile must be destroyed close to the ground, the likelihood is of both radiation dangers to the protected cities (requiring, again, fallout shelters) and damage from blast from either the nuclear-tipped ABM or the exploded enemy missile. This means elaborate blast shelters for ABM-protected cities.

Such a program could stimulate a Soviet response in the form of either an ABM of its own or a doubled or tripled missile force, on the theory that if the attack was big enough the ABMs couldn't stop it. The strengthening of the Soviet missile force might necessitate a strengthening of ours, to counteract it. A Soviet ABM might require larger missiles by the United States, and so a new arms race would begin. These are the reasons usually advanced for not building the ABM. On the other hand, a missile freeze might actually stimulate the ABM. As Clark C. Abt of the Raytheon Company writes:

The freezing of the number and characteristics of strategic offense and defense vehicles recently proposed for study by President Johnson's message to the Geneva disarmament conference is likely to encounter increasing pressure for procurement of anti-ballistic missile defense systems and their penetration aid countermeasures. There will be increased technological pressure due to advances in feasibility. There will be increased political-military pressure due to the increasing N^{th} country ballistic missile threat. Thus the proposed freeze and numbers and characteristics of offense and defense vehicles could come too late to avert a technological arms race between active anti-ballistic missile defense and penetration aids against such defenses. Such a race could destabilize the strategic balance by placing in doubt Soviet and/or U.S. strategic deterrent force effectiveness. It could also motivate the use of larger yield ICBM and MRBM warheads detonated at higher altitudes, as a way of evading the more effective decoy sorting at lower altitudes.

Such are the difficult issues at the Department of Defense. In making the decisions about deterrence—and all such discussions are governed by the principle of controlling an enemy "through fear," which means that war is to be averted by the enemy's regard for the consequences—the DOD is guided by several principles. One of them is that of uncertainty, and here the DOD takes a page from the book of realism. As Hans Morgenthau wrote:

The uncertainty of all power calculations not only makes the balance of power incapable of all practical application but leads also to its very negation in practice. Since no nation can be sure that its calculation of the distribution of power at any particular moment in its history is correct, it must at least make sure that, whatever errors it may commit, they will not put the nation at a disadvantage in the contest for power. In other words, the nation must try to have at least a margin of safety which will allow it to make erroneous calculations and still maintain the balance of power. To that effect all nations actively engaged in the struggle for power must actually aim not at a balance—that is, equality—of power, but at superiority of power in its own behalf. And since no nation can foresee how large its miscalculation will turn out to be, all nations must ultimately seek the maximum of power obtainable under the circumstances.

Maximum, or near-maximum, power is, to the DOD, entirely consistent with safety, under deterrence doctrine that force (especially nuclear force) is there for the express purpose of not having to use it. Accidental war would defeat deterrence, and the DOD has placed great stress on safety through many unilateral measures of arms control, such as the Permissive Action Link, barriers on runways used by nuclear-arms-bearing aircraft to prevent unauthorized take-off, deliberately difficult methods of activating nuclear weapons and so forth, all designed to prevent the sort of war envisioned in *Dr. Strangelove* and *Fail-Safe*. What might be called escalation by accident has also preoccupied DOD officials, who reflect deeply upon World War I, as presented in *The Guns of August,* as a sample of how a major conflict can begin beyond the will of the participants. DOD strategies lean heavily on ideas of stopping or reversing conflicts already begun. For this reason they try to preserve what Dr. Alain C. Enthoven, a Deputy Assistant Secretary of Defense, has called the "firebreak" between conventional and nuclear weapons.

"One of the great issues at the department over the last four years has been conventional forces," Enthoven says. "Some oppose the limited war build-up on the grounds that limited war capability subtracts from the deterrent, but I'm in favor of strong conventional forces so that we will not be forced to be the first to use nuclears. I've also emphasized the 'firebreak' between nuclear and conventional war: if you can contain a conflict by nonnuclear means, you may avoid a nuclear war. But it's very hard to judge the strength of your conventional forces in relation to the enemy's. I suppose that's one of the main reasons we haven't considered a doctrine of 'no first use' of nuclear weapons."

The DOD's emphasis on conventional warfare, plus its idea of controlled counterforce which requires an extremely tight chain of command, has led it, doctrinally, into clashes with those among our Allies who want nuclear weapons for themselves. The DOD's constant call for more divisions for NATO, if achieved, says Lawrence C. McQuade, "would enable NATO to respond appropriately and effectively to a wide spectrum of possible conflicts without being precipitately forced to choose between physical ruin through escalation or political ruin through accommodation. It would not *require* us to rely solely on nonnuclear or nuclear response but *allow* us to choose a course in the light of actual events."

Enthoven has also made visible the DOD's undoubted concern with the morality of its strategy. Before the Loyola University Forum for National Affairs, at Los Angeles, Enthoven said:

According to traditional Christian doctrine, the use of force to repress evil can be justifiable under certain conditions including the following: First, the use of force must have a reasonable chance of success. Second, if successful, it must offer a better situation than the one that would prevail in the absence of the use of force. Third, the force that is used must be proportional to the objectives being sought (or the evil being repressed). For this to be satisfied, peaceful means of redress must have failed. Fourth, the force must be used with the intention of sparing noncombatants and with a reasonable prospect of actually doing so.

It is interesting to observe that the potentially catastrophic character of thermonuclear war has forced practical decision makers, reasoning in a secular context, to adopt a set of criteria very much like those of the traditional Christian doctrine and to apply them to the design of the military posture of the United States.

. . . our defense posture is being designed to make war less likely and less destructive. I am not suggesting that we can make war and violence desirable. The question is whether we have a better alternative.

Tonight, I have defended our policies on the grounds that they make sense. Can they also be defended on the grounds that they are moral? Viewed with perspective, the two should be the same.

DIVISION OF DISARMAMENT

"The State Department, the Defense Department and the Joint Chiefs of Staff are three of the agencies with the heaviest responsibilities for carrying out our over-all security policy as defined by the President and Congress, and they must work together closely," says Paul H. Nitze. "Obviously, national security policy transcends the responsibilities of any one of these agencies or, indeed, of the three together. It cannot be narrowly looked at as 'foreign policy' or 'defense policy,' but must blend political, economic, military, psychological, scientific, cultural and other factors into a single cohesive national policy."

A noticeable omission from this list is an organization known as the United States Arms Control and Disarmament Agency, whose functions are probably less known to the average citizen than the CIA's. Originally, the ACDA was the idea of scientists attached to the Democratic Advisory Council's Committee on Science and Technology, and the first plans for it were laid out on the kitchen table of the geologist Harrison Brown in Pasadena, California. According to Brown, it was to be called the Peace Agency and, with a budget of a half-billion dollars a year, it was not only to have an elaborate program for peace research, as a sort of RAND-in-reverse, but also to intervene at almost every level of cold war policy-making to present the arms control–disarmament side of things. Some thought the ACDA should operate out of the White House as an executive arm of the President. It was, at least, to play a sort of adversary role to the DOD, to be, as former Deputy Secretary of Defense Roswell L. Gilpatric put it, "a countervailing force" to military influence, under the same checks-and-balances theory that operates throughout our government.

As it has emerged in practice ACDA has fallen short of being a countervailing force. It has, it explained in 1964, "the responsibility for the development of ideas and the proposing of recommendations to the President," but its role has not been easy. Its budget is small—six million dollars, on the order of 1/7000 of that of the Department of Defense. Officials have been frankly concerned lest it become a government-in-exile for the peace movement. It would be deplorable, said Robert A. Lovett, former Secretary of Defense, if the ACDA turned into "a Mecca for a wide variety of screwballs. It would be a great pity to have this launched and then become a sort of 'bureau of beatniks.' " Congress has never been enthusiastic. It refused to accept President Kennedy's suggested nomenclature for a Peace and Disarmament Agency and put a statutory limitation of ten million dollars on the organization.

Another fear was that ACDA would come to dominate the military. General Lyman Lemnitzer, testifying before the House Armed Services Committee in 1961, said, "The Joint Chiefs of Staff, in considering the draft legislation, did question the procedures which would be used in transmitting the recommendations of the Agency to the President, and wanted to assure ourselves that the Joint Chiefs of Staff would have an opportunity to study those recommendations and express opinion on them, much as we do on any other matters pertaining to the national security. . . . More specifically, we questioned whether the recommendations of the Agency would reach the President through the National Security Council, where Defense Department and Joint Chiefs of Staff have an opportunity to express their views."

Suspicious Congressmen and soldiers were no doubt reassured by the choice of William C. Foster, a Republican, as the Agency's first director. Far from being a unilateral disarmer, Foster advocated, in the *General Electric Quarterly* in 1958, increasing arms spending by the U.S. from 10 to 20 percent of our gross national product as a means of forcing increased arms expenditures by the Soviet Union, to deprive the Soviet people of "one-third of the already sparse good things of life they have" and hasten the downfall of the Soviet system. Foster also said, however, ". . . we talk of cold war and hot war. I prefer to talk about peace-fare instead of warfare. To accomplish our objectives a true peace-fare should be waged . . . and then the objectives can develop." And whatever lingering doubts he had seemed to have vanished in his new job. "He changed," said a former ACDA official, "from an interested to a committed person in the field of arms control and disarmament." Foster was meant to implant in Congress the confidence that ACDA was not run by wild-eyed peaceniks. Nonetheless, ACDA's troubles with Congress have continued. There has been intense opposition from a salient part of Congress. An effort against the Agency has originated primarily in the South and the West, claiming the ACDA is trying to give away the military force of the U.S. This effort may have more money behind it than the ACDA itself does. Some Congressmen have said that they get more mail on this subject than on anything else.

ACDA has its internal problems, too. It has been described as "the home of frustration" because of the amount of time spent on jurisdictional squabbling with other parts of the government, and on red tape. Turnover among ACDA's professional staff of 126 is high, one reason being that many ACDAers are on temporary assignment from other government agencies. Many of these recruits, even though they may work at ACDA as department heads, have little or no experience in the political, military or economic problems of arms control–disarmament. The ACDA, in short, has not been as strong as many people hoped.

The officials at ACDA recognize its problems and would like it to play a larger role. Some, in fact, believe that the ACDA ought to be represented in all foreign policy deliberations, so that arms control–disarmament implications would always be made apparent. "The trouble with ACDA is that it's limited itself to Geneva-type negotiations," said one ACDAer. "We ought to get in many other areas and have a voice in policy as a whole."

What sort of policy would ACDA advocate as a full-fledged counselor? GCD, for one, is not taken seriously here, the differences between the U.S. and the U.S.S.R. being simply too great. It's generally thought that while the U.S. is willing to stick by disarmament proposals it has made, the official American version of GCD is meant to counter the Soviet GCD scheme, which is regarded as propaganda. Officially, ACDA believes in staged disarmament, with inspection.

Although they will not say so in public, some ACDAers will tell you that they are not convinced about several aspects of U.S. military and disarmament policy. One of them is the need to maintain strong U.S. nuclear superiority through the strategy of counterforce. Another series of doubts centers around inspection. No one at ACDA would say that inspection was unnecessary, but some feel that substantial negotiated arms cuts could be made with only very limited inspection. Their theory is that violations, if any, by the Soviet Union would not endanger U.S. security, based as it is on invulnerable missile forces. Indeed, some who favor inspection for any, or most, possible agreements want it not so much from a national security point of view but to provide precedents for inspection when it is needed, as the U.S. and the U.S.S.R. approach more general disarmament.

Inspection is studied by the ACDA as part of what appears to be one of its two basic functions, the collection and examination of ideas for arms control and peace. Some of this work is "in house," but ACDA also spends four million dollars on contract research, much of it with the same study groups, like the Hudson Institute, which cerebrate for the Department of Defense. "Many of the signal ideas came from ACDA," Foster says, "like the nuclear freeze and the test ban." The ACDA has also managed to develop its own cadre of young, entirely dedicated, scientific specialists in arms control and disarmament. They may well be the first disarmament professionals in the history of the world.

The other important duty of ACDA is representing the U.S. at the face-to-face negotiations with the Soviet Union. Many ACDAers and other government people, too, believe that the Soviets are naïve on the problems. "Invariably," said a government official, "it's up to us to take the initiative. Four or five years ago in Washington you found almost no interest in the government on this problem and had to go outside for expertise. Now we have many very serious and informed people in the government. Only recently have the Soviets showed any sophistication at all, and their fear of inspection is still very profound."

The American view is that, given the ramifications and complexities of the disarmament problem, a high degree of both political and scientific knowledge is required for meaningful arms reduction, no matter what particular scheme is adopted. The Russians, according to ACDA, have stuck to sweeping disarmament proposals that fail to take into account the subtle strategic realities. The Soviet plan for disarmament calls, in the first stage, for the elimination of most strategic delivery vehicles and all foreign military bases, and the ACDA's contention is that it would leave the United States and its Allies in a strategically vulnerable situation.

But if the Soviet proposal does not seem to take in the political and military requirements as the U.S. sees them, neither do the American proposals always seem to show understanding of the Soviets. A central American concept, for instance, is that progress in establishing a UN peace-keeping force is a necessary feature to progress in disarmament. The United States proposal for a treaty, submitted in 1961 to the Eighteen Nations Committee of the UN, calls for, in Stage I:

Conclusions of an agreement for the establishment of a United Nations Peace Force in Stage II, including definitions of the purpose, mission, composition and strength, disposition, command and control, training logistical support, financing, equipment and armaments;

and in Stage III:

The Parties to the Treaty would progressively strengthen the United Nations Peace Force established in Stage II until it had sufficient armed forces and armaments so that no state could challenge it.

"To an outside observer," says Dr. Harold K. Jacobson, "at times this concept seemed to be the most essential and prominent feature of the American position." The American plan appears to resemble that for the UN police force that operated in the Congo. Jacobson says,

The USSR is now being told that it must contribute to [the UN Congo force] financially. It is being asked to pay for the UN operations in the Congo which have as one of their principal consequences blocked Soviet influence in the Congo. Is UNOC to be the model for the future United Nations Police Force? If it is, it seems to be that the United States is either proposing something the Soviet Union is bound to reject or is assuming that the conflict between the United States and the Soviet Union will so diminish that it is inconceivable that the interests of the two would clash if any future crises like that which arose in the Congo.

Jacobson is not blaming the United States for the failure of Soviet-American negotiations, but he is saying that the U.S. has not clarified its long-range thinking.

The United States Senate, furthermore, passed the Connolly Amendment restricting U.S. participation in the World Court, whereas the U.S. plan says that in Stage II of disarmament states must accept the compulsory jurisdiction of the International Court of Justice. American statesmen have often said that the United States desires a pluralistic world, one of diversity, and thus a world of sovereign nations. "It is somewhat difficult to square this image with that of a world in which the International Police Force is clearly superior to the military forces of any sovereign state," Professor Jacobson says. It is certainly difficult to square a UN police force with the objections of many Congressmen who fear that foreigners will be commanding American boys.

It is also difficult to reconcile disarmament with statements like that of Secretary McNamara's to a Congressional committee in 1963:

My position is a very simple one on disarmament or arms control: I think we should engage in such agreements if and when, and only if and when, we can do so without reducing our power advantage. It is perhaps over-simplified to say that the Soviets seek to dominate the present world but I believe that, and I think the only reason they don't dominate it today is, basically, because of the military and economic strength of the United States and, in my opinion, the only deterrent to their domination of the free world in the future will be the maintenance of that strength. . . . I foresee no period in the future, let's say in the remaining years of this century, when we can, under today's conditions, operate without a strategic nuclear force of the type we are proposing for this five-year period.

For the government idealists at ACDA, disarmament is a frustrating job. Caught among the pressures of Congress, the unwillingness of the Soviets to abandon any but the most sweeping goals, a small appreciation of and interest in the problems at home, the insistence on maintaining strong levels of arms by other government agencies and the limited powers of the ACDA itself, a clear American policy on disarmament has never emerged.

Mr. Coordinator

Many people refer to the excessive caution of the Department of State as though, were it unleashed, it could solve the country's difficulties overnight. "I came in with the idea 'Boy! Now we can really fix it,'" said Abram Chayes, the State Department's legal adviser under President Kennedy. "But foreign policy turned out to be a lot more intractable than we thought."

A number of reasons are put forth by the gentlemen of State for this intractability. The most obvious, though far from the only one, is the existence of large numbers of independent countries each with its own foreign policy objectives. The State Department must operate under the same uncertainty principle that governs the Department of Defense. Who is to know, State officials ask, if the next government of the Soviet Union will not share the hostile attitude of the Communist Chinese? "Almost any policy that involves drastic change in the status quo will be considered by any foreign office as involving too many unpredictable factors for comfort," Chayes says.

Another restraining force on the Department of State is domestic public opinion, for if ordinary Americans are convinced that Cuba is a menace, then State Department officials, themselves subject to the political system, must allow this belief to enter their policy calculations. (Dissident views, like Senator Fulbright's, nonetheless are not unwelcome at the Department of State. They may have no immediate effect, but they may widen the Department's radius of action later on.) Officials, too, speak of a bureaucratic lag between real changes in the world and changes in policy to keep up with them. And then the State Department may be restricted by the activities of other government agencies. Most notably, they refer to the subservience of diplomacy to military policy.

One force widely supposed to be governing on State Department thinking is not nearly so potent as left-wing critics claim, according to State officials: the influence of American business and financial interests abroad. (Defense Department officials, similarly, deny that the "military-industrial complex" decides the Defense budget.) Foreign policy, traditionally, tries to protect and expand a country's finance and trade, but State officials do not accept the view that narrow property interests are determining. "U.S. business interests abroad are a small factor in our foreign policy and maybe not as much of a factor as they ought to be," Chayes says. "The flag does not follow investments in a crude sense. In a larger way, American business abroad is important because it has weight. It's one of the ways we project ourselves and keep our ties. Business is virtually all that keeps the U.S. in, say, Ghana. So in this sense of a broader national interest we do try to help business."

At least as State Department people express them, the overseas goals of the U.S. are seen in the large terms of the country's position in the world. The Secretary of State has been described by a Senate subcommittee as " 'Mr. Coordinator'—the superintendent, for the President, of most major activities affecting our relations with other countries." As such, he is supposed to lay out the broader, governing concepts, and these have been sloganized by the Department as five U.S. foreign policy goals: "Security Through Strength," "Progress Through Partnership," "Revolution of Freedom," "Community under Law," and "Through Perseverance, Peace." Thus the Penelope of State weaves on the loom of diplomacy as she waits for the Ulysses of permanent peace.

Now governments have two kinds of policies: "declaratory"— the ones they announce—and "action"—the ones they intend to carry out. The action policies State spins fall into two general categories in terms of the American response to Communism: U.S. policies toward the developed nations of Europe and those toward the less developed nations. New ideas have been devised for both, and each is, or shows promise of being, highly controversial. To help solve the problems of NATO, the government has come up with the multilateral force. For the underdeveloped world, the strategy is known as counterinsurgency.

In lieu of disarmament, nations, it is presumed in Washington, will seek to augment their safety and prestige by nuclear arms. Some say that this trend must be opposed and the search for meaningful arms reduction accelerated. Some say that proliferation of nuclear weapons is more or less inevitable and, this being the case, the best policy for the United States toward Europe, where the problem is most immediate, would be to avoid the fragmentation of nuclear power by actively assisting a European "third force" to achieve it. (No one in the war-peace establishment, it might be noted, cares for the vision of a half-dozen or more independent European nuclear states.) The middle position, occupied currently by the American Government, argues that the U.S. should not relinquish its nuclear trigger finger at the present time, but that the U.S. must assuage, in greater measure than in the past, what it believes to be a European and, most important, a West German desire for a share in ownership, operation and control of strategic delivery systems. Its instrument for achieving both objectives is known as the multilateral force, or, to its opponents, the multilateral farce.

"It is natural," says Robert G. Neumann, director of the Institute of International and Foreign Studies at UCLA, "that a resurgent Europe, which has recovered its strength and confidence, should increasingly desire to play a more effective role in the management of the nuclear deterrent." In 1959 NATO commanders began asking what was to replace the Medium-Range Ballistic Missiles already located in several European countries and which were rapidly becoming obsolete. There were various reasons the United States felt it could not entirely resist the demand for new MRBMs. One of them was that the Europeans wanted to have a deterrent close at hand against the Soviet MRBM force aimed at Europe, which amounts to some 750 missiles today. European participation in such a force was desired by many Europeans. A second reason was equality, for, Neumann says, "Up to now the effectiveness of the movement toward European unity has rested on the essential equality among all participants," and both Britain and France were developing nuclear armaments, whereas the rest of Europe was without. The status quo, then, would result in what can be called nuclear discrimination.

Just what was to be done in this situation was by no means clear, however. One way was to assist in MRBM deployment under some sort of national arrangement, that is, with foreign countries owning and manning the missiles and use of the warhead being bilaterally controlled by each country and the United States. This is called, in the jargon of the war-peace establishment, "two fingers on the trigger" or the "two-key" system. It is used for large numbers of tactical nuclear weapons now in Europe. After considerable study it was concluded, however, that its extension to strategic weapons would be divisive in the West and unsettling to East-West relations. National manning and ownership of MRBM missiles with warheads mated to them, missiles capable of reaching the U.S.S.R., would have lent itself to the impression, at least, of proliferation and to Soviet charges of American warmongering.

"This brought the U.S. Government, by elimination, to the third alternative: providing MRBMs to our allies under multilateral manning and ownership," Neumann says. Here, too, there were choices. A multilateral force might have been land-based, but this was rejected because public opinion in Europe might object to nuclear arms close to their cities, and because of the difficulty of deciding which NATO countries to base the force in. Submarines were rejected as too costly, and this led to the idea of a multilateral fleet of surface vessels. The fleet, as presently planned, would consist of twenty-five surface ships, looking something like freighters, each carrying medium-range missiles. The first ship is to be com-

missioned in 1965 and completed in 1968, with the fleet in operation by 1969. The total price, about $2–2.5 billion in capital costs,
spread over five years, is to be apportioned among the participants,
the U.S.'s share and that of the Federal German Republic to be
about one-third each, with the rest spread among other participants.
At least part of the fleet would be on duty at all times, and its
strategic configuration would be such that, with the fleet spread out,
it could not be readily destroyed.

But nobody closely connected with MLF pretends that its purpose is primarily military, most Americans being convinced that
programmed U.S. nuclear forces are quite sufficient for any military
encounter. The MLF would substitute for some of these programmed forces, permitting a reduction in present U.S. plans to
build missiles. "Many Europeans simply feel that the U.S. monopoly is no longer fitting or acceptable for the long term. They
are not happy with the position of Europe within the alliance. They
want a larger role in the conduct of NATO strategy and in the
control over the nuclear forces. Their feeling is mainly a political
one," writes Robert R. Bowie, an MLF architect. "The purpose of
MLF," says R. H. S. Crossman, an English Socialist, is "to provide
an effective and credible deterrence of Western Europe by bringing the Germans into the picture but without conceding to them
the independent national army and national strategy which would
make an East-West settlement almost impossible."

An Italian writer, Ambassador Mario Toscano, chairman of the
Studies Office of the Foreign Ministry, sums up the arguments for
MLF. It would, he says, launch the building of Europe; prevent
the splitting of Europe; provide an effective reply to the independent policies of de Gaulle's France; channel the French and British
national deterrents into the MLF; solve the psychological uncertainty in Europe over U.S. strategy; bring Britain into a European
confederation; set down the basis of a U.S.–European partnership.

"The MLF is like malaria," said Henry Owen, deputy counselor
and vice chairman of the State Department's Policy Planning
Council, a youthfully gray-haired man, one of several known on
the premises as Mr. MLF. "Once you catch it you can't get rid of

it." Indeed, to American enthusiasts the MLF offers solutions to long-range problems. One of its core concepts is that of mixed manning, for the ten thousand men of the proposed MLF force would come from different countries and, it is hoped, would provide a precedent for the mixed manning of nuclear weapons, a basis for growing allied cohesion and a step toward the one Europe American policy people dream about. "Such a force," Bowie says, "could create new pressures and reasons for further progress toward European political unity and help in pulling the NATO members together rather than apart. If Britain joins at the start, there would be good ground to hope that the British national effort might ultimately be phased out. And in the decade ahead, when the three French missile submarines are being developed, probably with mounting costs, a French Government will have the same option, if they wish to adopt it." Implicit here is the idea that NATO must not become stagnant, that the MLF will be a recognition that the European community is still evolving in close relationship with the United States.

One further use has been suggested for the MLF, though others believe it is likely to produce the reverse results. This is the idea that the multilateral force, or the threat of it, will spur the Soviet Union to serious arms negotiations. "The Soviets may believe that they now hold Europe in hostage to their MRBMs," Owen says. "Once they have lost this one-sided advantage through creation of MLF, they may see more advantage in mutually inspected arms reductions."

To be sure, not everyone is afflicted with the bug of MLF. The MLF plan calls for a committee system of control, possibly some sort of "weighted majority" having the decisive voice, subject to an American veto, and, deterrence critics say, the arrangement would be subject to bureaucratic paralysis in an emergency. Not only this, they argue, but the MLF's potential inactivity might very well infect the American deterrent itself as uncertainty developed as to who would respond to what. (Pure deterrent theorists in the war-peace establishment always put great stress on clarity of purpose and, in line with it, a single center of command.)

To critics like Henry Kissinger, on the other hand, MLF will only serve to elevate the position of Germany, MLF's principal supporter, and divide Europe more than it is already. "For the issue before NATO far transcends military strategy," he says. "What is at stake is the organization of Europe, the domestic stability of major allied governments, and the future of the Atlantic community." To him, the MLF is a misguided attempt to keep Europe as an American satellite.

The danger in the multilateral force is that those who want effective control over their nuclear destiny will not long remain content with the projected arrangements, while those who go along for such motives as pleasing us, defying France, or keeping an eye on Germany will soon grow tired of the expense and will search for other options. . . . The multilateral NATO force is thus likely to combine the disadvantage of every course of action. It will not stop the diffusion of nuclear weapons; it may well accelerate it.

Kissinger, instead, favors "fostering a European nuclear identity growing out of British and French programs." This kind of multinational force, his critics say, would lead quickly to German nuclear arms (acquired from the French), set the example for still other countries to get nuclear arms too, trigger a Soviet increase in military spending and start the arms spiral to work once more.

A third set of arguments against MLF comes from those who contend that the Europeans do not want nuclear arms at all. "We've told the Germans they want nuclear arms so long that only now are they beginning to believe us," says a student of foreign affairs. (We come here to a moderately important distinction in the warpeace establishment, for when the peace movement says "the Germans" or "the French," it is thinking of the people, whereas government officials and advisers are likely to be referring to their opposite numbers abroad when they speak of "London thinks" or "Paris wants." "It's true that we're talking about a small group of people who do form policy, the elites," says a State Department official. "It's a gut feeling among these people that a self-respecting status comes with a responsible role in ownership, manning and control of nuclear weapons. This desire goes very deep in policy-making groups.")

The third set of critics, in and out of government, argues that the MLF is a serious threat to peace, making arms negotiations with the Soviet Union more difficult than they already are. How, they ask, can there be a true freeze on nuclear weapons with the MLF in prospect? (Pro-MLFers answer that nuclear arms for MLF would substitute for presently programmed U.S. forces.) "The MLF perpetuates the obsession with military response to rifts with the Soviets and between our allies, in an era which calls not for an arms polemic but for the progression of relationships between sovereign states," says a policy-maker of the Council for a Livable World. "Those who could promote a *détente* and ultimately a settlement in Europe must look beyond merely military alignments such as the pseudo partnership of the Multilateral Nuclear Force."

But the heart of the matter is whether the MLF will speed or slow nuclear proliferation. The critics are certain that it will assist the West Germans, in particular, to obtain them. The proponents say it will prevent, or at least slow, the process. It is clear the U.S. Government is determined not to allow the MLF to break up into national nuclear forces, but would it allow the MLF to evolve into an integrated, European-controlled force? Some say the government does not contemplate such nuclear sharing. Another way of thinking has it that the U.S. would relinquish control over nuclear arms only if and when a politically united Europe was well on its way to existence and it was clear that MLF would substitute for existing national European nuclear forces.

As well as anything else, the MLF illustrates some of the problems of government idealism, for goals that are equally desired turn out to be contradictory. Behind MLF is a vision with great historic implications, a united Europe that would cease warring with itself, strong and allied with the United States. This new Europe, by these lights, must be equal with the U.S. and is seen to require at least some role in ownership, operation and manning of nuclear weapons. By giving that role, the United States faces the possible failure of another desired goal, successful arms negotiations with the Soviet Union. The solution may come in one of two ways: either the Soviet Union also comes to realize that the MLF is safer in terms of its own interests than national European nuclear forces out of the control of the United States, or Europe decides to forgo the boon of nuclear arms.

If the United States seeks to stabilize the situation in Europe through the MLF, a little-known policy called "counterinsurgency" seeks to do the same for the nations of the underdeveloped world. "CI," I was told at the Department of Defense, "is the most important issue confronting us in the military field, now that strategic deterrence problems are under control."

Counterinsurgency, as such, is one of the few ideas in present strategic and foreign policy indigenous to the Kennedy administration, although many of the programs that have come to comprise the effort were already in existence under President Eisenhower. Guerrilla warfare, under Eisenhower, was a weapon to be used behind Soviet lines in the event of a general war, whereas to Kennedy the interest was not in guerrilla fighting but in fighting guerrillas. Cuba, Laos, Congo and Vietnam, it was thought, were all places that yielded the signal lesson that to avoid later, all-out U.S. intervention, earlier, remedial action must be applied.

Premier Khrushchev helped to focus American attention by a speech, in 1960, in which he declared that while general or local internation wars were to be shunned as being likely to lead to "thermonuclear rocket war," the Communists could not stand aloof from struggles for national liberation and popular uprisings. The Communists, he said, "fully support such just wars and march in the front rank with the peoples waging liberation struggles." This was interpreted in Washington as a direct challenge for the control of the underdeveloped world, and President Kennedy is reported to have said at the time of the Bay of Pigs that paramilitary activity was the coming thing and might well be the decisive factor in the East-West struggle.

The extraordinary nature of the effort that has evolved since then is suggested by the money being spent on it, an estimated $500 million, exclusive of Vietnam (which is considered closer to a real war, but which, nonetheless, is serving as a testing ground for counterinsurgency pacification efforts) and not counting the CIA, which is also committed to the program.

It is also suggested by the composition under the Kennedy and early Johnson administrations—what new form the Special Group might take is still in doubt—of the once secret Special Group for Counter-Insurgency (CI) set up in January, 1962, by the White House: the Under Secretary of State, the Attorney General, the Chairman of the Joint Chiefs of Staff, the Deputy Secretary of Defense, the Foreign Aid Administrator, the Director of the Central Intelligence Agency, the Director of the United States Information Agency and the President's Special Assistant for National Security, all of whom assemble once a week at the White House. The Special Group is charged with defining the problem, assaying the threat and assembling the means to combat it, its usual technique being to designate an "action agency" which takes responsibility for whatever action is decided on. The Special Group has no staff or elaborate machinery for making policy. Its function is to coordinate the various CI efforts and to decide where and when action is needed. If action is demanded, the Special Group is supposed to see that something gets done, whether it be road-building equipment airlifted to Thailand or tear gas dispatched posthaste to the police in Venezuela.

A member of the Special Group insists that CI aid is only given when requested by foreign governments and it has been chary of releasing information about the extent of American involvement on two grounds, one being not to tip off its CI hand to Moscow, the other being that some of the "host" countries are embarrassed about needing outside help to stay in power. It can be said, though, that serious American counterinsurgency work is being performed in Vietnam, Laos, Thailand, Congo, Iran, Bolivia, Colombia, Ecuador, Peru and Venezuela. In addition to these countries many more are being assisted in one form or another under the counterinsurgency program, and it's not too much to say that *every* non-Communist land, except the industrially developed ones, is thought to be a breeding place for Communist insurgency and thus a potential for American CI. The United States, at the moment, possesses complete plans, called Internal Defense Plans, themselves embodied in over-all country programs called National Policy Papers, designed to identify and prevent Communist-inspired insurgency in more than twenty countries in the Far East, Latin America and Africa, presumably with matching plans provided by the hosts, for persuading foreign governments to deal with their internal problems is a key feature of CI. "I'd like to see counterinsurgency plans for every developing country," says a Department of State policy officer. "Eventually, we will get them." CI, fundamentally, is out to stop insurgency before fighting begins.

The hard core of the CI program is the Special Forces of the U.S. Army, which has been tripled in the last few years to its present size of six thousand men. "In expanding the Special Forces the Army noted that the move was to create a weapon with which to aid the legal governments of allies against the criminal pressure which insurgent elements are bringing against them," said *Army* magazine. The Special Forces directly reflect the new emphasis of this decade, for until 1960 their sole mission was to engage in guerrilla warfare behind Communist lines in Europe should war occur.

Today, their role has been expanded to include teaching anti-guerrilla pacification operations. "Teaching may sometimes mean fighting," a Defense Department official said. CI is taught to American soldiers and others at four schools, the principal one being the Army Special Warfare School at Fort Bragg, North Carolina. There is also an Army Jungle Warfare School in Panama, and a counterinsurgency school in Germany which trains Europeans as well as Americans and whose particular focus is Africa. The fourth school is on Okinawa, and its concern is counterinsurgency in various parts of Asia. The schools, then, teach not only basic counterinsurgency but its various adaptations to three continents. Out of the 24,000 foreign military men who train each year in the United States, two to three thousand work exclusively in counterinsurgency. Foreign nationals also attend counterinsurgency schools abroad.

The Special Forces are augmented by what one counterinsurgency general says "could be twenty thousand Army men not counting anybody in Vietnam" of various specialties, such as communications and engineering. One hundred thousand civilian, diplomatic and military officers have also become trained in these techniques. In addition to the Army, the other service branches are also counterinsurgency conscious. The Marines are all trained in it, and the Navy has special counterinsurgency groups in the shape of underwater-demolition, SEAL (or amphibious), helicopter, medical and aerial reconnaissance forces. The Air Force has its Air Commandos and special groups for air warfare. No Army man today can achieve the rank of general officer in the U.S. armed forces without training in CI. "Where do you draw the line?" a CI specialist asked. "For instance, there is a military language school at Monterey, California. It isn't principally for CI, but it is used to train CI people."

The military establishments, too, have extensive research programs for counterinsurgency. The Army, the Air Force and the Navy each has such a program, and so does the Department of Defense. The total military CI research and development bill is said to be $50 million a year. Much of this is done under the DOD's Advanced Research Projects Agency, whose counterinsurgency program is called Remote Area Conflict or Project AGILE, the latter nomenclature intended to signify an ability to come up with rapid solutions to pressing problems. AGILE's budget is above $25 million for fiscal 1965.

The sort of problems AGILE tries to solve is how one defeats radio static during the monsoon season, or how to develop lightweight armor plating for a Styrofoam boat. It has developed spike detectors for use in the mud, and I was shown something called an anti-intrusion device which consisted of a hand-sized board on which was a small reel of filament thread, a buzzer and a light. The filament on the spool is one and one-half miles long. It is intended to be extended around a village or a strategic hamlet at night. When the filament is broken, the light on the board goes on or the buzzer sounds. AGILE is working on an aerial camera that will penetrate foliage, using the principle of spectrazonal photography, new kinds of flame warfare, a long-lasting battery for a portable radio transmitter, a special counterinsurgency (COIN) aircraft, lightweight weapons and ammunition for Asian soldiers who are smaller than our own, and ways to distinguish guerrillas from civilians away from a battlefield. Even rations have come under AGILE's scrutiny, its notion being that a counterinsurgency force is hampered by carrying live goats and chickens. It proposes to develop, instead, dehydrated rations which would be in accord with the national diet of a particular locality.

Under the counterinsurgency program, AGILE's responsibility, along with those of the research departments of the services, is to conduct research. The provision of weapons themselves is conducted through the Military Assistance Program partly as MAP's longstanding responsibility, but partly, too, in conjunction with the programs set down by CI. At this point, still another government organization enters the picture, the Agency for International Development, which, along with MAP, runs another facet of counterinsurgency, this one known as Military Civic Action. The budget for Civic Action is about eighty million dollars, half of which is being expended in Vietnam, and the other half around the world.

Civic Action takes for its premise the fact that military organizations are often in low repute in underdeveloped countries. They are also frequently idle and often make up a power elite which frequently overthrows the government. The American answer to this is several-fold. On the one hand Civic Action means encouraging the local military to engage in public works projects, such as dams, wells and roads, for which the Agency for International Development provides the support. It may even provide rations through the Food for Peace program. This sort of Civic Action is under way in many parts of Asia, Africa and South America. It may have a military function, as, for instance, constructing a road for easy troop access to the northeast section of Thailand, which is considered the heart of that country's insurgency problem. But roads also mean progress, and Civic Action's aim is to identify soldiers with development and not waste. It is meant, too, to encourage civic-mindedness on the part of the troops, and, further, to train soldiers for functions in civilian life, one of the lessons that Civic Action people constantly drone being that soldiers should have a limited tour of duty and then be sent home, to be replaced by new recruits.

This brief accounting by no means exhausts the American Government's activities on behalf of counterinsurgency. AID conducts still another program under the heading of CI, called Public Safety, with a budget of seventeen million dollars, to train the men of thirty-one police forces in twenty-one countries, hoping that a revitalized police will gain the confidence of the people and aid in controlling insurgency. The United States Information Agency, or Service as it's known overseas, is deeply committed, its function being to advise governments on what kind of propaganda to use both to counter that of the insurgents and to get support for itself. AID has a community development program under CI, and there is a program called Youth-Labor, whose objective is parallel to that of Civic Action for the military. Military Assistance Advisory Groups are involved, and the CIA is central to counterinsurgency. Its job is to discover, by infiltration or other means, the political views of insurgent groups, and to counteract them by any means, including the use of what is called "black" psychological warfare—that is, propaganda that appears to have emanated from the other side—and undoubtedly more extreme measures.

Overseas, counterinsurgency is conducted by what is called the "country team," comprised of members of the various departments involved in the effort. "The central task of any country team in the field is, of course, the preparation of an over-all U.S. program with respect to the country in which it is located," says a leading State Department official. "The whole of our counterinsurgency operation turns around the country team concept," declares Major General V. H. Krulak, former Special Assistant for Counter-Insurgency to the Secretary of Defense. The country team idea, which has been in existence only since the 1950's, is part of what has been called the new diplomacy, meaning the use of government disciplines from across the board, and the allocation of time and resources according to the needs of the hour, and not by a strict sticking to a government organization chart.

At home, the State Department runs a special four-week course in the "Problems of Development and Internal Defense" called the National Interdepartmental Seminar, held at the Foreign Service Institute in Arlington, Virginia. The students consist of high-ranking officials such as ambassadors and general officers from all U.S. agencies with major foreign affairs interests. The students are likely to ask what the counterinsurgency program has accomplished, and the answers will be these:

CI's proudest boast is that it saved the government of Venezuela from falling to insurgents in December, 1963. CI provided an airlift of police equipment, radios, billy clubs and what one official called "crowd stuff" to quell disturbances. It was aided by luck, for in a round-up of three hundred suspects one of them told about Operation Caracas, a plan to take over the capital. This disclosure also led to the discovery of the Cuban arms cache in Venezuela.

CI has prevented the outbreak of serious insurgency in Thailand.

CI has helped the "shaky" government of Iran.

CI has revolutionized the outlook of South America from external to internal defense.

CI, the government feels, has improved the credibility of U.S. power by making it better balanced, more flexible, more able to deal with problems requiring measured response.

The rationale for CI is provided by a State Department white paper called "U.S. Overseas Internal Defense Policy" (the State Department prefers the words "Overseas Internal Defense" to counterinsurgency, but President Kennedy liked the latter term), which defines Communist insurgency as an attempt to interfere with the modernization process. Any insurgency is dangerous because all insurgency provides the Communists with a foothold, although the government insists that it is not opposed to non-Communist revolutions. Insurgency is seen on three levels: inactive, a situation in which the U.S. concentrates on "nation-building" and equipping local forces to deal with future insurgency; existent, when the U.S. effort has a higher military content but the emphasis is still on nation-building and self-help; and active, when the U.S. response is almost entirely military, as in Vietnam.

To Walt W. Rostow, counselor and chairman of the State Department's Policy Planning Council, the Communists are the

scavengers of the modernization process. They believe that the techniques of political centralization under dictatorial control—and the projected image of Soviet and Chinese Communist economic progress—will persuade hesitant men, faced by great transitional problems, that the Communist model should be adopted for modernization, even at the cost of surrendering human liberty. . . . But it is one particular form of modern society to which a nation may fall prey during the transitional process. Communism is best understood as a disease of the transition to modernization.

To Rostow, underdeveloped nations, given help and guidance, can achieve the economic "take-off" and emerge as modern democratic societies only if insurgency is kept under control.

There is no doubt that although counterinsurgency borrows liberally from the domain of power politics, it also fits into the category of government idealism for it wants to reflect American notions of freedom and individual dignity to the darkest corners of the earth. One of CI's founding fathers, for instance, is Major General Edward G. Lansdale, USAF (Ret.), who has been involved in antiguerrilla work since the Huk suppression campaign of the early 1950's. "I have a deep, Jeffersonian faith in an informed electorate and responsive government," Lansdale says. "My own complaint with our counterinsurgency is that we have not worked hard enough to inculcate the democratic ideals." And he has told CI classes: "When your turn comes . . . serve in the spirit of American principles. As you do so, you will be right in the forefront—of giving the Communists a memorable licking—of helping the cause of freedom everywhere!"

Counterinsurgency is a striking example of the evolution of the U.S. in twenty-five years from isolationism to what U. Alexis Johnson calls "total global responsibility." Premier Khrushchev has stated the Soviet reaction when he referred to the U.S., sneeringly, as the "international constable." The constable's life may not be a happy one, for government officials realize the hazards involved in CI: that underdeveloped nations may fail to achieve the "take-off" rapidly enough, that the U.S. may have trained and equipped future guerrillas, and that CI-trained forces may be used by repressive governments to stay in power. The experimentalists would object that the U.S. has no business trying to run the world, and some in the peace movement doubt the long-run effectiveness of any policy that depends on armed force.

The critical questions that must be asked of American CI are these: In practice, can the government distinguish between Communist and non-Communist insurgency, or is such a distinction often impossible? Will our policy end by attempting to suppress any armed dissidence? And is the United States, in reality, prepared to exert the same effort in overseas economic development as it is to overseas internal defense? For if it is not, CI may turn out to be global waste.

The Big Picture

The American policy in the cold war is ultimately the responsibility of the President of the United States. The President, in turn, is subjected to a number of pressures, many conflicting: Congress, the public, the opposition party and government groups like the DOD and the CIA. Norman Cousins, editor of the *Saturday Review*, who had frequent access to the White House under President Kennedy on the peace issue, suggests how the policy process actually works. "The President of the United States," Cousins says, "occupies a position the central characteristics of which is vulnerability to pressures and whose object is to balance those pressures so as to move closer to his goals. He must attempt to get those pressures into equilibrium, for only then does his real freedom of action emerge."

The political balancing act required by American politics does not lend itself to a Grand Design, a long-range international plan to which our policy rigidly adheres, publicly or privately. Government is simply too complicated. Some, indeed, say that inconsistencies in policy are desirable because, if one fails, the government still has others. "Some idea of the future is necessary, but you can't make it too explicit," says Carl Kaysen, who was Deputy Special Assistant for National Affairs to President Kennedy, "because the situation changes. You're more likely to be wrong than right on what the world will be like in ten years."

If there is no Grand Design, there is still what might be called the Big Picture, Washington's vision of the world and the position of the United States within it. The most explicit rendition of the big picture is that of Walt Whitman Rostow, the State Department's Counselor of Policy Planning under Presidents Kennedy and Johnson, who has described his position as "one of the few places in government where the full range of policy problems can be perceived." Rostow sets forth a conception of the global interests of the United States. There is, he says, an American "style," a way of doing things, a form of life, which must be protected so that it may grow and flourish "in conformity with the humanistic principles which are its foundation." The protection of the American environment requires a recognition of the country's true position in the world. The United States, in actuality, is an "island" off the greater land mass of Eurasia. The object of our foreign policy must be to prevent any hostile group of powers from dominating either Eurasia or the areas adjacent to it, for this would threaten the United States. The loss of Japan or India or West Germany would directly threaten the American interest, Rostow says. We do not ask that governments model themselves after us; we do require that they be friendly.

"The legitimate American ideological interest is not that all societies become immediately democratic in the degree achieved in the United States or Western Europe, but that they accept as a goal the version of the democratic value judgments consistent with their culture and their history and that they move toward their realization with the passage of time," Rostow says in *The United States in the World Arena*. Another legitimate American objective is "to see removed from all nations—including the United States—

the right to use substantial military force to pursue their own interests."

The cold war, to Rostow, has been the gradual recapturing by the United States of the bargaining position lost immediately after World War II by Soviet encroachments in Eastern Europe. That objective, Rostow told a select audience in 1964, has been achieved. "We have passed," he said, "the Gettysburg of the cold war, the turning point. The Communists have overreached themselves and the tides of history are with the U.S." The object now, to Rostow, is to recapture the stability of the world order that was lost in 1914, with chaos ruling ever since.

Rostow defines three "gut" issues in the cold war: Communist goals for a world revolution, including the sending of arms across frontiers; the right of inspection for disarmament; and the principle of self-determination in Eastern Europe, including free elections in East Germany. The acceptance by the Communist bloc of these conditions will constitute a victory in the cold war by the United States. "Our objective," Rostow says, "is to win the cold war, if possible without a hot war. The cold war is not anywhere near an end."

The reward for our tribulations, Rostow says,

will be, simply, this: it will permit American society to continue to develop along the old humane lines which go back to our birth as a nation—and which reach deeper into history before that—back to the Mediterranean roots of Western life. We are struggling to maintain an environment in the world which will permit our open society to survive and flourish.

Such is the vision of the deterrers.

PART TWO

The Experimentalists

V

Experiments in Action

IN THE SUBTLE AND COMPLEX DEBATE UNDER WAY IN THE UNITED
States over what to do about the cold war the intermediate position
is occupied by those who can be called experimentalists and whose
hope is to find ways to end the arms race, reduce the existing level
of nuclear arms and, before too long, put nations out of the nuclear bomb business altogether.

Brokers in the precious commodity of time, the deterrers believe
that the best that can be had is a slow ebb of international hostility to be replaced very gradually by a more sophisticated world
order. The calendar for the deterrers reads 1965, and A.D. might well
stand for *animus dominandi*, signifying the continuity of historical
problems, the great difficulty of human change and the unwillingness of nations to surrender the artifacts of military power. The
experimentalist calendar, on the other hand, is likely to read A.H.
20—twenty years after Hiroshima—meaning that in that blinding
instant all previous bets were called off. Either history admits to
formerly impossible solutions or there will be no history at all. To
the experimentalists, change and flux are what they were to Hera-
clitus—everything.

For the experimentalist, the key word is "imagination." To
them, thermonuclear weapons must be done away with, even if
novel means are required. The risks of deterrence are too great for
the world to rely on it, and they call for other responsible measures
for keeping the peace. The experimentalists think that the deterrers'
talk of the "fine, internal structure" of war is a rationalization for

a poor argument. To them, a thermonuclear war would be all-out, and they constantly emphasize, as a means of dramatizing their contention that reliance on thermonuclear weapons must be abandoned, what such a war would look like.

Take, for instance, a book called *Nuclear Disaster* by Tom Stonier, a research biologist from Manhattan College. One reviewer said that Stonier's book "provides the most complete description available of the probable consequences of nuclear war and must be read by any citizen who seeks to have a full understanding of the revolution which began on August 6, 1945." The results of the thermonuclear war contemplated by Stonier are such that they affect man's ecological setting and permanently alter his environment. In the cities, the danger will come from firestorms such as that which ravaged Hamburg in World War II, where the temperature reached 1400 F. and higher. Not all experts believe that firestorms would occur after a thermonuclear attack, but Stonier, who does, says that all but the deepest blast shelters with an independent air supply would be worthless. Like ripples in a pool, the waves of terror would spread out.

Plague exists in the United States from the West Coast to the Middle West carried by rodents like prairie dogs and ground squirrels. At present, there are only a few cases a year, mostly among sheepherders, but, Stonier told me, "We don't usually realize how much social energy goes into controlling disease." After a thermonuclear war such energy would not be available and the barriers to bubonic plague would crack. Other ecological scales would be tipped as well. For example, insects are more resistant to radiation than vertebrates and could be expected to flourish in their absence, especially as the insects would have abundant supplies of dying vegetation to feed upon. As an example of what an insect plague might be like, a 1949 attack of bark beetles killed 400,000 trees in a Western forest. A fraction of the horde, falling into a lake, formed a body of dead beetles a foot deep, six feet wide and two miles long. Nor does this quite exhaust the horrors, for a thermonuclear war might affect the balance of weather and bring about a new Ice Age. The glaciers, which apparently came with frightening rapidity, covered most of North America with an ice blanket as much as two miles thick.

The experimentalists' tone is one of high alarm, but nonetheless they do not sound the peace movement's clarion call for general and complete disarmament. For one thing, the experimentalists are chiefly physical and social scientists with something of the caution of academia about them. (The list of academic and scientific peace groups is virtually endless: Psychologists for Peace, Behavioral Scientists for Peace, the American Psychological Association Committee on Psychology in National and International Affairs, Scientists on Survival and so on.) For another, they doubt that the peace movement's blanket call for peace will be effective, and for this reason the experimentalists have tended to focus on detailed plans for moving to peace one step at a time. Further, they are cautious about their major propositions—that deterrence doesn't work, that the Soviet Union is not a serious threat to the United States, that a real accommodation can be reached with Communist nations—and would test them as they went along. All this leads the experimentalists to gradualism. They would begin by reducing the country's nuclear armory.

THE MINIMUM DETERRERS

Among the first people to become interested in questions of nuclear public policy were the natural scientists who worked on the atomic bomb during the war and, having fallen under the spell of the nuclear *la belle dame sans merci*, are still in thrall. Scientists have continued to be an important force in government councils. "Never before," writes Richard Gilpin, "has the participation of scientists in the determination of public policy been as pervasive or as important as it is today."

Most scientists, like most citizens, are not involved in the strategies of war and peace, even though, it's been estimated, 60 to 70 percent of American scientists are tied to the defense effort, either directly employed by the government or working on government contract. Of these, an influential elite of one thousand has been posited, an active elite of four hundred, and an even lower figure for those who have been "consistently influential." Such scientists serve on one or several government councils, such as the Air Force Science Advisory Board or the President's Science Advisory Committee. It's quite possible for a "consistently influential" scientist to sit on a panel that discusses the technological feasibility of a particular weapon, another panel that considers its impact on arms negotiations, and then to engage in a private conference, such as the Pugwash Conferences, in which he comes out squarely against the device.

Perhaps because scientific influence has been pervasive, it has come under a good deal of criticism from nonscientists. The analysts, in particular, are disturbed at the scientists' presumption to be military strategists. "Many of the articulate scientists," writes Albert Wohlstetter, "especially when considering arms control agreements, prefer to think of harmony rather than conflict. The difficulty they have in contemplating countermeasures stems from hostility to the fact of hostility itself. In this way they slip more easily into the role of prophet and agent for a perfectly peaceful world."

The scientists, at least the ones who have spoken out, might be divided into three groups. The first consists of those, like Edward Teller, who believe that the cold war will continue and that the United States must not slacken in its search for greater military capability. This school is less influential than it was, but a good deal of American military policy bears its imprint. The middle group is headed by Dr. Hans A. Bethe, professor of physics at Cornell, and it believes in slowing the arms race. Of all the scientific groups, the middle or experimental position probably has the greatest number of influential scientists. The third or soft group believes in the complete elimination of nuclear weapons and is fond of phrases like the "abolition of war"; it is associated with the peace movement and is the antithesis of everything the "tough" scientists believe.

The middle and left group of scientists made their positions clear as early as 1946 in a booklet called *One World or None,* with such scientific contributors as Einstein, Bethe, Philip Morrison, J. Robert Oppenheimer, Harlow Shapley, Leo Szilard, Harold Urey and Eugene P. Wigner. To them, the meaning of the atomic bomb was just what their title implied. The problem, of course, has been how to arrive at this precious goal, and while scientists display differences of opinion they agree on certain things.

One of them is that the scientific community itself, with its emphasis on the internationalism of science and the brotherhood of scientists, provides a model of what the world might become. Another is that scientists deserve an important place in policy because they are more sensitive to the dangers. "More clearly than anybody else," writes Eugene Rabinowitch, the editor of the *Bulletin of the Atomic Scientists,* "scientists see the senselessness and tragedy of the present situation of mankind—the *reductio ad absurdum* by modern technology of the historical tradition of humanity divided into warring factions which threaten each other with armed might." (The "more clearly than anyone else" is the sort of statement that annoys deterrers.) The scientists, too, tend to believe that what stands in the way of peace is not the organic hostility of men and nations, but faulty communication. "I believe," said Sir Robert Watson-Watt, a British scientist who invented radar and who now resides in the U.S., "that it is no exaggeration to say that the whole range of human error is essentially due to defective communication from one mind to another."

The middle group of scientists puts its faith in cultural exchange, in getting to know the other side, in understanding—measures the deterrers see as short of solving the real political problems. The scientists believe in a purposeful trial-and-error attempt to solve the international crisis. They would begin by moving immediately to the military posture of minimum deterrence, with the ultimate objective of eliminating nuclear weapons from national armories.

Minimum deterrence, as we have noted, means a relatively small number of missiles. The force would be "hardened" in concrete silos or dispersed in submarines so that an enemy could not destroy all this force at once with the weapons he had available. Essentially, minimum deterrence means the abandonment of all, or most, "damage-limiting capability." To its proponents, it is the only way to move toward disarmament. Among these is Dr. Hans Bethe.

I had developed a good deal of sympathy for Dr. Bethe before I traveled to Ithaca to see him. He seemed always betwixt and between, with the big guns of the deterrers attacking him from one side as utopian and the peace movement laying siege from the other with charges that Bethe was not fighting hard enough for peace because he had not renounced nuclear arms. Bethe had served his country two times on the front lines as a disarmament negotiator at Geneva, and twice met failure. Soviet scientists had disappointed him; they had appeared to be negotiating sincerely, but it turned out that they had had unseen political instructions.

From America came the "big hole" theory, a contrivance of a RAND scientist named Albert Latter, with the scientific sanction of Edward Teller, which said that if tests were conducted in large caverns scooped out of hills or salt domes the explosions would be "muffled" and perhaps undetectable. Bethe found this eventuality extremely unlikely. Where, he asked, would one put the excavated dirt or salt so that *they* would be undetected? Nonetheless the thing *was* scientifically possible, Bethe decided, and he was obliged to tell the Soviet scientists so, even though it seemed to imply that the Soviets would go almost to any lengths to cheat. He hadn't liked suggesting this to the Soviets, Bethe said when he returned to the U.S., and for not having liked to tell them he was heavily criticized, too. Such, for Bethe, had been the perils of trying to find a way.

Bethe is a tallish man with gray hair and a gentle, unobtrusive face. "I'm really a soldier," Bethe said to me with a small sigh, and went on to list a number of government scientific panels to which he belonged, all of them concerned with military matters. "I'm an expert on atomic weapons and, slowly but steadily, I've been pushed from theoretical physics to applied. I did it first out of a sense of duty, but the worst of it is I've grown interested. I suppose I put in about a third of my total working time on defense matters."

Twenty of the top thirty theoretical physicists in the United States work as part-time consultants on defense matters, as Bethe does. Their fees range from $50 a day from the President's Science Advisory Council to $400 a day and more from industry, to which may be added yearly fees, retirement plans and stock options. Many scientists have come to depend on such emoluments to supplement their university salaries. "The more important the job, the less I get," Bethe said. "I could consult for industry on nonmilitary matters and make the same, but, unfortunately, I find the military work more interesting."

I asked Bethe if he had been disappointed by the Soviets in his contacts with them and he nodded vigorously. "My attitude has changed somewhat as a result of the Soviet 1961 test series. I was shocked by the magnitude of the tests and by the fact that the Soviets had played along as if they truly wanted to negotiate. Having initiated the moratorium, they must have used at least the last year of the negotiations to secretly prepare the largest series of weapons tests they had ever conducted. I suppose, in diplomatic war, you must expect this kind of behavior, and I suppose the Russians suspected us of preparing to test on our part. But in fact we had scrupulously refrained from any decision to resume testing. However, in spite of my disappointment with the Soviet Union in 1961, I believe the Soviets are very well aware that it is in their self-interest to live in peace with us. There is great hope in the gradual relaxation of the rigid attitude of the Soviet Union, and I believe we must do everything to encourage this relaxation. One of the principal problems of the Soviet Union is secrecy. I don't know if it is still true, but some years ago there used to be no telephone book and no published information on addresses. Now you can freely buy maps of the principal streets of Moscow. Secrecy in military matters has some justification—for instance, our Air Force has espoused the principle of counterforce for so many years, and so openly, that the Russians have good reason to hide the location of their strategic forces as much as possible. But their secrecy goes much deeper than that; it goes very much into their private lives."

We turned then to the minimum deterrent. "I would describe our present posture as a maximum deterrent," Bethe said. "Of course we could have still more missiles, more bombers, and could develop every newly suggested military plane and weapon. This would be the wish of those who would like us to plan for an essentially unlimited course of military action." Like Teller? I interrupted. Bethe nodded. "I myself am against counterforce, that is, trying to knock out the enemy's strategic war capabilities, like missiles, because this destroys the strategic balance. Besides, with hardened missiles, counterforce can essentially not work. If we give up impossible aims, we have just about as many weapons as we can possibly need even under very adverse circumstances. This is a maximum deterrent. I still like the idea of the minimum deterrent, perhaps two hundred missiles and bombers on each side, carefully controlled by treaty. We got to our present large numbers of weapons partly by running an arms race with ourselves. The idea that the Russians might get weapon X has had the same impact on us as if they actually had this weapon." Bethe paused and rubbed his head. "These weapons are so terrible, it's hard to imagine. Early during the development of the H-bomb, I once stood on a roof in New York. If one H-bomb hit us here, I thought, then none of the myriads of buildings I saw would be standing any more."

Between the deterrers and the experimentalists who believe in a minimum deterrent are several important differences. The deterrers declare that a large U.S. missile force should not be objectionable to the Soviets on the grounds that if the Soviet Union does not start a war the missiles won't be used in any case; and the large U.S. missile force plus tactical nukes makes deterrence possible by permitting the United States to "escalate" a conflict if the Soviets do start one. The minimum deterrers, on the other hand, believe that the size of the missile fleets is important because only by reducing it can either side gain the confidence to approach nuclear disarmament.

Herman Kahn has identified "Finite Deterrence" and defines it as "an expert version of the Minimum Deterrent, held by an expert who wants to look good to other experts." Those in the finite category, like the Hudson Institute's Donald Brennan, believe in having a minimum deterrent strong enough to have some damage-limiting capability by aiming at military targets, and some capability to control conflicts by threatening to raise the level of violence. Above all, finite deterrers want to avoid a cities-only war because of the destruction to life. Brennan says, "What constitutes an effective deterrent is the essential question. Many informed people believe that U.S. missile forces substantially lower would be as effective a deterrent as present forces. A few hundred missiles of sufficient reliability would kill a substantial portion of the Soviet population and the Soviets would regard this as unacceptable." Ultimately, Brennan hopes that nuclear weapons will be put in the same category as poison gas.

Dr. Jerome B. Wiesner, the President's Science Adviser from 1960 to 1963, has been probably the most highly placed advocate of reduced missile strength in government councils, and he once wrote: "Studies made independently by the U.S. Army and Navy have indicated that, even in the absence of [international] agreements limiting force size and permitting inspection, 200 relatively secure missiles would provide an adequate deterrent." Joseph Alsop, the columnist, reported that Wiesner opposed the spectacular rise in U.S. missile forces schedule under President Kennedy, and I asked Wiesner about this when I called on him at the Massachusetts Institute of Technology, where he is Dean of Science. He told me he had done so because "I don't think the controlled war strategy makes much sense. It's just stable deterrence at a higher level, and it just means more casualties if war breaks out. I don't see where it changes things quantitatively."

What Wiesner wants is stable deterrence at a low level of nuclear arms, and he is willing to accept nuclear parity—that is, a rough equality in the missile strength of the United States and the Soviet Union—as part of a major disarmament agreement. But Wiesner would arrive at this goal through negotiations, and, for him, inspection of test sites and production facilities are a requisite. Wiesner wishes current Soviet disarmament plans were more specific, and he is proud of American initiative in the creation of the ACDA, and the comprehensive disarmament proposals obtaining a limited test-ban agreement and putting forth the idea for a missile freeze, but he shares the experimentalist opinion that the United States has usually been too cautious in dealing with the Soviets. He believes that some of the Soviet bloc proposals also could serve as a starting point for further agreements.

"Several times during the Eisenhower administration I believe we could have had genuine, inspected disarmament agreements with the Soviet Union," Wiesner says, "but at the last minute, for reasons unknown to me, the American Government pulled back. This was unfortunate because military technology was easier to control then. I start with the fundamental premise that, whatever present political difficulties they may face, it is in fact to the Soviet advantage to disarm. I think we must create conditions where security lies in self-interest rather than trust. I do feel that if we make reasonable proposals they will eventually follow." For Wiesner, the important thing is not the size of the missile forces, however, but the discovery of a framework in which East and West can negotiate disarmament on a broad scale. And this implies more flexibility on both sides.

Pure minimum deterrers believe that the finite deterrers' extra missile "insurance," as it is called, interferes with disarmament. One such is Dr. David R. Inglis, a physicist with the Argonne National Laboratories in Argonne, Illinois, who says, "I want a situation more stable than the present one, and I fear that a minimum deterrent means we are stuck with making cities hostages. While this is in effect, there would be some likelihood that nuclear weapons would be used, but even under counterforce doctrine cities would probably be hit in the end anyway. Making cities the only targets is the sole way to begin reducing nuclear arms. The Soviets have accepted this in principle when they talk about a 'nuclear umbrella.' I favor a transitional deterrent, meaning cities-only, until nuclear arms can be turned over to an international authority."

An even more minimal deterrent is one proposed by the late Leo Szilard, who advocated a level of nuclear arms *"just sufficient* to inflict 'unacceptable' damage in a counterblow, in case of a strategic strike directed against [a country's] territory." He would give up

U.S. superiority in long-range missiles so that both sides would retain no more than forty. *"I believe,"* Szilard wrote, in italics, *"that it would be much easier to get the Soviet Government to accept very far-reaching measures of inspection for the sake of obtaining an objective that makes sense to them, than to get them to accept quite limited measures of inspection for the sake of any 'first steps' which would not offer any major direct benefits to Russia."*

Although the minimum deterrers, and for a variety of reasons, vary in their appraisals of how minimum the deterrent ought to be, Wiesner's two hundred long-range missiles is usually considered the maximum allowable in the minimum idea, as contrasted with a planned U.S. strategic missile force of over sixteen hundred by 1967. Most minimum deterrers would withdraw tactical nuclear weapons from NATO and Europe at once. (A question that troubles minimum deterrers is whether political isolationism would follow nuclear isolationism.) Many minimum deterrers, at the same time that nuclear weapons are being reduced, would raise the size of conventional forces, at least until a United Nations militia could be assembled. And while general and complete disarmament is not considered a bright prospect by the nuclear minimalists, it is still the long-range goal, which is to say that a disarmed world (except for the UN) is the kind of world the minimum deterrers consider reasonable and possible. (The deterrers have a difficult time imagining genuine disarmament.) To most minimum deterrers, the obstacles in the way of their reduced missile force, as far as the U.S. is concerned, are, as Bernard Feld, an MIT physicist, said, "entirely political, that is, based on questions of the electorate and our commitments to NATO and Germany. These problems could be solved, given the will."

The deterrers have rejected both minimum and finite deterrences because (a) they are based on a simple theory that fear of mutual annihilation is an automatic deterrent, and (b) they are not credible enough to an opponent who might be willing to absorb large losses himself if he thought he could win a war. The minimum deterrers answer (a) that mutual annihilation is an automatic deterrent, and (b) that seeking to make the deterrent credible at every level precludes arms reduction. Each position is seen by the other side as containing risks. For the deterrers, the risk in minimum deterrence is that credibility would be lowered and the possibility of war raised. For the experimentalist, heightened credibility means a greater risk of war through accident and arms race. For the deterrers, real credibility, in the end, rests on American superiority. And while the deterrers say that large numbers of U.S. missiles shouldn't matter to the Soviets because our intention is only to use them defensively, the experimentalists ask, "Why should the enemy believe our words? We don't believe theirs."

Between the two schools, then, the line is clear, the deterrers having little faith and consequently interest in disarmament, while the experimentalists will run some strategic risks to achieve it. Some experts, like Dr. Jeremy J. Stone, think that time is with the experimentalists. "An extrapolation of the strategic situation indicates that the U.S. strategic force will, over time, revert to a counter-city retaliation function only. This could make more acceptable the Soviet plan for a reduction to a 'mutually agreed and strategically limited' number of missiles."

The middle or experimental group of scientists have agitated hard for a softer American military policy that would blend with their long-range hopes. "To scientists," says Eugene Rabinowitch, editor of the *Bulletin of the Atomic Scientists*, which, along with the Conferences on Science and World Affairs (Pugwash), has been a principal platform for the experimentalists, "it is clear that in our times the world community of interest is a living reality, the only possible path into the future, whereas the traditional world of international strife is only pseudo real," based on the "shadow of once-meaningful concepts" like "national sovereignty, national security, victory and defeat." Rabinowitch calls for "a rebellion against rulers who, whether self-appointed or freely elected, consider it their right and duty to put the interests and ideals of the fraction of the humanity over which they rule above the interests of mankind as a whole and above the moral duties all men owe to it—rulers who ask, from those they rule, absolute and ultimate loyalty to the national power and to the faith or ideology for which they stand." "It is time," suggests a *Bulletin* contributor, "that a scientist be on top."

What a scientific president would try to accomplish is suggested by the Vienna Declaration of 1958 by the Conference on Science and World Affairs (Pugwash), in which East-West scientists agreed on seven points: (1) abolish wars; (2) end the arms race; (3) war would mean disaster; (4) bomb testing is a significant hazard; (5) scientific cooperation contributes to mutual trust and the flow of scientific information across national borders should not be impeded; (6) technological cooperation to help underdeveloped countries would contribute to peace; (7) scientists have a responsibility to educate their fellow men about the dangers of science used for military purposes.

The Pugwashers went a step further at the meeting at Dubrovnik, Yugoslavia, in September, 1963, at which they laid down a platform which is likely to be as far as scientific agreement can go short of actual agreements on the part of the U.S.S.R. and the U.S. A subsequent COSWA gathering, in India, broke no new ground. The Dubrovnik Pugwash emphasized the need for political stabilization in Central Europe as a prelude, said Bernard Feld, "to a disengagement of the NATO and Warsaw Peace forces and eventual peaceful negotiation of a more permanent solution." The conference called for: surprise attack controls posts in Europe, minimum deterrence, control and inspection by an International Disarmament Organization (though the conferees felt that the possibility of cheating has been greatly exaggerated), atom-free zones, extending the test ban and so on. The question that immediately arises is why governments have not accepted solutions that seem sensible to the scientists.

Eugene Wigner, himself a leading scientist, for instance, refers to the old days when scientists believed that the terrible nature of nuclear weapons would lead to the abolition of war, and wonders "why scientists so consistently overestimate the realizability of what appears to them the rational solution. It is in my opinion because they are not sufficiently aware of the phenomenon of the conflict of desires." Hans Morgenthau calls the scientific approach to world affairs "rationalism"—the belief that evil and political conflict come from ignorance and that the solution lies in the spread of knowledge. The scientists answer that the realist view of the world is itself an outworn creed. To them, as we have seen, international strife is only the lingering shadow of the past.

GRIT

How to arrive at the arms cuts suggested by the scientists has been the question for some of their counterparts in the social sciences. For them, the problem is finding ways to cut through the inertia and traditionalism embedded in world affairs to reach a genuinely peaceful world order. They propose to do this by tackling the problem of international psychology.

Seminal doctrine among the experimentalists is a plan called GRIT, short for the rather grandiose name of Graduated Reciprocation in Tension-reduction, the idea of a professor of psychology at the University of Illinois at Urbana named Charles E. Osgood. The proposal appeared in the *Liberal Papers,* a collection of essays sponsored by a small group of liberal Congressmen, and Osgood's paper was singled out for special abuse on the grounds that it meant "surrender on the installment plan."

It's characteristic of the experimentalists that they see the world in terms of its mental state, and when Osgood looks at the nuclear Pandora's box what he sees in there is tension, the cause of which is mutual insecurity. It is not the sort of inevitable, almost metaphysical insecurity Morgenthau has in mind, but one which will yield to treatment and education. High-level deterrence, in this view, is all wrong, because it is based on what Osgood calls the Neanderthal Conception of International Relations, the notion that armed force can stabilize the international situation, when all it really does is to heighten anxiety and produce new spirals of hate.

"Most Americans," Osgood says, "are filled with the basically irrational conviction that the only way to avoid military conflict with the Communist world is to prepare for it." What we are really doing is projecting our own fears into the enemy and, by creating a bogeyman, we perform acts that in themselves make the enemy more hostile than he would have been. Our notion that we are "good" and the enemy "bad" leads us to a double standard of morality, for an example of which Osgood singles out the U-2 incident.

Osgood does not believe that disarmament negotiations are likely to work because both sides suffer from a "biased perception of what is equable." He proposes, instead, a "peace offensive" based on unilateral acts to be carried out first by the United States. Such acts must have several characteristics. They must be clear enough to be perceived by the opponent for what they are; they must be accompanied by invitations to reciprocate; they must be carried out regardless of the opponent's intent to reciprocate—a key feature of Osgood's scheme and one, in his opinion, that distinguishes it from traditional bargaining; they must be done in a planned and previously announced sequence, over a period of time.

The kind of scenario Osgood has in mind is suggested by his GRIT proposals for Cuba. The U.S. publicly announces that our naval patrol of the Caribbean, designed to stop the exportation of Communist revolutionary forces, will also be used to protect Cuba from a counterrevolutionary invasion, and, in turn, we ask Castro not to molest our ships; we send medical supplies, and ask for the release of Bay of Pigs prisoners in Cuba; we send tractors; we gradually relax our sugar embargo, and ask Castro to negotiate for acceptable payment for nationalized American industries; we transform Guantánamo into an international university, suggesting that Castro reduce his armies; and so on up the line.

"The approach to disarmament implicit in GRIT," Osgood says, "is to give up the nuclear deterrents last. . . . I think we must retain the minimum nuclear retaliatory capacity necessary for deterrence, *and* for security in limited risk-taking, until international tensions have been reduced—reduced to the point where final elimination of the nuclear safeguards themselves can be achieved by successfully negotiated treaties."

The peace pressures in the world, Osgood believes, would force the Communist states to come up with reciprocal acts. This attitude presumes a particular view about the nature of the Communist states. Osgood says there are real differences between our way of life and the Communist way, and our policy must preserve our way. Nonetheless, Communist "practice does not jibe with theory. Just as technological and other developments have produced changes in our way of life—even though, being gradual, we often fail to recognize them—so are the technological revolution, universal education, and the race to catch up with the United States in material wealth gradually producing deviations from pure Marxist theory in the Soviet Union." The real enemy, Osgood thinks, is neither human nature nor Communism but nationalism, itself a manifestation of individual status-seeking based on insecurity. "To be feasible, any policy proposal must take this state of affairs as given, must work within the limits of the situation created by nationalism, and yet must also serve to eliminate it gradually as the dominant form of political organization."

Support for GRIT, or variations of it, has been widespread in the American academic community, and Amitai Etzioni, a professor of sociology at Columbia, used it as the basis for his own initiatives program which led to the formation of the American Faculty Council for a Gradualist Way to Peace, which lists such prominent intellectuals as Paul J. Tillich, Margaret Mead and Alfred Kazin on its letterheads. GRIT, indeed, is the bible of the experimentalists. But GRIT has also come under sharp attack. Robert Pickus of the peace movement, for instance, believes that Osgood is completely mistaken in his analysis of tension. To Pickus, tension is the necessary response of those who are threatened, as he feels the United States is by the Soviet Union. To Pickus, the United States ought to combat the Soviet Union through a far more aggressive program of peaceful initiatives, such as picketing the borders of the Soviet Union to force it to disarm.

Nor has GRIT escaped the sharp eyes of the sentinels at RAND. "There is," says Amrom Katz, "implicit in Osgood's work,

some set of assumptions about the character of the Soviets, their interest in disarmament, their goals and their methods. It is likely that I would disagree in most parts with the accuracy of these assumptions. Years ago, when I was young and problems were simple (or vice versa), I used to think that the lack of understanding between the U.S. and the Soviets was the big stumbling block that needed overcoming. I don't think so now. Better understanding of the Soviets, their goals, their methods and their style will not necessarily guarantee progress toward trust and disarmament. It may guarantee the opposite.

"Unilateral initiatives might be worth trying," Robert Levine says, "but only if managed by those with a healthy distrust of the Soviet Union. Managed ingenuously, the dangers inherent in the program's probable failure far outweigh the doubtful possibilities of its success." He adds what is the deterrer's ultimate condemnation of many experimentalistic notions: "This is not to argue that the program is a bad one—merely that when done in the way that it ought to be done, it is, like most panaceas, only in small part a novel idea."

Osgood himself has been described as "unquestionably one of the ablest living psychologists," and he is past president of the 25,000-member American Psychological Association. At Urbana, he doubles as professor of psychology and director of the Institute for Communications Research, among whose projects is peace research. I called on Osgood at the Institute and found him to be a dapper man in his late forties sporting a suede coat and shoes and a neat mustache and surrounded by mounds of books and papers.

Osgood told me that science fiction, with its superwars, had led him to take the peace issue seriously, and that he had started out as a unilateral disarmer but changed his mind because it wasn't feasible. "I've tapered off my peace work," Osgood said. "Not that I don't think the problem is just as serious. I think the test ban has changed things hardly at all. But I feel I've made all the immediate impact I could, and, besides, peace was taking up so much time I had none left for anything else. Now I'm studying ways to get around the language barrier. It's the sort of basic research that, in the long run, creates the context in which problems are more easily solved. So I haven't really given up peace work."

One of the big differences between the deterrers and the experimentalists is how they gauge the tractability of the world. The deterrers think it's harder to change than the experimentalists do, and therefore they are less attracted to supposedly new solutions. I asked Osgood about this and he said, "Yes, people have a tendency to use the word 'realism' for things that are really conventional dogma in disguise. They assume that the basic motive of nations is power, always power. All kinds of other motives are operating, and I question the assumption that power governs world affairs. The first step for developing a novel approach to a problem is to question the taken-for-granted underlying assumptions. If you don't, then you get caught on the same old framework and you're led back to the same old conclusions. I've convinced myself that psychological factors are a good deal of the difficulty and that many of our complex problems which seem to be external are really internal to America. An analogy to the international situation today would be a game of doubles, with one irrational player on each team whose object is to destroy the game. The irrational player, prompted by fear, wants to release his aggression, but the rational one wants to keep the game going."

This analogy, comparing individuals to nations, led me to ask Osgood whether he believed that nations act like people, for that assumption I had found implicit in his work. "I do," Osgood said, "and I think that you can't find a single writer on international affairs who doesn't personify either openly or through the back door. Our theories of international relations are implicitly theories of human beings. If that's the case, it's better to say so openly and see how well our theories stand up.

"There are at least three ways to look at international relations as fundamentally individual behavior. One of them is by the great-man theory—you know, that history is made entirely by great men, the notion used by the newspapers, which is nonsense, of course. The constraints on leaders are such that they can't make history by themselves. Another way to look at it is that, through the mass media, there is a great commonness of stimuli operating on everybody, including the leaders. That's nearer the truth.

"The third idea is a systems theory which says, in essence, that any adaptive organism will have inputs, outputs and so on, and that nations have analogous processes. I subscribe to this view. Information put into the system too rapidly will lower the ability to make decisions, that kind of thing. I got this idea studying suicide notes. The true suicides always displayed, in their notes, a higher degree of tension than the pseudo suicides who wrote notes but didn't do it. The true suicides showed markedly increased stress. Their systems were overloaded with it. Nations do the same thing. Too much tension overloads their decision-making circuits and they can no longer 'think.' "

"Would people's reading of international affairs be influenced by their own personalities?"

"Exactly. Those who see only power considerations are probably driven by power urges themselves. Extreme national fear, too, seems to reflect disturbances in individual psychology."

Was the United States driven by fear? "It gives every appearance," Osgood said. "Just why is a puzzle. Why are most Americans afraid to have their kids read various things? An underlying lack of faith in our own institutions, I'd say. One theory I have, and we've got some data on this, is the fear of poverty which is very dominant here. Our cross-cultural studies on eight national groups show that of them all the Americans and the Flemish show the greatest fear of not having enough to eat. Isn't that strange? The best-fed groups worry most about food. Our fear of Communism, even before World War II, has always been on an essentially economic plane—the fear of losing what we have."

I said, maybe we have something to be afraid *of*. "The Soviet Union is no more aggressive than any have-not country," Osgood replied. "We've got to expect that the source of aggression will come from the have-nots. I have to go back to what I said before. The reasons that Americans are so unsympathetic to revolutions like Cuba's is because of the fear of being reduced ourselves. Fat cats are afraid of change. And the tragedy is that it is based on a fallacy. Because if they get more, we will still have what we have— or more."

What Stands in the Way?

That the United States, its government leaders, and people must bear a large share of responsibility for international tension is an

idea common among the experimentalists and it is expressed in
various ways. One charge frequently heard is that American foreign
policy has misinterpreted the Soviet Union and, as a result, has
been far too rigid and even belligerent. This is the view of Dr. Fred
Warner Neal, professor of international relations and government
at Claremont Graduate School in Claremont, California. Neal is
far from exonerating the Soviet Union, whose policy he describes
as "often disruptive, obstructionist and uncooperative to the point
of paranoia." Nonetheless, "it is necessary to state that the responsibility for today's dangerous international situation must also be
shared in no little degree by American policy."

Neal's case is that Americans misread Marxist theory as practiced
in the Soviet Union. A revolution, according to Lenin, must be gen-
erated from within when the "objective conditions" are present.
There is no ideological compulsion to military aggression, nor does
Communism, of itself, necessarily mean Soviet domination, said
Neal in 1961, before the Sino-Soviet split. It is true that Lenin once
said he saw armed conflict between Communism and capitalism as
inevitable, but this was during the Bolshevik Revolution when the
U.S.S.R. was being invaded, when the Russians "naïvely believed
that the fall of capitalism was right around the corner."

For Neal, the distinction between political and military aggression is critical, for the assumption of Soviet military aggression is
what has propelled American policy down a tragic path, orienting
our policies against dangers that were not there, costing us precious
time in dealing with the social realities of the world, and pushing
the arms race to the brink of disaster. Neal quotes George Kennan
as saying, "Until we stop pushing the Kremlin through a closed
door, we shall never learn whether it would be prepared to go
through an open door."

The answer, Neal feels, is to cease and desist from demands that
the Soviets quit Eastern Europe, for we in no way ease the plight
of the people there. We should withdraw from our bases around the
Soviet heartland, and we should restrict our global interest to those
which really matter to our security. Disengagement, then, is Neal's
strategy, coupled with a firm demand that the Soviets recognize

U.S. "core interests," as, for instance, in South America. In peaceful competition in the underdeveloped world, the U.S. could fare well, better than at present when it seeks to enforce its will by military might.

"I do think the Communists have a very bad government," Neal says, "but no extreme commitment to military ideology. Much nonsense has been written about that. The idea that the Soviet Union had plans to invade Western Europe is utterly fantastic. The Soviet Union is more of a state than an ideological center for world revolution. It's wrong to think either that it's altruistic or a conspiracy whose whole object is to cause trouble. The notion that there is an international Communist conspiracy is also a fantasy. The Soviets can't even control Communist areas."

I wondered how this, in Neal's opinion, erroneous view toward the Communists had come into being. "My personal villain is Truman," Neal said. "His tradition was isolationism and therefore he was ignorant of the world. Couple this with American moralism and with our idea that here we had finally come graciously into the world only to have the Russians disappoint us and you've got the makings of our rigidity. The Russians are isolationist and highly moral, too. Truman is the epitome of the average man who looks to a primitive military solution to problems. Truman identified the Soviet Union with the Nazis, and this opened the way for McCarthyism. It really came down to a sort of Acheson-Truman-McCarthy doctrine. This identification of the Nazis and Communists has generally been accepted ever since by the government. The problem has been the lack of an independent opposition to this kind of thought."

Neal sucked on his pipe, and I asked him what his own independent opposition was in favor of doing. "I'm not in favor of doing anything that would jeopardize American security. No nation can ever trust another nation completely, and no one knows who will control the weaponry of other nations. For this reason I accept the necessity of some of our military strength. But an effort should be made to reduce those aspects of it that appear provocative. I would also like to make a better distinction between those areas in the world which are important to us and those which aren't. I opposed, you know, our Korean intervention, and I'm similarly against our involvement in Vietnam, on the grounds that neither constitutes our core interests. I think the domino or falling-blocks theory that if one country goes Communist its neighbor does is all bound up with the international conspiracy notion and plain silly. In some places of the world people might be better off with Communism, in some they would be worse off, and in some even though they might be better off I'd oppose it because the U.S. has a core interest there, such as Latin America. I'm in favor of the recognition of East Germany because it exists. There's no reason why the Alliance should fall apart if this is done. In short, I'm in favor of flexibility and protecting real, not imagined, American interests."

The belief that the United States has overextended itself and ought to pull back, giving its real international commitment only to a supranational organization, is widespread among the experimentalists, and it leads to a rather interesting crossing of party lines. Whereas people who might be thought of as conservative, such as Goldwater's foreign policy adviser, Strausz-Hupé, would actually extend American foreign entanglements, in the name of prosecuting the cold war, some of the liberally minded experimentalists would return simply to protecting the United States. One such is David F. Cavers, Fessenden Professor of Law at Harvard and a member of the Boston Area Faculty Group on Public Issues, one of whose purposes is to fight the fallout shelters program. He says:

A policy of progressive, if gradual, detachment from the responsibilities to other nations that we undertook in our successful effort to preserve the post-war world from political chaos would make it far easier for us and for them to accept the chances that a disarmed world would have to adjust to. At the same time it would permit a gradual thaw in our relations with our Communist adversaries . . . let me shamelessly assert my belief that political independence, the good ingredient in isolationism, is a virtue we sorely need to recapture and that, as we approach such independence, the acceptance and effectuation of disarmament will steadily become easier.

A school of war-peace thought virtually opposite from this is also to be found among the experimentalists, one of its representatives being Arthur I. Waskow, of the Institute for Policy Studies in Washington. For him, the United States, in the name of its heritage, ought to increase its international thrust and even intensify the cold war, only by nonmilitary means.

Waskow wants a minimum deterrent as the first step to disarmament, but he insists that the problem of military force must be seen in terms of military strategy, not peace movement moralism. He says,

the very act of examining disarmament as a military strategy produces a tone or flavor quite different from the traditional view of disarmament as a moral and ethical imperative. . . . Most of the disarmament moralists . . . confront the Establishment as an enemy, since they tend to oppose the state system, the use of violence as a means of coercion, and the domination of men or nations. . . . [But] the disarmament strategists are able to find an audience at almost every level of society. . . .

Waskow sees the experimentalists as disarmament strategists whose task it is to plot a careful course to a future without nuclear arms.

Waskow's notion on getting there is sharply different from Osgood's:

I suspect that initiatives that deliberately increase international tensions in certain spheres of policy could contribute to such desirable ends as disarmament. In particular, I feel that simultaneous initiatives aimed at eliminating American counterforce strategic capabilities and at increasing American political and economic pressures upon the Soviet Union might place the Soviets in a position where they would be forced to take the goal of disarmament more seriously.

Even after minimum deterrence and then disarmament had been achieved, the world would not be tranquil, and Waskow speaks of "disarmed disorder." The battle between nations and systems would continue, only by nonlethal means, and Waskow suggests, for instance, sending American Negroes trained in nonviolence to underdeveloped countries to lead anti-Communist revolutionary struggles. "And so the conflict of states might be settled through economic, political and psychological 'wars' that did not involve arms and killing. Americans, using their courage and ingenuity, should find such a world not easily won, but exhilarating to fight for." Waskow wants the United States to win the cold war, and what stands in the way, for him, is American unwillingness to experiment with nonlethal equivalents of military force.

The experimentalists' concern that the U.S. is a cold war force has also caused them to worry that the country will continue in the arms race because the economic penalties of disarmament will be too severe. "There has been considerable resistance to making [disarmament] studies," writes Professor Emile Benoit of Columbia, "based on the notion that disarmament is impossible to attain, and that such studies may create overoptimism and lead to a relaxation of vigilance or increased resistance to bearing the heavy burden of big defense."

A few governmental study groups are working on the problem of "reconversion," as it's called, and many of the defense industries employ small staffs to work on arms control and disarmament, partly to investigate new product lines and partly to act as a kind of disarmament barometer. I talked to a good many of these men and found them, contrary to popular stereotypes of defense industry people as eager to arm and rearm, prepared to accept disarmament gracefully. Some think the defense industries should diversify, others are frankly pessimistic about the ability of the giants to survive, and still others cogitate bold schemes. One such is an arms control expert from Raytheon, Dr. Thomas O'Sullivan, who proposes that defense industries, uniquely equipped as they are to handle new problems, become loosely organized, task-solving enterprises, willing to take on almost any job and provide the research, the people and the production, whether it be for weather control or better organization of hospitals.

But it's probably a sign that substantial disarmament is unconsciously considered a long way off that few full-fledged economics-of-disarmament experts have emerged in the U.S. Benoit is one of the few who have, and he is now directing a Ford Foundation-financed program that he calls RIEDAC, standing for Research on the International Economics of Disarmament and Arms Control. This is a successor to a program called READ (Research on the Economic Adjustments to Disarmament), which was financed mainly by the Carnegie Corporation.

Benoit's disarmament model, created in 1961, assumes a cutback in U.S. armed forces personnel from three million to one-half million by 1977, "with a cutoff in the production of bombers and liquid-fuel rockets and tactical nuclear weapons by 1968, of solid-fuel rockets and nuclear fuel by 1971, and of conventional weapons by 1974." In the first three years following an agreement to disarm, U.S. defense expenditures would decline by $17 billion and ultimately by $46 billion, which, in Benoit's view, would be partly offset by an annual $7 billion U.S. contribution to an international force for inspection, police and deterrence. Another $7 billion would be plowed back into civilian space and atomic energy programs; thus, in fifteen years, Benoit sees a net reduction of $32 billion in U.S. defense spending.

Benoit believes the basic obstacles to a satisfactory adjustment are psychological and political, not economic. The United States can surmount the economic perils of disarmament *provided* no attempt is made to achieve a surplus in the federal budget and retire the national debt. He points out, as a few Senators and Congressmen have, that, in sharp conflict with current beliefs, real federal expenditures for nondefense goods and services were, on a per capita basis, 42 percent lower in 1961 than in 1939. Benoit says that new types of public works and welfare programs may be necessary, such as a large research and development program. "However," he points out, "if we enter tomorrow into an age of jet travel, space exploration, cheap nuclear energy, Telstar world communication, advanced miniaturized electronics, etc., it will be largely attributable to the spillover from past defense-financed R&D and grants to higher education. In my opinion, the economic contribution from all this to civilian life will pay for the whole defense program many times over, so that, paradoxically, one could argue that the defense program, rather than being a heavy burden, really costs us nothing." The point, to Benoit, is that the U.S. must not try to cram itself back into the old predefense type of economy, but strike out into something new. The development of "an effective prosperity and growth policy should be given top priority."

Benoit and other economists do see serious problems arising from "structural" unemployment, for example, in areas like Arizona and California where 20 to 30 percent of the labor force is in defense industries. Here, Benoit feels, the answer will be in diversification and area redevelopment, again involving the use of government money. It may be, too, that inspection itself will prove to be expensive, so that many defense industries might well become inspection industries (although it must be added that other experts do not feel inspection will prove to be expensive). But his main suggestion is that the defense industries, even if it takes federal subsidies to do it, begin to work on such problems as "water conservation, improvements in productivity, planning and implementing urban redevelopment, commutation and other transport systems, weather control, improved aviation facilities and traffic control, industrial development of the oceans, establishment of world-wide communications networks, large-scale production of teaching machines and programs for the eradication of illiteracy, and the world-wide transmission of development skills, etc., etc. If these tasks were performed by the companies now holding defense contracts, this would be no more 'socialistic' than the defense program is now." The defense industry, Benoit says, "constitutes today one of the major concentrations of truly creative and innovational brainpower in American life . . . it is mounting . . . great and ambitious programs which exhibit and continually amplify our capabilities to apply science to the achievement of men's goals. Our nation's prestige and influence, as well as its economic progress, will increasingly depend on its success in using the type of productive capabilities which defense industry has nurtured. . . ."

Benoit laments that more is not being done on the economics of disarmament by the U.S. Government. "There is no one in the government really empowered to take charge of it," he told his visitor. "We need a new kind of authority capable of redirecting resources released from defense efforts. Many people think the problem is too remote to think about. They overlook the possibility of rapid change—but with another Cuba, or with cities blowing up and nobody knowing why, I think the situation could change over-night, and I'm afraid some such event is the most likely way that disarmament may arrive. A principal danger in arms cuts is that if we cut back without a supranational enforcement authority to safeguard the peace and if we should then have to rearm there would be a terrific right-wing reaction. Major arms cuts will be safe only if you build up a supranational enforcement agency at the same time that you disarm."

A corroborating opinion is voiced by Arthur Barber, a Deputy Assistant Secretary of Defense who works in both arms control and reconversion problems. "The real question," Barber says, "is how you allocate resources, and that's a political issue at heart. We can get plenty of money for a moon shot but not for education or hospitals. It's a failure in our political system that by and large Congress and the people will pay only for programs that have not been tried. A supersonic transport or oceanography, yes, but money for our existing needs, no. We could solve many of our problems with money, but people cry socialism. We must clarify the distinc-tion between federal subsidy and federal control. Washington would be willing to give up control if the programs were fairly monitored."

That American thought and institutions contribute to an un-willingness on our part to relax tensions is the theme of a responsible group of intellectuals centered around *The Correspondent*, a maga-zine published by David Riesman, the sociologist, Erich Fromm, the psychologist, and H. Stuart Hughes, the historian. "In the mak-ing of twentieth-century American foreign policy," writes Staugh-ton Lynd, in its pages,

an impressive series of such figures have stepped into government from a background not of business, but of corporation law: Richard Olney, Elihu Root, Robert Lansing, Henry Stimson, Dean Acheson, and John Foster Dulles, to name only a few of them. There are men whose devotion has been to the society as a whole, as that society's interest is perceived through the lesson of the experience of its upper class. They are the men ready to say, as President Kennedy said in the aftermath of the Cuban invasion, that "our system" will be defended at any cost. The type of economic motive I am attempting to suggest has a difference . . . from that ordinarily associated with Marxism. It is the stance not of grasping men, but of men who feel themselves on the defensive.

A lively flow of social criticism is maintained by *The Correspondent* for its four thousand readers. The picture of the cold war one gets from its pages is that everybody is on the defensive in one way or another. If the Americans feel economically threatened, the Soviets are an emerging society, backwards in many respects. "Soviet diplomats . . . felt that their manners, their clothes, their whole style was inferior to that of the well-tailored, tall and elegant aristocrats of the West," Riesman says. He reports that in Vienna, President Kennedy's mother, Rose, said loudly about Khrushchev, "How small he is!" "Khrushchev, immediately alert, asked an interpreter what she had said; the remark was translated, and he stiffened visibly."

The contributors appear to regard the Russians as self-conscious hicks with a deep feeling of inferiority. Threats only make them belligerent. But instead of understanding this, the Americans overrespond. For this, *The Correspondent* blames, on the one hand, the "toughs," that is, the militants, and, on the other, the American personality itself. Roger Hagan, *The Correspondent's* editor, lists six characteristics of an American style: self-righteousness, punitiveness, bewilderment, the myth of a pure past, projectivity (attacking in others what we feel exists in ourselves) and a sense of emptiness. "Perhaps this is the real irony of American history," Hagan says; "in spite of their totalitarian background, the Russians have more faith in politics than we; in spite of the liberal intellectuals in our leadership, we believe less in the life of the mind and the power of ideas than [the Russians do]. They deter war, we deter the external forces of darkness."

The Correspondent bears the unmistakable stamp of the romantic sociology of David Riesman, author of *The Lonely Crowd* and a ranking American intellectual. Riesman, Fromm and others have helped support *The Correspondent* with their own funds since its inception. "More and more of my time has gone into trying to keep up with the march of events and to efforts to understand these in historical perspective," Riesman says. He sponsors a Harvard student peace group called Tocsin. He also carries on, with the aid of a portable dictaphone, a far-ranging correspondence, much of it on foreign policy subjects, and he is willing to do almost anything to help either students or peace, though Riesman draws the line when it comes to writing articles for popular magazines or being interviewed on television, even when the emoluments offered are relatively handsome by the standard of a professor's salary.

Riesman is a self-confessed amateur for peace, but he says, "Until a serious effort is mobilized for peace, amateurs will probably have to be relied on for new ideas in the field of defense and foreign policy." Riesman sees dangers in totalitarian Communism, but he, like the other experimentalists, is concerned that the American response in the cold war has been misguided, and his hope is that "the practicality of ethical considerations may become more widely understood, and that discussions of deterrence and its alternatives can be enlarged, and more differentiated modes of thought encouraged." His enemy is the cold war itself, which, he feels, is "a distraction from serious thought about man's condition on this planet."

Riesman makes clear that he is no pacifist. "I'm opposed to pacifism not because I like war or cannot imagine living in a warless world, but because I regard pacifist techniques as unrealistic." (Riesman enjoys quoting a suggestion that if we wanted to show the Soviets we were serious about threats, say, to Berlin, he would have the Secretary of State call in the Soviet Ambassador, shoot him and send him home in a box. This, Riesman says, would be preferable to a nuclear strike, but it seems to shock officials who hear of it.) But though he is not repelled at the thought of armed deterrence of war, he is appalled by the inability of the Soviet Union and the United States to break out of the cold war, which he compares to sibling rivalry. He is especially appalled by the failure of the United States, as the older brother, to take the initiative.

Riesman's analysis of the cold war is really an extension of this point. For the failure of the U.S. he has many explanations, for instance, a nostalgic desire to cling to a confederate past on the part of the right wing (about which Riesman worries considerably); the need for the American male to prove himself by being "hard"; a certain schoolboyishness that Riesman finds evidence of in such military establishment vocabulary as doing one's "homework" and "military posture"; and the American style, about which Walt Rostow talks so glowingly, but which, to Riesman, suffers from an inadequate formulation of alternatives, a tendency to oversimplify, and "a certain callous lack of sympathy for the sufferings of others." Riesman concludes, "What I am suggesting here is that it may be easier in the short run to contain the Soviet Union than to contain our own allies or the American energies mobilized behind the cold war."

"I know I will be misunderstood," Riesman says somewhere, and, indeed, like many experimentalists he does not quite make explicit what he is driving at. The reason is, perhaps, that Riesman is not really presenting an analysis of international relations, but one of internal, domestic relations. If the U.S. improved itself as a society, it would become stronger, more self-confident and less defensive, Riesman thinks, and its reaction to the Soviet Union would therefore be firmer, more consistent and more likely to influence their behavior in the direction of nuclear disengagement. In this view, clearly, the Soviet Union and its allies in the Communist bloc would respond positively to the actions of a mature United States. Riesman thus explores the cold war through the instrument of the American character.

Riesman is a slight, dark-haired, bushy-eyebrowed man with a round face and prominent spectacles. I asked him about himself, and he told me that he had started out in life as a lawyer, was legal secretary to Supreme Court Justice Brandeis, and worked for a while in the office of the District Attorney of New York City.

During the war, Riesman handled contract negotiations with the government for the Sperry Gyroscope Company.

"I was always very interested in society and my commitment to law was never deep," Riesman says. "After the war, I started to teach at the University of Chicago, but I don't have any other degree than in law—no master's, no Ph.D., because I never took time out to get them. I was too busy educating myself retrospectively. I became a sociologist because I found my closest kinship with the sociologists. I couldn't have been more surprised about the success of *The Lonely Crowd*. My interest in the comparative study of whole societies has influenced my thinking on foreign policy and vice-versa."

I asked Riesman where he stood in the great debate and he said, "Oh, I'm wildly experimental, all right. I'd like to see the United States and the Soviet Union undertake a joint industrialization of China, and I once suggested, not entirely facetiously, that the United States bombard the Soviet Union with nylon stockings and refrigerators, to force the Soviets to put more effort into consumer goods and less into arms. That may sound materialistic, but I tend to defend materialism, at least insofar as it is superior to fanaticism. I'm not totally opposed to nuclear weapons; I see nuclear arms on the whole as a kind of storm cellar, but I don't want any soft missiles and no deployed tactical ones either."

I admitted to a certain difficulty in getting a "fix" on Riesman, who nodded and said, "One reason why it's hard for people to locate me politically is that I was a conservative, though not so much any more. I felt, and still do, that private property furnishes support for civil and cultural freedom. I was never an admirer of Roosevelt, and I never thought of the Soviet Union as the wave of the future or omnipotent. I was a Tory even when some of my friends were radicals of various persuasions. I've tried to take a balanced attitude; I have a considerable fear of Communist China, and of incendiary powers getting hold of nuclear weapons, but on the other hand, when it comes to the Soviet Union, I have a greater, though not a complete, trust.

"We have never had a very clear picture of the Soviet Union.

The main sympathizers here were those who were down on America, and among the opponents were those who had swung violently to the other extreme. Their attitudes were reinforced by the refugees who came here, by Niebuhrian pessimism—I'm suspicious of the present fashion of emphasizing basic malevolence and original sin, though, of course, the potential is all there—and by the many Soviet experts who have continued to insist that nothing has changed basically since Stalin, and that Khrushchev was only a cleverer and more adventurous Stalin. Then, those Americans who went to Russia weren't markedly good observers. I went there in 1931, after having learned some Berlitz Russian, and what I decided was that many Americans knew so little about America and American history they had no basis for comparison. They knew nothing about our own problems of before the Civil War, with steamboats exploding and railroads falling apart. They had no idea what we were like, so they thought the Russian Revolution was a flop. So educated opinion here swung violently against the Soviet Union to where it came to meet popular opinion, which has never been anything but suspicious and which, even now, won't really admit that the two countries were once allied.

"In emphasizing the psychological and cultural aspects of the cold war on the American side," Riesman went on, "I don't mean to overlook more strictly economic or military factors but rather to emphasize themes that tend to be neglected or treated by simplistic assumptions about American or Soviet character and society.

"My view of the Soviet Union is the same as it is of any society—that it is capable of radical change and that it's not the same Soviet Union today as it was yesterday. Violence, for instance. Read Chekhov and you see that Russia was a world of thugs. Soviet society, by comparison, is much safer. The United States, similarly, is much less violent, and one reason violence is shocking to us is that it has become *outré*. I think that the S.U. and the U.S. have great influence on one another, and a great sadness of the cold war is that opportunities offered by one side are not grasped by the other. In this, I attribute much blame to the U.S. We've started on a track and it's hard to divert us. We have a tremendous amount of drive here, and through the cold war we've found a way to externalize it. I think it's too bad that we can't find the means to use the enormous and healthy American energy to our domestic ends."

Riesman, it's plain, is not offering a program so much as an impressionistic portrait of what ought to be done. For the experimentalist grand design, I turned to the idea of world government.

THE GOAL

To be sure, some experimentalists do not find in a world government an agreeable conception, on the grounds that either the cold war remains to be fought (nonviolently) or that a world government is a potential oppressor itself. Nonetheless, the dominant spirit among experimentalists is for stronger world organization in one form or another, to be supported by a world parliament with stronger powers than the UN and backed by the fists and arms of a world police force.

The world governmentalists themselves by no means present a united front, being divided, roughly, into "minimalists" and "maximalists." The maximalists advocate, in the near future, a real world government (though perhaps a federate one) with a world congress given binding power in many areas over individual states and, conceivably, a world president elected at large. The minimalists are undecided as to whether to effect changes through improving the UN or starting a new international agency to go with it, but on the whole they stand for the sort of world government whose sole responsibility would be the preservation of peace and the development of backward countries, leaving a more comprehensive world order for evolution to take care of. The minimalist position, represented by the American Association for the United Nations, the United World Federalists, the World Peace Through World Law Center in Washington, the World Rule of Law Center at Duke University and so on, is the dominant voice in the world government movement, and its intellectual leader is a Harvard professor of law named Louis Sohn.

In 1958, Sohn and Grenville Clark, a well-known lawyer, published *World Peace Through World Law,* a detailed plan for revising the UN charter and establishing effective institutions for the prevention of war. At the outset, the authors make clear that neither the arms race, an indefinite "balance of terror" nor diplomatic maneuver will ensure peace, but that universal and complete disarmament is required, along with law-enforcing agencies to maintain it. To enable the United Nations to achieve its basic task of collective security, Clark and Sohn want to equip it with new peace-keeping machinery embracing not only an effective inspection system but also a strong military force.

The plan implies deep changes in the international environment at the outset, for five-sixths of the nations of the world, representing five-sixths of the population, would be required to ratify it, meaning that Communist China must be a signatory. Assuming that she becomes one, peace would then become the property of the UN General Assembly, which would be given definite legislative powers in this field, and, accordingly, the UN representation would be revised, with the four largest nations given thirty votes each, the next eight fifteen, and so on down to small nations with one vote. Representatives to the UN General Assembly would eventually be elected by popular vote. There would be, in addition, an Executive Council replacing the Security Council, with seventeen nations chosen by the General Assembly, always including the big four, on which the veto would be abolished in favor of a complicated procedure which would still leave the larger countries strong powers to say nay or *nyet.* What the authors call the "disarmament process" would be supervised by an Inspection Service with the right of access and verification, and would take at least twelve years, at the end of which no national military forces would remain, but only a United Nations Peace Force build-up as national forces went down. The UN Peace Force would be empowered to enforce the procedures adopted by five-sixths of the nations even on those who did not join the UN. There would be a Nuclear Energy Authority to buy up fissionable materials, and an Outer Space Agency to see to it that space stays peaceful, too.

The UN Peace Force, as Clark-Sohn envisage it, would consist of between 200,000 and 400,000 men, drawn from all the countries of the world and dispersed to avoid concentration on the territory of any nation-state. It would be backed up by a large reserve, and it would be empowered to use nuclear arms under extreme circumstances, though they would be strictly in the custody of a civilian authority. The peace force would be under the immediate leadership of representatives from only the smaller nations, although directions would come from the Executive Council and the General Assembly. Strong provision is made for an international judicial authority to settle disputes, and the authors propose, as an integral part of the scheme, a World Development Authority to foment the economic development of the poorer countries, on the theory that peace will not be secure in a world divided into nations fat and thin.

Clark and Sohn have since come up with another proposal, for a World Disarmament and World Development Organization that would be affiliated with the UN but which would not require revision of the UN Charter. Any nation, even those not in the UN, such as both Germanies, both Vietnams and both Koreas, would be entitled to join, and there would be a world representative body and world executive along the lines the authors suggested for the UN. The bill for the WDWDO would be about $75 billion a year, $15 billion for peace-keeping and the rest for development, to be paid for by a national tax of 3 percent of each country's gross national product, or about $18 billion for the U.S. This tax would be taken directly by the UN (as, say, withholding taxes are taken now) so that no state could easily renege.

This setup has certain advantages from the standpoint of international acceptance, one being that the UN Charter needn't be tampered with, and another that, in effect, the world would get a bicameral legislature, with the General Assembly and the WDWDO assembly functioning at once. Both plans are limited to the preservation of peace. "All other powers," Clark says, "should be reserved to nations and their peoples. This definition and reservation of powers is advisable not only to avoid opposition based upon fear of possible interference in the domestic affairs of the nations, but also because it is wise for this generation to limit itself to the single task of preventing international violence or the threat of it. If we can accomplish that, we should feel satisfied and could well leave to later generations any enlargement of the powers of world organization that they might find desirable."

What Clark-Sohn and others claim is that GCD is too narrow a concept, and that it cannot possibly function without machinery to handle disputes about interpretations of law and demanded changes. They postulate that the two dominant theories of international relations—the balance of power theory, now deterrence; and collective security, the UN—are no longer adequate to meet world needs. They are implicitly saying that under the theory of the social contract the individual gives up certain rights to the state which guarantees his protection in return, and when the state can no longer provide that protection the individual may break that contract and sign a new one with the only organization that can so do, a world authority. They also presume that such a change can occur peacefully.

We come here to one of the typical debates in the war-peace establishment, as set down in the pages of the *War/Peace Report*, between Clark and Herman Kahn as to whether a peaceful change to world law is possible. "I am perfectly willing to assert that the natural state of man is an empire of some sort," Kahn says, and goes on to postulate that while world government is inevitable it will most likely come by one side conquering another, and here Kahn finds support in Reinhold Niebuhr, who is of the same opinion. To Kahn, a peaceful transition appears too difficult because of the hurdle of how to distribute voting power so that small, and potentially unruly, nations will not gain control of the peace force, impose a high income tax on the developed nations and other unpleasant consequences. Nor, to Niebuhr and Kahn, does world government necessarily mean world community; rather, under the stress of a seriously differentiated work community, the world government would fall apart.

Kahn, Clark observes in reply, is somewhat baffling in showing that what must, and inevitably will, happen cannot happen, for which Clark accuses Kahn of dogmatism and says that his opponent "lacks experience" with drastic change. "It is a curious phenomenon," writes Clark, who has practiced law since 1906 and is in his eighties, "which I have often observed that in this period of rapid change, younger persons tend to be more skeptical of revolutionary developments than older people who, without being any more imaginative, have simply had more opportunity to observe changes which in their youth were scoffed at as beyond reach." And, Clark says, Kahn underrates the human capacity to find a way out of a serious position when conscious of the danger and under sufficient stress. Clark admits that framing a world constitution may be more difficult than, for instance, launching the United States of America, but he pleads for "constructive ability," which he finds Kahn lacks.

The key element here, it seems, is whether a limited world government would encourage the cohesion of states, or whether such international institutions must await the development of an enhanced international political community. The fear, on the one hand, is that a premature world state which then dissolved into warring units would be almost impossible to reconstruct, and, on the other, that with no international state at all the world may be condemned to the present unstable nuclear situation. Clark and Sohn have elected to make a moderate step in the direction of world order through their peace-keeping plan.

I took up some of the aspects of the Clark-Sohn proposals with Louis Sohn, Bemis Professor of Law at Harvard, who turned out to be a medium-sized, amiable man with a bald head and eyeglasses enlaired in a small law office which looked as though he had half the books from the law library out on loan. I asked Sohn how he had become interested in world law, and he said that he had been born in Poland and gone to school there and had decided, at an early age, that international affairs were "all that really mattered." His father, though, thought that Sohn ought to have a practical grounding, so Sohn studied both law and diplomatic relations. In reviewing a book about American law, Sohn discovered that the United States managed to survive with forty-eight legal systems, plus that of the federal government, and this convinced Sohn that different legal systems could be successfully merged into one whole.

Sohn arrived in the United States in 1939, and worked his way as a bus boy through Harvard law to his doctorate. During the war, Sohn worried about the next war he perceived on the horizon and the international organizations that might be able to deal with it. In 1944 he met Clark, and the two of them set out to examine the whole field of international law and present a proposal of their own. It took Clark-Sohn from 1944 until 1957 to write *World Peace Through World Law*, and they are still at it, with new proposals and revisions.

"One theory we wanted to show," Sohn said, with a slight accent, "was that there was an evolution. We were trying to point out article by article how you could do what we suggested without destroying the present structure of the UN, and that there were precedents for everything we said. I actually put down on paper the precedents for one of our proposals that took two pages in the book; the precedents for the two pages came to 120 pages. And we also wanted to make our plan understandable to the public, which meant trying to find relatively simple, not-too-technical language.

"We can't rely on our present UN," Sohn went on. "It's makeup must be revised to cope with new problems. The veto must go and the big powers need more of a vote to compensate for the loss of the veto. The UN can't rely on its present financing either, for it almost collapsed on this issue. Most important, we need the best first-strike policy, which, of course, is disarmament."

As Sohn sees it, genuine disarmament would have to be accompanied by genuine peace-keeping machinery through some sort of international arrangement. Arms negotiations can begin outside the UN, but, sooner or later, they will have to come within it. In the meantime, he is all for the U.S. and the S.U. taking the first steps, and he is a consultant to the ACDA and has served with the American negotiating team at Geneva.

I asked Sohn whose fault it was that the negotiations had stretched out for so many years with so little results. Sohn thought a second and said, "The U.S. proposals have too much inspection in proportion to disarmament and the Russian proposals do not have enough inspection in proportion to disarmament, and that is the trouble. Neither side has been ingenious enough to find proposals that would enable them to agree on the minimum inspection needed for each disarmament step. One of the basic troubles is that we put so much effort into the test ban only scraps of energy are left for thinking through the next stage.

"And then we may have oversold complete and general disarmament. Even after we've passed through minimum deterrence I would still leave some military force for the big powers for the foreseeable future. The U.S., say, might cut back to the forces it had in 1932." And if the Soviets wouldn't agree? "It's necessary to do what it is necessary to do," Sohn said. "Both sides have an interest in increasing their security by diminishing arms. We can devise methods to persuade the Russians. I am optimistic about this. By 1970, I think we will get pretty far down the line." And China? "Perhaps China could be persuaded. Maybe there would have to be a joint U.S.–S.U. blockade of China."

Others, less optimistic than Sohn about the UN, like Strausz-Hupé, have suggested strong regional arrangements like the Atlantic Union to take the place of a world government. About this, Sohn said, "If we had six or so strong groups in the world, it would be like 1984. It would be the old balance of power situation, only this time with nuclear-armed superblocs. That thought makes me tremble. I don't like Clarence Streit's idea of a white Atlantic Alliance either, for that would divide the world into two camps. One vague possibility I can see is an Atlantic world that also includes some Asian and African nations, but, generally, I don't feel alliances like this work except under enormous pressures. So I have to fall back on Clark-Sohn."

I wondered how and when Sohn thought even a limited world government would happen, and he said, "I think Kahn's quite right on this; it's very likely to happen after a crisis, of which I expect many more. Cuba would have been an opportunity for a step forward, and we may need more Cubas. Not that I want them, you understand. The other possibility is by evolution, and while I'm not clear as to which way it will come, I do anticipate some kind of world government by the year 2000 or 2100. If we have to wait until 3000, there won't be any more world. We owe it to ourselves to have some plans in our back pocket so that when the crisis does come we'll be ready for it.

"One shouldn't be discouraged by the slowness—it took the United States a long time to evolve to its present form. I'm not worried either by complaints that our proposal is too technical, and not operational, because I realize that you only start with a blueprint and after that you will need a lot of dirty, difficult compromises. I think our proposals are right in principle, but they may change in practice. I'm a pragmatist, you know. I think the advocacy of some people in putting new ideas in concrete form is the way change happens. You can never tell when something will germinate, but if you do good work, it will someday be useful to somebody even if it's not acceptable now. That's what I think, anyway, and I guess it has sustained me over the years."

The experimentalists are in agreement on a number of ideas. All want a minimum deterrent as a first step to more general disarmament, and all feel the United States can contrive positions and negotiate them in a successful manner with the Russians. A "no first strike" policy is called for by most experimentalists. All place a considerable degree of blame on the U.S. for the cold war, higher, certainly, than most deterrers do, and the explanations for this are too great a U.S. reliance on military force, an inflexible foreign policy, a dogmatic electorate and an unwillingness or inability to experiment. Few experimentalists believe in the precepts of realism and its notions of an implacable urge for power on the part of nations and individuals, and, in line with their more genial conception of human nature, experimentalists, for the most part, take a view of the Soviets which, while not precisely rosy, can probably be best described as tolerant. Neither military force nor deterrence, to the experimentalists, is likely to be effective in the long run, and the answer to the flourishing of nuclear arms is not to make them

safer, through arms control, because the instability will persist, but
to do away with them as rapidly as possible. At the same time, the
United States ought vastly to increase aid to underdeveloped countries and to press for a supranational agency to enforce disarmament
at once.

To accomplish such goals, the experimentalist credo says, experiment. Offer one thousand of the most important Communists
from underdeveloped countries a six-month, all-expenses-paid trip
to the United States, to win them over; put a nursery in the lobby
of the UN; distribute freely American surplus food over the world;
buy the machinery from obsolescent American factories and give it
away; begin a joint U.S.–U.S.S.R. disaster corps for international
relief; urge young people to join "the army of your choice," as we
now urge people to attend "the church of your choice"; stop the
"brainwashing" of populations by their governments, including
that of the U.S.

Have the UN sponsor international achievement contests so that
nations can reveal their good sides to the world. Initiate cooperative
trade policies, research programs, loan programs, agricultural programs—have a sustained policy of "massive reconciliation." Don't
rely on newspaper reporters to provide the truth about others; go
see for yourself, or send truth squads abroad to get at it. Form a
council of the best minds from East, West and the neutrals to solve
disputes. One writer suggests an Intellectual's Manifesto:

Intellectuals, Scientists, Scholars, and Academicians of the world,
unite; we have nothing to lose but our ideological blinders. The problems besetting the world are too serious to permit our work to be beclouded by dogmas or narrowly conceived national interest. . . . Let
us begin to replace dogmatic, ideological assertion with an open-minded,
objective, factual test of our theories and hypotheses about economic
development, social change, and the development of creative, responsible people. Only by so doing will our common objectives of creating
a saner, comelier, and more amicable life be achieved.

To such high-minded sentiment one deterrer is likely to answer
"Bosh!" To him, experimental analysis is too subjective, too full of

projections of the experimentalists' own attitudes, to be of use to policy-makers worrying about contingencies and public opinion. Inherent in the experimentalist argument is the idea that international difficulties are based on misunderstanding and poor communications, and therefore *no* overwhelming obstacles prevent solutions. The deterrers doubt both halves of this proposition. They answer that the experimentalist solutions have been, and are being, tried, to which the experimentalists say, "But not hard enough."

VI

Peace Research

HAVING TO LIVE YOUR LIFE WITH A GAME LEG, YOU HAVE TO SOME *extent compensated for this handicap by your ability to lead people. At times, however, when something occurs placing you in a bad light your old feelings of inferiority and lack of confidence appear, leading you to do something impulsive to cover the wrong. In your eyes you are always right. Further, you are an emotional person often caught up in enthusiasm and optimism or pessimism of the moment. To you, your country is very important—you desire to increase its power and prestige in the world. Because you dominate people naturally and easily you are often not satisfied with other governmental officials who are too independent of you. . . .*

This is a sample from what is called an Inter-Nation Simulation Game as played at Northwestern and a few other universities where peace is undergoing research. You are a high school student and you are playing the role of the Central Decision Maker (CDM) of Dube, a country in deep dispute with its rival Colo over bases in space and control of the moon. Although great care has been taken to disguise the fact, the historical circumstances are reproductions in futuristic dress of the situation that existed in the summer of 1914, and you have been chosen for the part you play because your personality appears to resemble that of Kaiser Wilhelm II, the CDM of Germany-Dube. As it sometimes works out in these games, Dube's CDM takes his country to war, indicating to the researchers' cautious satisfaction how the personality of leaders has its impact on actual events, how leaders are subject to extreme tensions, how military threats may cause those tensions and escalate a threatened nation into war.

One of the originators of Inter-Nation Simulation is Dr. Harold Guetzkow, a professor of both psychology and political science at Northwestern, who explains the purposes of the exercise. "I call ourselves idea-builders," Guetzkow says. "The trouble with working in international relations is that you're handicapped because you can't experiment with history. So we have tried to create it, using a combination of people and computers. We want to use matched personalities not only because we want to be historically accurate, but also so that we can deliberately put in different personalities to see what would happen then. We tested about eight hundred people in our experiment on World War I to get the right twenty-four. The game took a week. The results have been congruent with historical fact. We had a fellow who played Lord Grey, and he wanted to call a peace conference during the game. We didn't know it at the time, but Lord Grey actually did try to call such a peace conference in 1914.

"We have two purposes," Guetzkow goes on. "One is teaching, to demonstrate how the international system works. You get the feel of it in our game. The other is research, for we would like to be able to predict the outcome of future events, and some years ago we began studies along these lines. One was on the proliferation of nuclear weapons, the 'Nth country' problem. Our simulation showed how the 'world' was different after the spread of nuclear arms. The external threat to a bloc was reduced, but the threat internal to each was increased. In other words, the cohesiveness of each bloc went down, and the number of states which acted independently increased. The outcome presaged what is happening today with France, with alliances going to pot."

"Was there 'war'?"

"One-third of our 'worlds' had thermonuclear war," Guetzkow said with a trace of sadness. "One of them was so extensive the simulation simply stopped."

Inter-Nation Simulation is one facet of a new and increasingly broad field of study known as peace research, or the peace research movement. Writes Donald L. Michael,

In the last few years, there has gradually grown a new state of mind in some whose profession it is to study man's individual behavior and that of his institutions. What once were, for example, simply studies in international affairs, political science and the psychology of decision making are now viewed, in a few quarters, as peace research. In the past, scholars in these fields might have been motivated to seek knowledge and understanding, or to improve our capability for conducting world affairs in traditional ways. Today, the professional peace researchers seek to discover the criteria and conditions for viable alternatives to the coming annihilation toward which traditional perspectives and operating styles are driving the world.

The flavor of peace research is experimental, but those engaged in it are not, at least consciously, out to formulate policies, plans and proposals. "I'm interested in the research, not where it leads," one peace researcher said. The idea is to investigate, at all levels, the causes and results of war, and the spirit of peace research scientists is not dissimilar to that, say, of Louis Pasteur confronted with the problem of anthrax. It is neither an action nor a pacifist movement, but one that sees its function, as the economist Kenneth Boulding puts it, in devising social systems that have the property of "stable peace." There is no doubt that some of peace research's devotees believe that they are unraveling, for the first time, some of the secrets of the mystery of war, and some think the field should properly be called "war-peace research."

Peace research is really so new that even those close to it have no clear idea of how to appraise the early results. Although a little of what's now called peace research went on before World War II, it was not until the late 1950's that the movement began to be organized, as it is now, into peace research centers with teams of scholars of different academic disciplines. Probably the first of the peace research centers was started by the psychologist Theo Lentz of St. Louis in 1957, called the Peace Research Laboratory. On its heels came the Center for the Study in Conflict Resolution (an unwieldy title dictated by the fear that peace was a subversive term), Creighton University's Center for Peace Research, begun by a Jesuit priest, the Institute for Communications Research at the University of Illinois at Urbana, the Institute for International

Order and so on. In addition, there are now peace research societies
and funds both American and international. For unknown reasons,
peace research is headquartered in the Middle West, and unknown, too, is how a peace research group decides whether to call
itself an institute or a center.

Peace research differs from the work of established "think factories" like Hudson and RAND. Its idea is to go beyond deterrence,
and, then, peace research is not generally investigating military
strategy and techniques in support of policies. Some government
money for research, however, comes from the Department of Defense and the Arms Control and Disarmament Agency. Another
$500,000 or so annually is put up by an unusual organization
known as Project Michelson at the U.S. Naval Ordnance Test
Station at China Lake, California, where behavioral scientists in
earshot of screaming jet engines are studying the psychology of
deterrence, usually reaching the conclusion, common among peace
researchers, that it is not an effective way of controlling the actions
of people or states.

The question with which peace research begins is whether man
has an instinct for bloodshed and fighting. (Peace research is not
necessarily original research, but may also apply to earlier findings
reorganized or reappraised against the background of thermonuclear war.) Eleanor Leacock expresses the prevailing view among
anthropologists: "Man is a fundamentally peaceful, cooperative
animal. He is curious, inventive, gregarious. If those things were
not true, he would never have evolved into man." While refusing
to more than suggest that there may be some parallels between the
behavior of man and the rest of the natural world, anthropologists
draw supporting evidence from patterns of animal behavior.

What we have previously interpreted as aggression among animals may be forms of cooperation. Vertebrates, for instance, may
actually try to prevent conflict by staking out defensive territory
from which, by spits and growls, other animals are warned. ("Nature" films emphasizing brutal conflict between animals may reveal
more about the audience than about the animals.) Even when
conflict between animals of the same species occurs, it is often a

ritual form of battle ending in defeat but not death. Except for man, and for ants and termites, organized war is unknown in the animal kingdom. Indeed, many forms of cooperation are common to higher forms of life and may make the difference between successful and unsuccessful evolution. The important point to many anthropologists is that sociality is the line human evolution has taken, and it is what has permitted the evolution of human beings.

Man's instinct for self-preservation is working against him today, some scientists think, on the theory that self-defense means nuclear self-defense and racial suicide. But most appear to believe that he is not condemned by nature to any special style of behavior. According to the psychologist Morton Deutsch,

Man's makeup may always contain the psychological characteristics which have found an outlet in militarism and war. There is no reason, however, to doubt that these characteristics can find satisfactory outlets in peaceful pursuits. Aggressiveness, adventurousness, idealism, and bravery will take a peaceful or destructive outlet depending upon the social, cultural, and political conditioning of the individual and upon the behavioral possibilities which exist within his social environment. Some may assert that war provides a more natural, spontaneous, or direct outlet for hostility and aggressiveness than any peaceful alternatives. Such an assertion is based upon a fundamental misconception of war: war is highly complex, organized social activity in which personal outlets for aggression and hostility are primarily vicarious, symbolic, indirect and infrequent for most of the participants. . . . War is defined to be such a good outlet *only* because of our cultural conditioning: the military toys children are given to play with, the identification of heroism and bravery with war in so many novels, TV dramas, and films that we are exposed to . . . the definition of patriotism in military terms.

If this view is correct, then war is a highly conditioned social activity, and it ought to follow that some societies are less warlike than others, and, indeed, some societies do not make war at all. ("What!" said an Eskimo, informed about war, "you mean you kill people you don't even *know!*" During World War I, Eskimos offered to send missionaries.) It seems that even in societies that do fight wars enormous pressures are required to make people willing to engage in military activity. T. Abel reports that warlike attitudes on the part of the population are likely to follow, not precede, the outbreak of hostilities.

Do the American people want war? A survey by the Institute of International Order asked, "Do you have any doubts about the desirability of peace?" and 81 percent responded "No." "Do you think there's any use in working for peace in spite of the current international situation?" "Yes," said 94 percent. "If world peace was established, could our ideas compete successfully with Communism?" "Yes," said a resounding 73 percent. "Do you think there will always be wars?" "Yes," said 55 percent.

Why will there always be wars if there is no enthusiasm for them? One answer given by peace researchers is called the self-fulfilling prophecy, a mechanism which is defined as a set of beliefs causing one to act according to what one expects to happen, thus setting in motion events which bring about precisely what one sought to avoid. This logic was used by a representative of the American Psychological Association in testifying against the shelter program before Congress.

The self-fulfilling prophecy occurs in both the U.S. and the U.S.S.R., both of which have "mirror images" of each other, according to Urie Bronfenbrenner, a social psychologist from Cornell. Each holds the other to be an aggressor, attempting to impose his will on the rest of the world; each thinks that the government of the other exploits people; each is convinced that the mass of the people is not sympathetic to the regime; each thinks the other cannot be trusted; and each thinks the policy of the other, in the nuclear age, is mad. Reinforcing the mirror image, it is thought, is social conformity which makes everyone think like everyone else, and the tendency of diplomats and reporters to interpret events in line with its side's image of the other. Assuming the other side is aggressive, one becomes aggressive oneself, and the images flashing back and forth in this hall of "twisted mirrors" are such that "even deliberate efforts to reverse the process are reinterpreted as evidences of confirmation." The hazard to the U.S., Bronfenbrenner says, is that, reacting to our image of the Soviets, we dramatize our aggressive stance and bungle the opportunities to present ourselves as a nation "committed to peace, human values, and the economic and social welfare of the world." The way out of the mirror-image trap, he says, is for one party or the other *"to be willing to accept what it regards as an unacceptable proposal."*

Misperceptions are considered a key feature of war by the peace researchers. How pervasive misconceptions are, say the researchers, is suggested by a study by the now defunct Committee for the Application of Behavioral Sciences to the Strategies of Peace (ABSSOP). It examined two rival groups in San Francisco. One was called OASIS, standing for Organization for Atomic Survival in Suburbia, and the other People for Peace. Each had about twenty-five members and each lived in the same town and had roughly the same income, social standing and so on. OASIS stood for bomb shelters, while People for Peace opposed shelters and wanted a positive program for peace. People for Peace described itself as radical, OASIS as conservative, and each believed the other to be quite different in spirit from itself.

In fact, the conservative OASISites supported Medicare, federal aid to education and the unification of East and West Germany as a United Nations protectorate. Even more mystifying to the researchers, OASIS thought that People for Peace was more conservative than itself. People for Peace, for its part, was convinced that shelter-builders must necessarily be conservative. What interested the researchers was that the two groups could have such extensive misperceptions about the other, when so many of their attitudes were the same. Such misunderstandings, peace researchers conclude, are a sample of what happens internationally in a bigger and more important way.

Peace researchers have also conducted a number of sociological surveys of the American attitudes toward the cold war and the Soviet Union. From one of them Andrea Modigliani concludes:

The public is aware of and knows the consequences of nuclear war almost to a man. A sizable fraction is in a state of some anxiety concerning this . . . people *do not* need to be told more gory facts about nuclear war . . . there is a dearth of information about Russia and Communism. This plus an understandable fear leads to a vicious circle whereby all Russian actions are perceived negatively, thus constantly worsening an already black image. In the end, people's concept of Russia is completely divorced from reality. While we can easily agree that life under Soviet rule means the absence of certain important human rights, it is hard to take so dark a view as the 45 per cent from my sample who claim that "any American would rather be dead than live *even for a year* under Russian domination."

Game theory is used by Anatol Rapoport, biologist-mathematician-semanticist of the Institute of Mental Health at the University of Michigan, to draw a profile of American male college students to see how much they are willing to trust. The preliminary findings are not encouraging. Among the players, despair was greater than hope, greed more common then repentance, revenge outweighed forgiveness, but trustworthiness outweighed deceit. This was not considered to violate the other findings, however, because, a Michigan game theory researcher explains, "In the American business ethic if you have something working for you, you stick with it. But beyond keeping agreements that work the ethic says expect no quarter and give no quarter. Therefore our profile shows a high degree of distrust."

Rapoport's idea is to find the conditions under which cooperation is encouraged, such as increasing what game theory calls "the payoff" and making the processes of the game (life) visible at the outset. "Imagine," Rapoport says, "that three men have to divide a dollar by majority vote. One says to the other, let's take a half buck each and freeze the other out. The third comes to the second and says, I'll give you seventy cents and we'll freeze out the first. At this point the first is forced to offer the second eighty cents, at which point the third and the first conspire to freeze out the second, and so on, until it becomes apparent that the only solution is to divide the money and flip for the extra cent." Game theory's inference is that conflict is virtually inevitable in many situations because of the perceived short-range advantages of noncooperation, so that cooperation requires a high degree of understanding. This has led Rapoport to suggest that each side in an international bargaining situation be required to state the position of the other side to the other side's complete satisfaction before it advocates its own.

Peace research's objective is to attempt to get outside of the confined perspective of nationality in order to see the problem as a whole. This was the idea of probably the first of the modern peace researchers, the late Lewis F. Richardson, an English meteorologist and Quaker who tried to reduce wars to mathematical terms. Richardson's book, *The Statistics of Deadly Quarrels*, treated arms races as economists treat price wars, as processes that could be measured with the proper indexes. Richardson thought that it ought to be possible to find objective factors governing the occurrence of wars, which was what he meant by a deadly statistic.

He looked, for instance, at three hundred wars in the nineteenth and part of the twentieth century and discovered that they were distributed as though by chance, with no evidence that they were happening either more or less frequently, though they did appear to be getting larger. Since, during this period, the world's population had increased, Richardson was able to rule out population as a war-causing factor, and he could find no evidence that any one nation was inherently more warlike than any other. He did conclude that nations got involved in wars in proportion to the number of states with which they had common frontiers. Richardson, in short, was trying to go beyond the explanations for wars offered by statesmen and historians and get at the external realities.

This is also the objective of the economist Kenneth Boulding of the University of Michigan and one of the founders of its Center for the Study of Conflict Resolution. Boulding studies conflict as a social process capable of being analyzed. Wars, for instance, are a function of units called milorgs (for military organizations) attempting to establish supremacy over other milorgs through various means short of war and failing to do so. Boulding says:

Conflict processes are neither arbitrary, random, nor incomprehensible. In the understanding of these processes lies the opportunity for their control, and perhaps even for human survival. We cannot claim that our understanding is deep enough, and much work yet needs to be done, but it can and must be claimed that the understanding and, therefore ultimately, the control of these processes is possible.

Conflict is the theme of one of the most highly touted experiments in peace research, the "conflict project" of the Stanford Studies in International Conflict and Integration, headquartered, fittingly, at Harmony House on the Stanford campus. The Stanford project is working with what it calls "psycho-politics," and I asked the project's director, Dr. Robert C. North, how he had come to it. "My own field is political science," North said, "but I began to feel, by 1957 or so, utterly frustrated in my understanding of international relations. The conflict mechanism seemed to work in ways my own discipline did not help me comprehend. So I decided to attempt to find out what the tension cycle was all about, using methods of analysis borrowed from psychology and, later on, computers.

"One of our first projects was an attempt to measure hostility in World War I. We got five thousand or so relevent documents and studied them exhaustively. Our basic assumption is that no utterance is meaningless though we may not know what the meaning is. We look for patterns of emotional changes, consistencies and inconsistencies, *sequiturs* and *non sequiturs*, frequently repeated words and themes, differences between word and action, and so forth. We are looking for clues to misperceptions and choices arising under extreme tension. For instance, in the summer of 1914 the Kaiser started out convinced that a world war at that time would be disastrous. We studied what the Kaiser scribbled in the margins of his papers—he was a compulsive scribbler. The notes looked about the same until July 29, 1914, at which point they became erratic, so much so, to judge by them, the Kaiser had what amounted to an emotional breakdown on the thirtieth and became something less than rational. It was during that time that he invoked the Schieffelin Plan for the invasion of West Europe. Once set in motion it was difficult, if not impossible, to stop the war machinery.

At almost every major turning point during those crucial days decision-makers in Europe were subject to irrational perception and impulse and a high degree of emotion."

The greater the tension, the study concludes, the greater the tendency to confine decisions to a handful of people, to perceive ever narrower fields of possible action, to select information according to preconceptions and to heighten the redundancy of communication. Changes in tension levels were found to correlate with economic indicators such as flows of gold, rising wheat futures, and so on.

"Our aim," North went on, "is to go a step beyond wetting your finger and holding it to the wind. Using computers and a kind of emotional dictionary of loaded words in speeches, we hope to be able to compose fever charts for conflicts. We have done that for the Cuban crisis of October, 1962, and other comparatively recent conflicts. We're aiming at formulating a more or less scientific background for political decisions, introducing somewhat more control and guidance. Decision-makers might be aided in making judgments about, say, the effect of American intervention in North Vietnam on India, China, Russia and so on before it happened.

"National leaders are subject to tension and projection even as you and I, and we are trying to measure it. One of our conclusions from the World War I study is that threats produced tension and the tension reduced leaders' abilities to think clearly. We view the cold war as a high-tension—but very real and very dangerous—situation on which whole societies are caught in psychological binds."

Another conclusion of the Stanford project is that under some circumstances the larger, more overwhelming and more immediate the deterrent threat of its opponent appears, the more likely is the state to take precipitate and even desperate action. Unless the state is encouraged to perceive some acceptable alternative it may undertake the very action that was intended to be deterred.

"We are not trying to say that threats should never be used," North said, "nor that all would be peace and sweetness and light if they were not. We believe that the evidence from the Cuba crisis of 1962 suggests that Kennedy used the biggest threat of all successfully—though not without risks. What we want to find out—as objectively as possible—is what kinds of action (including threats) are *most likely* to stimulate *what* responses in various kinds of circumstances. We are not pushing any special kind of strategy, peaceful or otherwise, but rather we are trying to find the patterns of behavior which seem to repeat themselves through history, some leading to consequences of large-scale violence, some to other consequences. The leader should at least know what kind of response his actions are likely to evoke from his opponents. We think this is a hard-headed approach."

The results of the opposite of deterrence threats, friendly actions, have also been studied by peace researchers using the Inter-Nation Simulation Game at the Western Behavioral Sciences Institute at La Jolla, California, with American Navy personnel as subjects. First, the researchers directed the country Omne to increase its military expenditures, keep Utro, a country from the opposite bloc, out of an international organization and stress the stability of the status quo. Tension markedly rose. At this point Omne's CDM announced a tension-reducing strategy to the *World Times,* challenging Utro to join it in specific steps for peace. Tension dropped, but Omne encountered severe difficulties with members of its own team and its allies, and Utro continued to arm. It took, in fact, six "years" (meaning research days) before Utro began to respond with arms reductions of its own, and, as it later developed, Utro's CDM had been, during this period, considering world domination as the only means to peace. Studies like this, says Lawrence N. Solomon, one of the psychologists who conducted it, don't "prove" anything except that such research may be a valid tool for international studies. Nonetheless, the psychologists have high hopes that war can ultimately be predicted and controlled.

Peace research, says Johan Galtung, is meant "to provide us with the discipline that collects and unifies man's knowledge of the conditions of peace, broadens it, makes it more valid to serve as the basis for this emerging profession," and, Boulding says, it "may turn out to be one of the most significant movements of our day."

At least four objectives are listed by peace research: to foster emotional closeness between peoples, to improve the accuracy of perceptions, to reduce fear and to discover better means of settling disputes. The peace research formula is that neither men nor nations are inherently warlike, that they are subject to elaborate misperceptions of others, that they respond to threats by fear, tension and counterthreats, with a loss of rationality, all of which results in war, and that the process may be halted if it is recognized in time. Friendly initiatives may then restore the peace. The spirit of peace research is summed up by Kenneth Boulding:

We are like a man in a car with inadequate brakes who attempts to solve this problem through prayer or taking tranquilizers or by issuing threats against the manufacturer instead of going to a garage mechanic who can operate in the system in which the trouble lies. The social scientist is the garage mechanic of social systems. He may not be a good mechanic, but he is better than nothing. For a car without brakes it is better to have a bad mechanic than a good preacher or even a good politician.

One of the noticeable aspects of peace research is that much of it is conducted by psychologists. As Boulding says, "Contrary to some popular belief, it may well be that the psychologist has the least to contribute to peace research of all the social scientists. This is because peace is essentially the property of the *social* system. . . . It is particularly dangerous to generalize from special psychological theories . . . into the social system at large." Because the psychologists, or those using psychological theory, can't really prove that social systems obey the same psychological rules that people seem to, peace research often has an anecdotal quality.

And many feel that the peace researcher is not the only mechanic around or necessarily the best. The peace movement, for instance, argues that peace will only be found through changes in the social system, not in attempts, say, to lessen conflict spirals in the present one. The deterrers, for their part, argue that war (like peace) is a delusive term, for what we are dealing with is a spectrum of violence that must be controlled through the threat of force. Peace research, to the deterrers, underestimates the power urge in men and nations, and the deterrers object to peace research's assumption that the American people and its leaders have been operating under a collective delusion toward the Soviet Union, when, in fact, the U.S. attitude represents an accurate reading of the evidence.

In the war-peace establishment, such disputes are without end.

PART THREE

The Peace Movement

VII

The Survivalists

PEACE IS A JOURNEY OF A THOUSAND ARGUMENTS, AND STILL IN search of answers to the problems of the nuclear age, I turned to the ideological agglomeration known as the American peace movement.

Whereas the experimentalists concentrate on means, the peace movement is really concerned with ends. It might agree, for instance, to minimum deterrence as the best of a bad lot of defense policies, but it is not really interested in deterrence, strategies and arms, but peace. If the deterrers can be loosely identified with political science, and the experimentalists with science and social science, the peace movement is the camp of morality, philosophy and religion, where earthly concerns are judged in accordance with ultimate standards.

One of the difficulties in assaying where the peace movement stands is that, like the Department of State, it has both a "declaratory" and an "action" policy. Declaratorily, much of the peace movement emerges close to the experimentalist position of gradualism. In action, the peace movement, for the most part, would move faster and farther than the experimentalists would toward the goal of permanent peace. In tone, the peace movement, though it sometimes tries hard to control it, is angry at the government of the United States for its conservatism in foreign policy, which, it feels, has brought us close to the brink of thermonuclear war. Another characteristic of the peace movement is that, since it is operating in the realm of ends, it attaches great importance to ideologies. The result has been that the peace movement is split into dozens of rival doctrines and sects. The one principle on which peace people do agree is the efficacy of education and mass action for a warless world.

Mass action for peace, in the shape of societies, centers, propaganda publications and so on, is now nearly 150 years old, having come into existence simultaneously in the U.S. and Europe after the Napoleonic Wars. There was no need for a peace movement before. One of the republican rights secured by the French Revolution was the right of everyone to be conscripted, and it was in opposition to *mass* warfare that *mass* action for peace was born. But the groups that comprised the peace movement differed in that while all were opposed to war the commitment of some was absolute and to others it was contingent on circumstances. The result was that the peace movement could never decide which wars not to fight.

"The almost complete collapse of the peace cause in the face of the Civil War is a striking example of what would happen again and again," says Roy Finch in the magazine *Dissent*. "The Civil War looked 'different'; it looked like an 'exception,' one war at least that could be justified." Its purpose was noble, to free slaves, and in terms of the war-peace theory of the time it wasn't a war at all, but a rebellion. World War I, for much of the peace movement, was again an exception—the Carnegie Endowment for International Peace turned its offices over to the government's propaganda agency—and if, by 1933, the peace movement could command twelve million followers, most of them faded away when confronted with the exceptional circumstances of World War II. "It is," Finch says, "a melancholy tale—125 years of attempts to build peace on the shifting sands of popular emotion."

Contrary, then, to what one might expect, the peace movement usually appears to flourish inversely to the danger of war. In periods of relative peace the movement is often at its strongest, but when war seems near the relevance of national objectives reasserts itself. There have been exceptions, such as the resurgence of peace movement strength that followed the Berlin crisis of 1961, but generally against this popular tide the peace movement has always fought unsuccessfully. Today the peace movement has what would seem on the surface the best issue it ever had, nuclear arms, and yet the bulk of the people have chosen to seek protection in military strength and thus voted against the peace movement. The most touted of modern peace candidates, H. Stuart Hughes, professor of history at Harvard, polled only 2.5 percent of the vote when he ran for the U.S. Senate in Massachusetts in 1962, and Hughes did better than most of the others. President Johnson, after his accession to office, saw representatives of almost all organized groups in the U.S. Significantly, he neglected the peace movement.

Is there a peace movement? Robert Gilmore, executive secretary of Turn Toward Peace, estimates that there are about fifty thousand people who constitute a peace "hard core," plus about a half-million others who appear on membership lists and may participate sometimes in peace projects. To this figure may be added several sizable religious groups, like the Mennonites, who because of a religious belief in pacifism may be said to exist on the fringe of the peace movement, and an unknown but probably sizable number of congenital nonjoiners and nondoers who sympathize with the peace movement but who have an aversion to what W. H. Auden calls "the flat pamphlet and the boring meeting."

The peace movement, then, does have some organizational following and some popular appeal. It has also been a propaganda "countervailing force" and contributed decisively in diverse fields like civil rights. Most important, the peace movement has been a contributor of ideas to the war-peace establishment, and though the deterrers may frown at the peace movement's arguments, it is, nonetheless, forced to take them into account. "Despite irrational elements existing within and around the peace movement," says A. E. Wessel of RAND, "it deserves serious consideration and cannot be dismissed merely as one more lunatic fringe group."

There are now so many peace groups that even experienced peaceniks can't keep track of them. The *International Peace-Disarmament Directory* (it has gone *that* far) lists fourteen hundred of them here and abroad, though many of these are aligned with the Communist nations, and nonaligned or anti-Communist U.S. peace people would rule them out of the movement. About a dozen organizations contain the bulk of the American peace movement. Half of these, including the Women's International League for Peace and Freedom, the American Friends Service Committee, the War Resisters League and the Fellowship of Reconciliation, emerged after World War I and survived World War II. The other half arrived in time for the cold war: the United Nations Association for the United States, formerly the American Association for the United Nations, which combined with the U.S. Committee for the United Nations; the United World Federalists, the National Committee for a Sane Nuclear Policy (SANE), the Committee for Non-Violent Resistance (CNVR), Women Strike for Peace, student peace groups and so on.

All these groups have a common aim, to reach the people, and yet they are divided in ideology and approach. "Peace organizations fall into various categories," writes Alfred Hassler, executive secretary of the Fellowship of Reconciliation.

The lines are often blurred, the same people may be found in positions of leadership and influence in several groups, and overlapping frequently occurs, but the categories exist and have meaning nevertheless. One broad division of this sort is between pacifists and nuclear disarmament people. The pacifists, for religious or other reasons, oppose all war and assert the relevance of nonviolent reconciling actions in resolving war-breeding disputes. The "nuclear disarmers" focus their attention on the danger of nuclear war, and work for nuclear disarmament as the essential step for human survival.

These two broad groups may be called "survivalists" and "radicals." Survivalists are those who, whatever their personal beliefs, are pragmatists about peace and the peace movement and hope to find a program that will be politically acceptable. The changes they seek are therefore somewhat marginal compared to those asked for by the radicals. The survivalists try to reach the public by education, propaganda and by reasoning with it. For their part, the radicals disagree with the survivalists' central idea, that a mass movement encompassing different ideologies can be effective. To them, the hope lies in the principles of nonviolence and serious changes in the internal social organization, usually away from centralization. The survivalists seek policy changes within the existing order, while the radicals hope for alterations in the very consciousness of human beings. The radicals are more inclined to follow Christ and try to teach by personal example. An organizational chart of the peace movement looks like this:

SURVIVALIST

Right: not terribly critical of U.S. foreign policy; critical of the Soviet Union; advocates stronger UN leading to a world state. UNA, UWF.

Center: critical of both U.S. and U.S.S.R., hence "nonaligned"; concerned with nuclear crisis; general and complete disarmament the goal; nuclear pacifists, generally, but pragmatic. SANE, WSP, WILPF.

Left: critical chiefly of U.S. U.S.S.R. is no threat, hence Red scare prompted to justify high arms expenditures. General and complete disarmament the goal.

RADICAL

Religious Pacifists: pacifism, nonviolence, unilateral American disarmament if necessary, but hopefully not necessary. Nonaligned. AFSC.

Religious-Secular Pacifists: religious pacifist base but, generally, sweeping changes in social order toward utopian socialism. Nonaligned. CNVR, FOR, WRL.

Anarchist-Pacifists: nation-state responsible for ills of world, hence abolish it. Nonaligned.

The groups on the right of the peace movement ("right" here is hardly "right" by John Birch Society standards) are those which more radical peace groups hardly consider in the peace movement at all, so gentle has been their deviation from U.S. policy, but it is commonly said that the memberships of the UNA and the UWF are a good deal more dissident than their organizations' policy papers show. In any case, the UNA and the UWF, with seventy thousand and eighteen thousand members respectively, stand for a new world order through a stronger UN. Both maintain that if American policies were consistently judged in terms of their impact on the universal, as opposed to the national, interest, some of those policies would have to be changed.

The UNA has a tax-exempt status as an educational organization instead of one devoted to political action, and it has tried to educate the American people and its leaders to accept the UN and give it wider powers. The UNA, for instance, has come up with the novel suggestion that the UN be given jurisdiction of the sea bed beyond the continental shelves both as a source of revenue and as a means of forestalling international rivalries. It emphasizes that world interest would be better served by the United States if it did not by-pass the UN so often, as it has largely done in the case of Southeast Asia.

Although UNA and UWF have thought of a merger (just as UWF is discussing one with SANE), UWF is somewhat more avant-garde. Its battle plan for peace would begin by repealing the Connally Reservation limiting American participation in the World Court and proceed by stages to replace national armies with a UN police and inspection force. Leaders who urge war would be subject to arrest. It might be noted that the archetypical world tucked away in the UWF heaven is radically different from that of today, but not so radically different as that offered by those who urge decentralizing the state itself. Ultimately UWF wants limited world federal government.

One of the problems of the UNA and UWF is that their plans seem realistic only in relation to the willingness of great states to put their war-making power under a world authority. Congress, for its part, has shown no enthusiasm for this, and neither has the Soviet Union, which declares that even a police-power federation of capitalist and socialist countries is incompatible with Socialist objectives. (China isn't even in the UN, of course, and for the UNA and UWF, admission of Red China to the UN is a long-run objective.) These peace groups hope that eventually everybody will see the logic of their ideas. "Sooner or later," says UWF's Marion McVitty, "the Soviet Union and China will have to turn to the UN as the only means of protecting themselves from each other."

A guiding spirit of UNA and UWF is Norman Cousins, editor of the *Saturday Review*. The extent of Cousins' commitment to peace and the peace movement can be gauged by the fact that he puts almost every moment into it. A few years ago, he sold the *Saturday Review* to the McCall's Corporation, one of his principal reasons having been that he was tired of asking people for money. Fund-raising in the peace movement can be a full-time job. Cousins' personal contributions since have run deep into six figures and, in giving to peace, at one time he almost destroyed himself financially.

Cousins disproves the rule that peace people are isolated and without influence. He was instrumental in persuading the philosopher Albert Schweitzer to issue a peace appeal and he was consulted on several of President Kennedy's speeches, among them the American University speech which some feel was a turning point in the cold war. Cousins' sponsorship of conferences between the American and Russian intellectuals gave him a standing in the Soviet Union, and at one point he acted as a kind of unofficial liaison for President Kennedy with Premier Khrushchev during the test-ban negotiations.

Khrushchev, at this time, was under attack from Soviet hardliners and the Chinese for being too soft, and after a lengthy conversation with Khrushchev at a resort on the Black Sea, Cousins decided that, for Khrushchev, the test-ban was a watershed. If the negotiations had failed, Cousins is certain that Khrushchev would have returned to the hard line. Khrushchev was doubtful that the U.S. wanted a test ban. It was Cousins' job to convey to the Soviet leader that Kennedy was honestly interested. After that, the negotiations proceeded successfully.

Cousins is a medium-sized, supremely energetic man of fifty, with a boyish face, an intense expression and a rapid delivery. A printed warning stands near his desk: "The Critic Judges Himself in His Criticism." I asked Cousins how he saw himself in the peace movement, and he said, after a long moment, "It's extremely difficult for a man to look inside himself and give an accurate accounting, but I guess I can say that I'm not a sectarian nor have I ever been anything clearly defined in my life. Maybe my role in the peace movement is as something of a switchboard operator, keeping the lines of communication open among some of the principal groups, like UNA, UWF and SANE. I've attempted to be a peacemaker in the peace movement. But you can't push unity too far when people aren't ready for it: it results in false unity and weakness."

The switchboard, for Cousins, was completely lit up a few years ago in one of the more difficult situations the postwar peace movement has encountered. It is still important today because the scars still exist, and it also shows how the divisions in the world at large are reflected in the struggles of those who agitate for peace and reconciliation. The New York chapter of the National Committee for a Sane Nuclear Policy, in 1961, was about to hold a mass rally at Madison Square Garden when the Senate Internal Subcommittee, through Senator Thomas E. Dodd of Connecticut, told Cousins that the treasurer of the Garden rally had been an active Communist. What followed, Cousins told me, "was the most pulverizing experience of my life."

Cousins and Dodd, as it happened, were old friends, Dodd having been president of the Connecticut chapter of UWF while Cousins was national chairman, and Dodd wanted Cousins to know in advance that the Subcommittee intended to release the news before the rally. Cousins argued that this would be hitting below the belt. "You know the National Committee is not a Communist organization." Dodd agreed to hold up the news, and Cousins called a meeting in his office, consisting of some of SANE's leadership, the accused man and SANE's lawyer. SANE's by-laws provided that members of the Communist Party were not welcome in the organization. "I told the man that if he had no connection with the Communist Party I would lay down my life for him. He wouldn't say, so I asked him to resign. The decision was later backed up by SANE's executive board."

Immediately after the rally Senator Dodd issued a statement attacking SANE for allowing itself to be infiltrated by Communists. SANE's response is worth repeating, for it sets forth the issues clearly:

As a matter of democratic principle and practice we resent the intrusion of a Congressional Committee into the affairs of an organization which during its entire life has acted only in accordance with its declared principles. . . . The Committee [SANE] itself is entirely capable of carrying out its principles and guaranteeing that it will not permit their betrayal or subversion under any pressure from, on the one hand, investigations directed to its hurt or, on the other hand, by the actions of its local chapters or their leaders.

SANE then passed a resolution requiring that its groups sign a charter that provided "persons who are not free because of party discipline or political allegiance to criticize the actions of totalitarian nations with the same standards by which they challenge other nations will not be welcome." This led, in turn, to the separation from SANE of the New York chapter, as well as the resignation of several important SANE people, among them Linus Pauling, the chemist, and the radical pacifist A. J. Muste.

Muste's position was the civil libertarian one, for he felt that SANE was wrong to take measures which, to him, smacked of McCarthyism. Muste, like Cousins, is opposed to a united front with the Communists, but he believes that a clearly stated nonaligned position is enough to keep the Communists out or to change them should they choose to come in.

Cousins and other SANE officials eventually obtained assurances from the Subcommittee that the rights of witnesses would be respected, and Cousins feels the hearings were aboveboard and fair. "My trouble was the moral strain which had to do with those individuals who didn't understand the nature of the Communist Party and resisted the kind of restriction on Communists which we were imposing," Cousins told me. "You simply can't run a peace organization in which some people fall silent whenever the Soviet Union is criticized. I, for one, would not work with the

Communist-led World Peace Council nor would I be part of a united front with the Communists in the U.S. I also feel accurate labeling is essential and in some cases obligatory in a democracy. However, the situation is less clear than it was, for while formerly the American Communist Party was entirely a creature of the Soviet Union, just as there is some development toward independence within the Soviet Union, there is a similar trend in the American Communist Party."

Cousin's own peace politics are a blend of UWF—his principal interest in the peace movement—and the philosophy summed up by Albert Schweitzer as "reverence for life." Cousins' appeal is a broad-gauge one to man, to give up his reliance on the "inadequate shield of nuclear deterrence," to accept the dictates of one world with a UN police force. He attempts to persuade by showing the sheer moral logic of conciliation. "If there is a conflict between the needs of this generation and the needs of later generations, the needs of the later generations come first," he says in his book *In Place of Folly*.

If there is a conflict between the security of the sovereign state and the security of the human commonwealth, the human commonwealth comes first. . . . With these first principles in operation, the people can create a mandate for government. Such a mandate would enable the nation to put first things first. The nation can declare that, even in its self-defense, it will not engage in a war that would destroy the rest of the world. Neither will it hesitate to declare that it would rather die than be the first to use chemical, biological, or nuclear weapons on human beings.

This paragraph is illustrative of the differences in the war-peace establishment because it contains the kind of strategic ambiguities which the analysts pounce upon as examples of their contention that the peace movement does not know what it is talking about. When Cousins says "even in its self-defense, it will not engage in a war that would destroy the rest of the world," it sounds as though he means unilateral renunciation of nuclear arms by the United States. But then he says, "be the first to use," which appears to permit the use of nuclear weapons in retaliation, though not in a first strike. I asked Cousins which he meant.

"I recognize the gross inconsistency in the position because I don't want to say what I would do in case of a nuclear war," Cousins said. "There ought to be somebody outside the government able to talk against the weapons without having to justify them. But, to get to particulars, the reason, perhaps, for the contradiction is that we are dealing with two separate and distinct worlds. The first world is the old world in which nations have certain conditioned reflexes, where they act or react, knowing that their national interests ultimately have to be upheld by force rather than by any objective instrument or agency or court. It is the world of armament races, balance-of-power arrangements, threats, ultimatums and showdowns.

"The second world is a world with entirely new contours shaped by new facts: the fact that the world has become a geographic unit in most essential respects; the fact of instant communications; the fact of obliterative weapons. These facts have yet to serve as the basis for a reorganization of the nations into a new kind of ordered relationship.

"The problem, therefore, is how to move from the first world to the second. It will not be done overnight. We can't pretend the first world doesn't exist. We have to live in it until we create the kind of structure that can fit the second world. The apparent contradictions, therefore, are the result of the fact that we approach some problems in the context entirely of the first world and other problems entirely in the context of the second.

"When I say that I believe the United States should announce in advance that it will not be the first to use nuclear weapons, I do so not just out of moral fervor but out of a conviction that it is necessary to avoid, so far as it is within our power to do so, any impression that we are trigger-prone. We must do everything we can to keep a potential enemy from believing that he has to hit us first because of what he considers to be a probability that we are considering a first strike.

"If, on the other hand, we also announce that we have no intention of defending ourselves, even if we are hit first, the result may well be to increase the likelihood that we may be attacked.

"Not until the nations act adequately on the facts represented by the second world, the new world, will it be possible to avoid all the inconsistencies and paradoxes that are inherent in having one foot in each world."

The survivalist wing of the peace movement confronts an agonizing moral and intellectual dilemma. On the one hand, either for pragmatic reasons or not, they are opposed to unilateral American nuclear disarmament. On the other, many of them are what are called "nuclear pacifists," a term often used to describe SANE, meaning that while they will not unilaterally disarm nuclearly, they will not use nuclear force either. "Many of our people would have trouble pushing the button under any circumstances," says SANE's Donald Keys. As I'd learned from Herman Kahn, the possession of a deterrent necessarily implies its use, for were there no possibility of using nuclear weapons they would hardly be deterrent. This ambiguity on the part of the nuclear pacifists has led the analysts to conclude that they are unilateral disarmers in disguise.

The peace movement's response to this is that deterrence theory does not face its own ambiguities. It is one thing to threaten to use nuclear weapons; it is quite another to push the button if a large portion of the human race will be destroyed and enormous casualties incurred by oneself. The deterrers' answer is that controlled counterforce war will reduce casualties. The peace movement says that such a war cannot be controlled and, even if it could, twenty or forty million casualties is too high a price to pay for virtually any rational objective.

But the deterrers, after all, are out to prevent just such a war. Deterrence, they say, deters simply because of the possibility of enormous casualties. The peace movement cannot actually prove that this is not so. For this reason it has longed to meet the deterrers on their own strategic grounds, and in a fashion understandable to people. It has found such an argument in the doctrine of "overkill."

"Overkill" is the controversial theory of a professor of industrial engineering from Columbia University named Seymour Melman who has a plan for reducing the U.S. military budget to about $34 billion independent of disarmament agreement, and he also hopes for even sharper cuts based on negotiations. Melman's estimate is that the United States in 1964 has the capacity to overkill Soviet cities of over 100,000 population 231 times, assuming a 95 percent loss of major aircraft and 75 percent loss of major missiles. Melman concludes that American nuclear power is far in excess of what it needs to be because of "overkill," which has been rather horribly described as "pouring another bucket of gasoline over a baby that is already burning."

To Melman, "The military budget is based upon technologically obsolete military strategies and strategic speculations that are of doubtful validity. Further enlargement of strategic striking power which is now being effected seems to be based on the assumption that persons and societies can be destroyed more than once." Melman's figures themselves have been interpreted as being of doubtful validity. The Air Force in 1964, for instance, released (on taxpayers' money) a sixty-page rebuttal which accused Melman of being "intoxicated by the exuberance of his own verbosity" and even referred to his "modest military background." Melman's overkill is based on "Hiroshima units" of the nuclear equivalent of twenty thousand tons of TNT. Melman assumes that a one-megaton bomb produces fifty times the explosive power of a one-kiloton (or Hiroshima unit) one. Actually, one megaton has only sixteen times the explosive power of a kiloton bomb, and the figure can be reduced to seven in terms of destructive power because the size of cities varies.

Further whittling came from Charles J. Hitch, the Controller and Assistant Secretary of the Department of Defense. According to him,

As the Soviet Union continues to build up its ICBM forces, our manned bombers on the ground will become increasingly vulnerable to surprise attack. That is why we have increased from one-third to one-half the proportion of the bomber forces to be maintained on 15-minute ground alert, the warning time we expect to get from our ballistic missiles early warning system. This point Professor Melman completely ignores in his calculation. In all prudence, we can only count on those bombers maintained on a 15-minute ground alert, and that means about half the B-52's and B-58's shown in Professor Melman's table.

"What are his [Melman's] attrition assumptions based upon?" asked a RAND specialist, Amrom Katz, in *Air Force and Space Digest* magazine, referring to the "Road to Meltown." "Who attacks first? The United States? The Soviet Union? . . . Is there any mention of alternative target systems—of partial response? Any thought of damping out war? Nary a word." Katz goes on to suppose that

ninety per cent of our military forces were struck, and that the reliability of the remainder is thirty per cent, and of that thirty per cent, local defense in the Soviet Union can knock down seventy per cent— we are now down to a force over the Soviet Union of but one per cent of everything we had. In terms of our Melman unit (the overkill statistic) we are down to but two times, and, if the entire Soviet bloc is considered, by Melman's own statistics, we have no overkill at all!

I took up these figures with Melman, a member of SANE's executive board. Melman feels that his critics use implausible arguments, such as the Soviet Union's ability, with less than two hundred long-range missiles, to strike 90 percent of our forces, which he describes as a "malicious fantasy." No one, he says, knows what a nuclear war would look like, but using his own "reasonable assumptions" about how much of our striking force would be hit, and the attrition rate of the remainder, the U.S. still has a vast overkill capacity.

"But the whole argument is outmoded," Melman said. "Ideologies are still around long after circumstances require them. Ideologies become the intellectual properties of men and their careers and acquire a life beyond the need for them. The obsolescence of ideas in this business is fantastic. Fantastic! You've got a bunch of smart cynics out at RAND, with strategic myopia. I deny that my case isn't good because I haven't got the facts; nobody is an expert at this because nobody has run a nuclear war. And I don't buy a lot of *their* arguments. For instance, that Soviet secrecy stands in the way of a U.S. reduction. We've hemorrhaged the Soviet security system, as McNamara's detailed statistics on Soviet forces show. I don't accept the counterforce-countercity discussion either. You can't use counterforce without destroying cities. It's all city war.

"But I'm not really interested in criticizing various defense strategies. All these strategies have become 'no win' because there is no winner in a nuclear war. I want a 'win' policy. I feel appalled that we have a technological cornucopia here, and instead of it being used to end poverty for mankind, our technological ingenuity is being poured without stint into the cold war. I think there is a basic strategy better than the military way for the safety and freedom of society. I want a peace race." Melman would compete with Communism by taking 10 percent of the gross national product, about the same as that being used for defense, and carry out a program of world industrialization. The Soviet Union, to compete in a peace race, would be forced to take disarmament seriously.

Melman appears to omit from his figures some of the considerations of strategy, especially that of counterforce, which weigh so heavily at the Department of Defense. Even so, I wondered, do we have an "overkill" capacity? I turned to Dr. Jerome Wiesner for an answer. "Melman and Katz are talking about different things and in a sense they are both right," Dr. Wiesner said. "Melman totals up all of the nuclear explosives available to the United States and finds that it is much greater than is needed for our strategic missile and bomber forces, even the largest proposed strategic force. This certainly represents the potential for an enormous overkill. But only a fraction of our nuclear material is used for strategic weapons. More of it is tied up in air defense weapons, antisubmarine weapons, and a vast array of tactical nuclear weapons. A large amount, too, is tied up in production facilities, reactors, pipelines, and so forth. I happen to believe that we have overstocked here, too. In any event, Melman concludes correctly that the U.S. nuclear stockpile is many, many times the size needed to maintain an adequate deterrent force. Katz creates a new strategic force by reducing the present U.S. force level by Melman's overkill ratio and finds a strategic force too small for comfort.

"I think the criticism of Melman is correct—that he does not sufficiently take into account the destruction of our own forces and their reliability—but on the other hand, the picture is not so black as it is pictured by Katz. I believe we do have an overkill capacity, but in my opinion it's to be counted in factors of a few times rather than the very large numbers Melman uses. From a national security point of view, the important thing is to reduce force levels on both sides rather than debate the absolute level of the force we create unilaterally. I would agree with Melman wholeheartedly when he argues that buying unnecessary military force needlessly diverts money from other vital social needs."

"Overkill," no matter what figures one attaches to it, ties in nicely with peace movement tactics, which are not to argue the merits of one strategy over another, not to concentrate on required force levels or questions of national security, but to arouse the people to the danger of thermonuclear war and to urge peaceful solutions to international disputes. It relies heavily on peace propaganda, such as that produced by the National Committee for a Sane Nuclear Policy.

SANE, with 25,000 members, was created especially to combat nuclear testing, but it has since broadened itself into a policy organization trying to deal with a range of questions. "We believe," said Homer Jack, its former executive director, "that modern war does not work and that other methods are needed to allow change, yet keep the peace, in the modern world. Here we differ from some organizations which oppose war primarily on religious grounds."

SANE's publicity has always emphasized crisis, and its ads have displayed skull-and-crossbones on milk bottles or the concerned face of Dr. Benjamin Spock, the famous pediatrician and SANE's co-chairman, staring ruefully down at a child. "The next time mad-ness strikes, couldn't it be The Bomb instead of the bullet?" SANE asked shortly after the assassination of President Kennedy. To avoid such an occurrence, SANE recommends a sweeping change of policy: disarmament, an understanding with Cuba, disengagement in Europe and Southeast Asia, no MLF and an end to nuclear deterrence. On the one hand, SANE opposes virtually all U.S. cold war policies, but on the other it regards itself as a valuable adjunct to the government in getting support for disarmament measures and in gaining Congressional approval for them. (One unanswered speculation in the war-peace establishment is whether peace groups actually bring right-wing groups into existence, as a kind of political deterrence.)

SANE is as worried as a munitions maker about the present lull in international tensions, not because it is opposed to tranquillity, but because it thinks that people will mistake a momentary calm for the real goals of peace and disarmament. "My fear," says Norman Thomas, six times Socialist candidate for President and SANE co-chairman, "is that we will do none of those things that have to be done while there is time: recognition of Communist China, a realization that you can't try policing the whole world without running terrible risks of escalation into a world conflict and so on. We are bound for war if we don't get out of the present drift. It is nonsense for people to say that war will never happen because we'll be destroyed. The use of threats means you run the risk of war. I would bet on a world nuclear war in thirty to forty years if we keep on drifting. I'm blue about the failure to think into these problems. It's an ironic situation in the United States: almost everyone is for peace but no one wants a peace society."

Thomas has been part of the peace movement for over fifty years, and I asked him if he thought it had changed. "Oh, yes," he said. "It's far more sophisticated now. There is a deeper understanding of the trouble. Few peace people now think that simple disarmament will create a warless world. We all know that there must be international controls, that economic factors will have to be taken into account, and many of us realize that it's by politics that we'll have peace or war, no matter how much goodwill gets diffused.

Most of us also recognize that the Soviet Union is a problem." I asked Thomas why the American peace movement was such a battlefield of ideologies. "It's hard to get good people to cooperate, and if they're very good they're inspired either by Karl Marx or God and they feel they can't let either one down." Thomas chuckled.

The resident psychiatrist of the American peace movement is Erich Fromm, a round-faced man with rimless eyeglasses and a well-adjusted mien. Fromm analyzes himself for forty-five minutes a day (the analytic hour) in order to rid himself of bias when he views the world. He told his visitor, "I'm a nuclear pacifist, certainly, and if I had to decide, I think the greater security for the U.S. would be in unilateral disarmament because I think the Soviets would disarm, too. I think the chances for nuclear war are greater than those against it, and we haven't much time. But I'm aware of the fact that as a political issue in the U.S. unilateral disarmament is no good, so for practical purposes I'm for universal controlled disarmament."

Fromm has used psychiatry to investigate the cold war and come up with a distinction that is widely quoted in peace circles between the possible and the probable. That it is *possible* that the Soviet Union will risk nuclear war is quite different from saying that it is *probable,* and it is the paranoid who mistakes the latter for the former. "I submit that our political thinking suffers from such paranoid trends. We should be concerned, not with possibilities, but rather with the probabilities. This is the only sane and realistic way of conducting the affairs of national and well as individual life." Policy-makers, we have seen, feel they must consider possibilities as probabilities in order to safeguard the national interest, as they construe it. And it must be noted that deterrers turn Fromm's analysis around: to them, nuclear war is a possibility which Fromm converts to a probability.

But I was curious to know how Fromm accounted for the fact that societies were willing to risk mass destruction. He started off by saying, "I see the U.S. and the Soviet Union as quite similar in many important aspects due to the common features of large-scale, centralized industrial production, and they will be utterly similar in twenty years. What I most regret about both in the last analysis is the loss of spiritual life in large-scale-production societies. There is a trend toward the love of the inorganic, to gadgetry, and to a deep emptiness in life. Have you read the *Manifesto of Futurism?* No? Well, it was written in 1909 by an Italian named Marinetti, and it expresses very well the affinity between contempt for life and the admiration of the mechanical." Fromm showed me the *Manifesto,* part of which said:

We shall sing the love of danger. . . . We declare that the world's splendor has been enriched by a new beauty; the beauty of speed . . . a roaring motor-car is more beautiful than the *Victory of Samothrace.* . . . We wish to glorify war—the only health giver of the world. . . . We wish to destroy the museums, the libraries, to fight against moralism, feminism and all opportunistic and utilitarian meannesses. . . . We shall sing of the great crowds in the excitement of labor . . . of the nocturnal vibration of arsenals and workshops beneath their violent electric moons . . . of bridges leaping like gymnasts over the diabolical cutlery of sunbathed rivers; of adventurous liners scenting the horizon; of broad-chested locomotives prancing on the rails . . . of the gliding flight of aeroplanes. . . .

Fromm looked at the *Manifesto* a moment and said, "If we're sure that men are wolves, that they need to destroy, to use force and violence, then our resistance to this brutalization will die. Is man basically evil, or is he good and perfectible? I take the view that man hasn't got a fixed nature, but a fixed contradiction between his animal nature and his self-awareness. It forces him to seek a solution, either in progress or regression. Two types of regression are narcissism and necrophilia, both of which make the world disappear, one by self-inflation and the other by death. The other choice is freedom through life, and freedom is something one must constantly widen, through proper choices, through keeping in mind the regressive side, yes?"

Necrophilia, of course, means obsession with the dead. Fromm went on to say that people, as part of their uneven and incompleted development, were mixtures of the necrophilous and biophilous, the latter meaning love of life. Necrophiles, he said, are unaware of their death-loving orientation. They harden their hearts in such a way that the death-love appears to be a logical and rational response.

"Why do the bulk of the people accept their potential incineration without protest?" Fromm said. "Because they are attracted to death and hence do not fear destruction. Forms of necrophilia are widespread. True necrophiliacs are a small minority, but in difficult circumstances small minorities have been able to frighten the majority, to appeal to the necrophilia in them." Did he mean some of those I have called deterrers? Fromm nodded vigorously. "'The wise man,'" he said, quoting Spinoza, "'does not contemplate death but life.'"

"Life," I was beginning to see, is the true theme of the survivalists, and it looms large in the hearts of those to whom tradition assigns the role as spokesmen for peace, the women. The smaller of the two chief women's peace groups, with a few thousand members, is the Women's International League for Peace and Freedom (one of whose founders was Jane Addams, winner of the Nobel Peace Prize in 1931), which believes in international order, worldwide disarmament, the maleficent influence of the military-industrial complex in the U.S. and the benefits of a pacifistic spirit in international relations. WILPF prefers the more modest route of education and nongovernmental representation at official councils.

Its younger sister organization is Women Strike for Peace, at once the pride, envy and shame of the peace movement—pride because WSP, with perhaps fifty thousand adherents, has proved capable of organizing mass support more than any peace group; envy because other groups would like to have WSP's typical turnouts; shame because many peace organizations feel that WSP, by its chaotic approach and its steadfast refusal to go much farther than "life" for a program, fails to tackle the issues of war and peace in a systematic manner, which, other peace people feel, has cast doubt on the movement's professionalism as a whole.

Indeed, there is something helter-skelter and *ad hoc* about the whole charming affair. WSP and its international affiliate—inevitably, WISP—has no officers, no dues and no membership lists, but is rather a collection of committees with mimeograph machines. It is closer to *Lysistrata* and its sex strike against war than a professional peace organization. The women describe themselves as "angered by the failure of nuclear powers to end the threat of nuclear destruction."

But the reasons the baby-carriage-wheeling demonstrators of WSP do not have a program lies in their appraisal of the cold war. The women say, ask the major powers to lay down their nuclear arms, and if they lack a program for doing so, it can be for only one reason: the problem between the United States and the Soviet Union is fictitious, and therefore requires no complicated formula for solution. If the Soviet Union is "no problem," then the United States has largely imagined the need for nuclear arms. This is by no means the same as saying that WSP, as the House Un-American Affairs Committee tried to suggest, is aligned with the policies of the Soviet Union. It is saying that when one perceives no serious problem to exist, then one hardly feels the need of a complicated means of solving it. To the WSP, what stands in the way are traditional, business-as-usual, power politics.

If any one person can be said to be the mother of WSP, it is a Washington housewife and mother named Mrs. Dagmar Wilson, a short, attractive brunette somewhere in her forties. I brought up the question of a program. "Don't ask me about those complicated things," Mrs. Wilson said, with a wave of her hand. "We're interested in the broad perspective of peace. We rather deliberately do not understand the intricacies of the situation, for we want to concentrate on the goal. Communism? A stuffy old doctrine. It's a pity we have such a blind terror of it because Communism is out of date. 'East' and 'West'? It's where you happen to live. 'Free world'? A meaningless term. War? It's a bad habit, like smoking. We have to give it up. War is the fanaticism of powerful people and governments. We do not want unilateral disarmament. We want universal, general and complete disarmament. We only want both sides to live up to the ideals they have expressed. America's fear of Communism has put our backs to the wall. Our foreign policy is no longer related to real things."

There is a clear demarcation among the survivalists between those who do consider Soviet foreign policy a real difficulty, such as UNA, UWF and SANE, and those, like WSP, who consider the Soviet Union an excuse for not dealing with the real issue, power politics.

A point of view on the cold war more detailed but not dissimilar in many ways from WSP's is offered by Dr. Linus Pauling, winner of two Nobel prizes. For the first, awarded in 1954 for chemistry, Pauling was widely applauded as being perhaps the most eminent native-born American scientist, while for the 1962 Nobel Prize for Peace, awarded in 1963, a national magazine went so far as to call the prize "a weird insult from Norway" and "an extraordinary insult to America," although other magazines and newspapers expressed editorial approval of the award. No one in the peace movement is more embattled than Dr. Pauling.

Pauling is a tall, rangy man in his early sixties, with a sometimes hesitant way of speech, a gentle manner and blue eyes that appear large behind his glasses. His face, though mobile and alert, often bears the look of scholarly detachment, and two feathery wings of white hair float beside his head, giving rise to suspicions that Pauling has not had a haircut since the Nobel Peace Prize. Pauling buys good suits, but he buys them in lots, like test tubes, and after that they are engaged in an experiment to see how long they can go without a press. Pauling is quiet, amiable, even diffident, and his rumpled bearing suggests a man of the laboratory more than one of the political platform.

Despite appearances, Pauling has been an aggressive and relentless campaigner for peace, and "peace work," as Pauling calls it, has increasingly taken over from the laboratory. Pauling resigned from the California Institute of Technology at Pasadena, where he has taught chemistry since 1922, to join the Center for the Study of Democratic Institutions at Santa Barbara, and while he intends to continue with science, peace is much on his mind. Pauling has lectured tirelessly to audiences he estimates at 25,000 a year, plus those he can reach on radio and television. His book *No More War!*, which he dictated into a machine in eight days, is one of the best-known productions of the peace movement.

He has given his name and high scientific prestige to the whole gamut of appeals by which peace groups try to reach the public, and he has participated in, and sometimes organized, peace conferences, even disrupting a few in the opinion of some. He has sued, unsuccessfully, the governments of both the United States and the Soviet Union to prohibit nuclear testing, and he has carried placards before the White House. Peace has seen him take up arms against a sea of passport troubles, bouts with legislative committees and disputations with fellow scientists and his nominal allies in the peace groups. "As one of the most passionate and effective campaigners against nuclear testing he helped create a climate of awareness and concern that impelled the world towards [a test ban]—and enabled the American public to accept it. His task," the *Times* of London said, "has not been easy."

Pauling's position is stated in *No More War!*, his emphatic declaration that war in the nuclear age is useless as an instrument of national policy:

> *We are truly forced into abandoning war as the method of solution of world problems, the method of resolution of disputes among nations. . . . We need to begin now to make international agreements. . . .* It is proposed that the great world problems be solved in the way that other problems are now solved—by working hard to find their solution—by carrying on *research for peace.*

His paradigm is science: "Science is the search for the truth—it is not a game in which one tries to beat his opponent, to do harm to others. We need to have the spirit of science in international affairs." Reinhold Niebuhr, a critic of this view, characterizes it by saying, "The contest between nations, in which their pride and morality is at stake, is reduced to the dimension of a problem of natural science, which can be solved if disinterested specialists devote themselves to it."

I visited with Pauling and his warm and friendly wife, Ava

Helen, whose peace work has been in lockstep with his own, on several occasions. The back of the door at his laboratory at Cal-Tech, I noted, was covered with cartoons, one showing a missile leaving a naval vessel and a sailor standing by an instrument panel, peering at a Coke machine in the corner, and saying, "Woops! I must have pushed the wrong button."

"I used to feel there was some limitation on my mental capacity because I found it hard to accept conclusions about world affairs that seemed to be accepted by other people," Pauling told me seriously. "I was essentially apolitical in the 1930's and not really concerned with social issues—I voted Republican until 1928 or 1932, I don't remember which. Only rather late in life did I reach the conclusion that I had as much ability to think about world affairs as other people did."

Pauling believes fiercely that war must be abolished, that the means for this are at hand with modern weapons, and that what stands in the way is traditional power politics. "National power," he said, "is becoming meaningless if associated with the institution of war. We must reassess its significance. The old concept of power used to be tied up with military might that could be beneficial to nations that used it. That's no longer true."

Pauling's view as to how the transition away from war is to be accomplished appears to be broadly educational. His principal identification with the peace cause has been over the issue of nuclear testing, against which he battled long and hard. The question of how dangerous atmospheric testing is has never been completely settled by scientists. One school, represented by Edward Teller, has maintained that the health hazards from testing were small, and if one wanted to compensate for increased radiation one should put lead roofs on houses and cut down on the maximum permissible dose from X-rays. To Pauling, the hazards are extreme, endangering the lives and health of literally millions of people, born and unborn. Some scientists who agree with Pauling still feel that he has pushed his statistics too far.

I took up this question with what I hoped would be a neutral authority. Dr. Francesco Sella, Secretary of the United Nations

Committee for the Effects of Atomic Radiation. Sella said, speaking unofficially, "The difficulty arises from the way the risk of any effect of current levels of fallout is expressed. If, for instance, you consider the probability that an exposed individual would be affected, the figure will be extremely low. If, however, you multiply that figure by the number of persons exposed, the expected number of affected people may be staggering. Either means of expressing the risk is equally legitimate from a scientific point of view, but the psychological weight may be quite different and lead to assessing differently issues in which questions of policy are involved." To Teller, the risks had to be taken in view of the greater danger from the Soviet Union. To Pauling (and the United States Government in signing the limited test-ban treaty), the human sacrifice occasioned by nuclear testing was too great.

Pauling has also campaigned against the present size of American nuclear stockpiles as being immorally large, and he has joined a committee that seeks a "triple revolution": in Negro rights, unemployment because of automation, and peace. But, except on specific issues like stockpiles and testing, Pauling does not involve himself in what he calls the "details." I asked him, for instance, how he would settle issues such as the one over the *Autobahn* approach to Berlin. He dismissed this dispute as "puerile," and went on, "It isn't my function to get into specifics. That is for statesmen. It's my job to point out the goal that we have to reach, not the path that we have to follow."

"What are your ideas about disarmament?" Pauling is frequently asked by polite listeners who expect him to advocate the unilateral disarmament of the United States. He replies that he is not now, and has never been, a unilateral disarmer. "Nobody would accept unilateral disarmament. Besides, there are military leaders in both countries who might take advantage. I'm in favor of a negotiated disarmament and inspection. I might be a tough bargainer myself in a negotiating session. But it's wrong to say that the Soviet Union doesn't want peace. What stands in the way isn't the Soviet Union, but the difficulty of finding a course for the world to follow that doesn't rely on war or the threat of war."

Pauling has criticized both the United States and the Soviet Union. He blames us for the economic exploitation of the underdeveloped world and the failure to permit progressive systems to operate. He once shocked a Pugwash gathering of scientists by suggesting a resolution condemning Soviet nuclear tests, "a move," a participating scientist said, "that was plainly impossible for Soviet scientists to accept. Our whole point was not to do anything that would prevent the Soviets from coming back."

To those who have suggested that Pauling is a Communist he has retaliated with libel suits, and two newspapers in recent years have presented him with substantial checks, plus retractions, for suits settled out of court. "I'm not a Marxist," Pauling said, "because I haven't studied it enough to take a position. Anyway, I would probably contend that any position blueprinted a hundred years ago isn't close enough to the modern world to be one I could accept."

None of this makes Pauling sound terribly controversial, and yet he is. More than anyone else in the peace movement, Pauling has been subjected to attacks from people in the government. Senator Joseph R. McCarthy called him a Communist (as a result, Pauling was denied a passport three times in the early 1950's), and in 1960 the U.S. Senate Internal Security Subcommittee demanded that Pauling furnish information about a petition he had circulated, signed by eleven thousand scientists on both sides of the Iron Curtain, demanding an end to nuclear tests. Pauling refused to give information on who had helped him gather names, and he made it clear that he objected to the inquiry on principle, as violating his constitutional rights and being an attempt to discredit himself and the petition.

Pauling's problems with the government, on the one hand, have been matched by his difficulties with some in the peace movement on the other. He is not, by many accounts, an easy man to work with on the endless committees which constitute peace movement policy groups. But his heinous sin, to the anti-Communist survivalists, is that he works with pro-Communist peace groups. In 1963, for instance, Pauling and Mrs. Pauling visited several countries of South America to lecture about world peace and to talk with representatives of the governments; during part of the trip they were accompanied by several members of the World Peace Council, which is described as Communist led. "My wife and I collaborate with essentially all peace groups," Pauling says, "although we do so in our own way, as individuals, because we don't want to become involved in organizational details. I think the goals of all peace groups are the same, and I feel it's illogical to say that we advocate getting along with the Soviet Union and, at the same time, be unwilling to have any contact with the Soviet peace movement." To which Robert Pickus, of Turn Toward Peace, answers, "Our problem is to open and strengthen communication with the Communist world, but there are better ways to do that than participation in their organizational and propaganda effort. We want a freely independent base from which to conduct the discussion." Pauling answers, "I think there is protest in the Soviet Union, only it works differently."

This schism in the peace movement reflects the larger stubborn division in the world at large, and, to some extent, it may undermine Pauling's argument that peace is a matter of settling the details. To Pauling, however, the test ban was the first step in an inevitable process toward the recognition that the dangers of thermonuclear war are insupportable by any doctrine.

His role, as he sees it, is that of a scientific reconciler between East and West, and, as such, he is inclined to debunk the merits of the East-West struggles. Here, Pauling feels the American anti-Communist peace people are a divisive force. He feels, too, that his persistent efforts as a conscience-at-large to the nuclear age have been successful as a first step. When Pauling got word of the Nobel Prize for Peace, his family and close friends provided three magnums of champagne and a half-dozen posters with such legends as "For Whom Nobel Tolls" and "Pauling Puts Pace in the Peace Race." "I think the peace workers have won out!" Pauling told his visitor, and literally beamed.

The far left in the peace movement is not represented by any major peace group, and individuals of this persuasion are either not peace movement members or they are sprinkled through the other groups, always in the minority. Many people in the peace movement believe that the United States aids and abets the cold war through its support of reactionary governments, and that we have failed to ally ourselves with progressive forces for change. The center group of survivalists, however, accompanies this accusation with the charge that the Soviet Union has fomented the cold war as well. For those on the left, the cold war is almost the sole responsibility of the United States. It favors disarmament as the natural part of a policy of friendliness with the Soviet Union.

Spokesmen for the far left are publications such as the *National Guardian*, a weekly newspaper with a circulation of 28,000, and the magazine *Monthly Review*. "We're an independent radical publication," the *Guardian*'s editor, James Aronson, and Russ Nixon, general manager, said. "We stand for independent political action in contrast with the Communist Party, which believes in working in the mainstream. Our origins are in the Wallace-for-President movement in 1948, but we've never been an official organ of anything. We stand for the acceptance of the existence of Socialist states. We don't make a fetish of denouncing them because they are not pure examples of Socialism, but, of course, we reserve the right to be, and have been, critical of them. We want good relations with Cuba, the Soviet Union *and* China, and we think all countries have the right to national self-determination. We're related to the class struggle, which we believe exists, and we do relate to one side, that of Socialism, in the cold war, for which we hold monopoly capitalism mainly responsible, that and Washington's desire to maintain the *status quo* in the world. We feel we are working for the best American interests in a world that is rapidly becoming more progressive than the U.S."

That the class structure is the determining factor in the foreign policies of capitalist countries is also the view stated in "The Theory of U.S. Foreign Policy" by Paul M. Sweezy and Leo Huberman in the *Monthly Review*. "Thus we see that in the case of mid-20th-century America," they say, "the thrust of domestic class interests imperatively demands the cold war and the arms race, and it becomes the primary task of foreign policy to provide the necessary justification. From this it is but a short and logical step to the policy of global anti-Communism with all that it implies." The purpose of U.S. foreign policy under "monopoly capitalism" is to provide for the maintenance of a huge military establishment, which is the only way to keep the economy going other than an expanded New Deal which is unacceptable to the ruling class.

But while it may work at home, the U.S. is losing the cold war overseas. The rational policy for the U.S. is to junk its doctrinaire anti-Communism, negotiate a settlement by recognizing Communist China, encourage Japan to become a neutralist power, disengage in Europe, permit underdeveloped countries to follow their own economic destiny (the authors suggest that "a frank recognition of the inevitability and legitimacy of revolutions aimed at social reforms" would bring moderate revolutionaries to power), and institute a strongly planned progressive economy at home. The authors do not believe that the nature of the capitalist system will permit such events to happen. Instead, they suggest, the United States will succumb to "military fascism." The authors deny that to end the cold war the United States has to change its form of government to socialism.

This essay was written in 1960, and while the sort of historical process they suggest is necessarily long-range, one would have expected to see, if the analysis were sound, more of a deterioration in the U.S. world position in the intervening years than has occurred. There is no reason to believe, as the authors suggest, that the loss of fairly substantial overseas investments will cause a collapse of the U.S. economy. The American investment loss in Cuba, for instance, was one billion dollars, or one-tenth of total Latin-American investments. Evidence is lacking that American "class" interests demand an enormous military establishment and the foreign policy to go with it. Nor do many people in the peace movement believe with the left that the Soviet Union (or China) represents the wave of the future.

The survivalists, to sum them up, believe in strong changes of one kind or another in U.S. policy, but not in its social structure.

Even the minority, left position does not say that peace requires a Marxist United States. The survivalist goal is general and complete disarmament, which it would like to get to as rapidly as possible because, if not, the peace movement sees only the end itself.

VIII

The Radicals

THE PEACE MOVEMENT RADICALS, THE FINAL CAMP IN THE WAR-peace establishment, are without doubt revolutionaries, not ones armed and ready to storm the barricades, but ones who nonetheless seek a revolution in human affairs.

As we have seen, the tendency in the war-peace establishment is toward ideological proliferation, and this is nowhere more true than among the pacifists. They would do well to issue a pacifist glossary and clear matters up once and for all. Pacifists, for instance, differ in their commitment to nonviolence, for while some are what are called "police pacifists," meaning that they tolerate the use of force and even violence by legally constituted authorities in the interests of protection and order, other pacifists abjure the use of armed force on any level. Some pacifists would take arms themselves in protection of their family and themselves; absolute pacifists would refrain from doing even this. Some pacifists, while refusing to engage in violence, may do service to a state engaged in the violence of war; others prefer to go to jail. Some pacifists are religious, some secular, and while a degree of anarchism is inherent in pacifism, some pacifists are clearly more anarchistic than others.

"Distinctions are often made, too, between the personal ethic of non-violence and its political significance," writes Mulford Q. Sibley.

Thus certain groups—like the Mennonites—think of it as a personal religious commitment and, in fact, argue that it cannot be a strategic instrument of politics. Groups of this kind passively obey the state so long as it does not require them to perform positive acts that run counter to their non-violent professions. Taxes may be paid, but there can be no active participation in office and no entering of the army—both of which are regarded as participation in violence. Non-violence of this kind is sometimes called "non-resistance"—although the terms used vary. "Resistance" is anathema, reminding one as it does of war.

Nonresistance, or passive resistance, pacifists are to be found in such groups as the Mennonites, the Church of the Brethren, Jehovah's Witnesses and the Society of Friends (Quakers). There may be a great many others scattered throughout many religious groups. A study of the Methodist Church about five years ago found 250,000 pacifists, most of whom can be assumed to be of the passive, nonresisting variety. Religious pacifists of this kind accounted for most of the six thousand C.O.s who went to jail in World War II (Jehovah's Witnesses provided, alone, two-thirds of them). It might be noted here that there could have been a great many more jail-going C.O.s had not draft boards felt that they were a stigma on the community and sought to defer them on other grounds. "Many conscientious objectors," says Lee D. Stern of the Fellowship of Reconciliation, "were deferred on mental grounds since many boards felt that the position of C.O. itself indicated some mental defect or aberration."

The textual basis for religious pacifists is found by them in the Bible, under the injunction "Thou shalt not kill" and in Christ's bidding to "turn the other cheek." This is by no means the only interpretation of these Biblical teachings. James E. Dougherty, Catholic theologian and a forward strategist, argues to quite a different point:

Generally speaking, the Church has always approached the problem of military power with circumspection. Recognizing that nowhere in the Gospel is military life censured, the Church is not at all sure that the meanings of the Scriptural passage on which the pacifists rely so heavily (e.g. "they who live by the sword shall perish by it") are incontestably conclusive. Did Christ disdain the use of force because He wished to indicate the intrinsic evil of physical power as a means to a moral end, or because of the nature of the unique spiritual task which

He had to perform? Granted that He did not wish to see His Church depend upon any kind of power except that of the spirit, is it clear that He condemned the tendency of States to rely upon the instruments of force for the maintenance of *their* security? . . . The organized political community, charged with safeguarding a human common good which has its primary meaning within the historical order, cannot seek its perfection in the same way a person can; it cannot turn the other cheek.

The pacifist answer to this tends to be mystical. The Quakers, says Howard H. Brinton in *The Peace Testimony of the Society of Friends,* "have employed arguments based on the direct insight of the soul into the nature of Truth and Goodness, an insight interpreted as a revelation through Divine Light and Life. According to this view, a certain way of life is intuitively recognized as good and with this way war is seen to be incongruous."

Most pacifists (the secular ones being in the minority) take off from a religious base, but the distinction that concerns us most here is between *nonresistance* and *nonviolent resistance.* All pacifists can be considered radical, since they urge that society divest itself of one of its chief instrumentalities, the use of force, but the nonresisters are less radical, both in technique and spirit, than the nonviolent resisters, who seek to actively influence the political process. The NVRs are in the peace movement, while the NRs often are not, and the NVRs often regard the NRs as weak and defeatist. (Gandhi, whose satyagraha, or "soul-force," was NVR, tended to be contemptuous of NR.)

The NVRs' means and ends may be the same—the achievement of nonviolence through nonviolence—but, for the most part, the modern NVRs look to broader patterns of social change. Their spirit is that of Joan Baez, a folk singer evidently in a high tax bracket, who refused to "volunteer the 60 percent of my year's income tax that goes to armaments," because, as she said to the Internal Revenue Service, "I do not believe in war. I do not believe in weapons of war." The NVRs agree with Aldous Huxley that "The best way of dealing with typhoid is not to cure it, but to prevent its breaking out. Pacifism is to war what clean water and clean milk are to typhoid; it makes the outbreak of war impossible. But though mainly preventive, pacifism is also . . . a technique of conflict—a way of fighting without the use of force."

A breed of pacifism that has managed to combine both NVR and service is that represented by the American Friends Service Committee, whose goals may be roughly stated as the establishment of nonviolent institutions but with no pre-established political base. Not all Quakers are pacifists, but the AFSC can be considered the action wing of those who are. Nonetheless, it is independent of the Society of Friends. It is one of the oldest, and certainly the richest, of all peace organizations, with a budget of some four million dollars a year. (Not all of this is spent for peace, though, for the AFSC also works in such areas as disaster relief, strike relief and integration.) The AFSC was established in 1917 for the purpose of securing legal recognition for conscientious objectors, and having secured this it has been active in peace work ever since, with goodwill missions, a peace intern program, a peace corps of its own and peace education. For its peace work, the AFSC, with the Friends Service Council of London, received the Nobel Peace Prize in 1947.

"Pacifists don't have a Pope," I was told by two smiling gentlemen, Clarence E. Pickett, secretary emeritus of the AFSC, and Stewart Meacham, head of AFSC's peace program. "For this reason we allow for a wide range of individual consciences. Some pay income tax, some don't. Some feel the state has no right to command, and following this dictate they would rather go to prison than serve the state in, say, a military noncombatant function. Others feel, 'Well, there's a war on, people are in need, and I'm willing to serve the world but not to kill.' Quakers, on the whole, do this kind of military service."

"We would certainly deny that the Bible indicates one moral law for the individual and another for the state," Meacham said. "There is a single moral law for both."

"Pacifism," Pickett said, "is a way of life that you try to apply to all areas of life. One of the troubles with trying to describe it as a doctrine is that it's really more of an achievement than a doctrine. You really don't know how good a pacifist you are until you're in a situation where you might be able to use nonviolence. And you might fail."

"Theoretically," Meacham said, "pacifism means no physical violence. We take that to include everything that rejects other people. The pacifist does not shut anybody out."

What was "bearing witness"? I asked.

"It might be a number of things, from nonpayment of taxes to not signing the loyalty oaths on passports," Pickett said. "Bearing witness includes any or all pacifist actions and means standing up for one's conscience with the purpose of influencing others to do the same."

None of this sounded very otherworldly to me, I said, and Pickett said, "Oh, dear, no. There are otherworldly pacifists for whom it is essentially a matter of obedience to God, and the question of relevance to the power struggles of our time is quite beside the point. To us, on the other hand, God and service are intertwined. One encounters God *in*, not out of, the sectarian world—in experience."

Cuba? I said, thinking of cold war experience. Pickett eyed his hands. "Most pacifists were impressed with how Kennedy's show of force stopped the Russians in their tracks. Was there any way to manage that situation otherwise? I realize we are dealing with a real problem, we pacifists. Cuba is the most difficult question the pacifist has to answer. I think I would have to say that in the short run force works. Where it fails is in the long. You see, we were encouraged by our success in Cuba to use force elsewhere, in Vietnam and Laos. The use of force in one place leads to its employment in others, and, in the end, it fails. In renouncing force we would run terrible risks, but it's the only way I see light at the end of the tunnel."

One of the sharp changes that have occurred in pacifist thought is its attempt to break with the popular image of pacifists as being weak and ineffective. The modern pacifist wants to show that he is a muscular fighter, and that his ideas are realistic. "The non-

pacifists are the visionaries; they are the 'impracticable idealists'!"
writes George A. Coe. Deterrence or "through fear" theory comes
in for considerable pacifist abuse. "The non-violent resister believes that a large part of the activities of the state are founded on
a mistake, namely, the idea that fear is the strongest and best
sanction for group action and association. He believes that fear is
divisive and therefore cannot be the foundation for permanent
unity and strength," says Richard Gregg.

He believes that in the family and in education it has now been
realized that fear is not a sound basis for action. There we find substi-
tuted the more positive and growth-stimulating forces of intellectual
curiosity, wonder, love and cooperation. The non-violent resister looks
forward to a time when a similar realization will come in regard to the
larger associations of states. He believes that non-violent resistance will
probably be an important means in reaching this realization.

The principles of non-violent resistance can be applied to diplomacy
as well as war, for the two are closely allied. Compared with war, non-
violent resistance is a safer and more effective instrument of policy.
By its use the entire military and naval expenses of all nations can be
eliminated.

What can be called the utilitarian view of pacifism is also stated
in an AFSC document called *Speak Truth to Power*, which, says
one of its authors, Robert Pickus, "parts from one stream of
pacifist thought in its recognition of the existence of evil and the
need to resist it actively. It does not see peace-making as the attempt to reconcile evil with good. It speaks directly to the problem of inevitable conflict. But it insists that the traditional power
framework within which men seek to deal with conflict is futile
and self-defeating." *Speak Truth to Power* tries to identify the real
enemy. "Man's curse lies in his worship of the work of his hands,
in his glorification of material things, in his failure to set any limit
on his material needs. This idolatry leads him to lust for power, to
disregard human personality, to ignore God, and to accept violence
or any other means of achieving his ends." The choice, the authors
say, is to continue "to deal with international problems on the old

basis of military power and attempting to deal with them on the new and revolutionary basis of non-violence."

Nonviolence leads the pacifists to one of their principal and most controversial stands: the unilateral disarmament of the United States. To W. H. Ferry, of the Center for Democratic Institutions,

> By unilateral disarmament I mean that I believe that this country should lay down its arms, scrap its warplanes, missiles, and submarines, disband its troops, and leave itself only the organization and weapons needed for local police and for normal patrols of its borders. . . . Unilateral disarmament would be a great nation's attempt to turn away from technology toward wisdom, away from armed force toward new conceptions of politics and power.

The bulk of world opinion will go immediately to the side that decides to end the thermonuclear arms race once and for all.

Another pacifist, Mulford Sibley, proposes a unilateral initiatives program similar to that of Robert Osgood, but unlike the experimentalists Sibley would move to unilateral disarmament even if no counterinitiatives forthcame. Osgood's program offers inducements to the other side in the form of mutual tension reduction, a sort of deterrence-in-reverse. Sibley puts little pressure of this kind on the opponent who knows that we will go on disarming no matter what he does. But Sibley has a deterrent of his own. For him, the entire population would be trained in nonviolence, with leaders attending a now nonviolent West Point and Annapolis:

> No one can guarantee, of course, that the existence of a population disciplined in the techniques of non-violent resistance would prevent invasion, nor can we be sure that, in a disarmed nation such as we are assuming, the "enemy" would not bomb American cities. All we are maintaining is that under conditions of unilateralism and its context, the certainty of organized non-violent resistance would do far more to "deter" invasion than threat of retaliating in kind.

Another unilateralist, Robert Pickus, couples the approach with a strong attack on the Soviet Union, which he regards as the antithesis of a nonviolent state. Pickus thinks that American disarmament, including an end to the draft, ought to be accompanied by nonviolent initiatives of the most muscular sort—mass picketing of Soviet embassies, the attempt to send in large peace teams which, if refused, would then picket the Soviet borders—to compel the Soviets to disarm. Nonviolence, for Pickus, is meant to be tension-producing, to "coerce" nations and men to abandon the rule of force.

"The pacifists," says Reinhold Niebuhr,

have a simple answer. Let us simply renounce the use of such a weapon, together with our enemies if possible, but alone if necessary. The answer assumes that it is possible to summon the human will to defy historical development with a resounding no. But where is this "human will" which could rise to such omnipotence? Unfortunately, we do not have moral access to the Russian will. . . . Could we possibly, as a nation, risk annihilation or subjugation for the sake of saying no to this new development of destruction?

For Niebuhr, men, on both sides of the Iron Curtain, are too poor, too ignorant, too selfish, either to summon this mass will or to respect those who could.

Niebuhr, in fact, has been a persistent critic of the pacifists, and he has put the same challenge to them a number of times and in a number of different ways, to reconcile the claims of love and justice. He says,

The difference between pacifism and non-pacifism is more profound than the question of the use of force or "violence." . . . The Quaker attitude toward political questions puts "power" and "love" in contradiction to each other. This contradiction leaves out the whole problem of the attainment of justice. . . . Power is not evil. It may be put in the service of good ends . . . only if one adopts the principle that it is better to suffer injustice than to resort to force can one wholly disavow the use of force . . . statesmen, responsible for the values beyond their own life, do not have this option.

To this charge of irrelevance and others like it the pacifists have responded in a number of ways. One of them is by participating in, and often forming the leadership for, survivalist peace groups that are nonpacifist and in which the pacifist, by not insisting on a platform of nonviolence, tries to work effectively within the popular consensus. One such group is Turn Toward Peace, which is an amalgamation of some seventy important labor, church and peace organizations, most of which are nonpacifist. TTP shows its pacifist bent only insofar as it supports alternatives to military policy.

Cognizant, too, of the possible irrelevance of their thought, many pacifists have engaged in intense personal searches for the truth. One such is Robert Pickus, founder of a group of peace centers in California and a founder of TTP. Pickus is a Jew, and if not precisely a religious one, at least a Jew steeped in Jewish cultural traditions. During the war, Pickus served in the OSS in Sweden, where he posed as a cultural attaché to the American Embassy. One of his jobs was to keep in touch with European political refugees. "Before that I thought perhaps that violence was not the right commitment, but I hadn't encountered pacifist thought. In Sweden, I met a whole generation of men who had been defeated from Spain on, and their failure made an enormous impact on me. They had all been willing to use violent methods, and I thought the whole failure of Europe could be summed up in the inability of violence to succeed in achieving good ends."

After the war, Pickus went to the London School of Economics on a Fulbright scholarship and then decided to take the long way home, hitchhiking across Europe. Then, in a kind of antipodal intellectual frenzy, he hitched by air to India, where he traveled the roads on foot, stayed at refugee camps and studied Gandhian philosophy. "I was still trying to find out what the good man ought to do. I learned much about human nature, its depravity and infinite capability. I saw power as the ability to cause pain, and I felt that there had come alive in the world a current that said, it needn't be this way. When I came home I joined the Friends." Pickus' idea in pacifism is to find an approach that neither kills nor submits.

There has been some attempt, too, to justify pacifism in terms of science. "The strongest ground for hope is the existence of many successful examples of both individual and group nonviolence. If it works sometimes, it should be possible to make it work more often," says Dr. Jerome Frank, a psychologist. "Man is a very modifiable creature, and his behavior depends a lot on his past training. Dr. Scott, an animal psychologist, has shown that mice can be trained to fight or not to fight. And if mice can be trained, why cannot man?" (On the other hand, why?)

Probably the most significant answer offered by pacifists to charges of irrelevance is to deny what Hans J. Morgenthau insists is a "permanent discrepancy between the assumptions of perfectionist ethics and the actual conditions of human action." That is, if pacifism is "the way," and yet it seems irrelevant in the world, then pacifism must create the conditions for its own relevancy. For this reason, modern pacifism is out for social action.

"The peace movement," A. J. Muste has said, "is in a period of transition, a period of groping for a valid analysis of the conditions under which we live. This is true for all sections of the movement, East, West or essentially unaligned."

Almost everyone in the peace movement believes that something is wrong with it, or its analyses. The world is perhaps not better as a result of deterrence, but neither is it appreciably worse, and all those dire predictions that used to emerge from peace movement Cassandras—that American policies were made to order for Communist expansion because deterrence doesn't work, that the U.S. would succumb to a military dictatorship, that American principles have been undermined and our morality debased—do not appear to have come true in any very visible sense. Many of the peace movement militants are now in civil rights, as if to prove that either the need or the results are greater there.

"I do not know of a single organization devoted to peace or related concerns . . . that has a sense of moving ahead on a clearly defined program," Muste says. To Paul Goodman, "The peace movement is at present astoundingly negative: 'strike for peace' means merely 'refuse the Cold War.' The most popular slogan is Ban the Bomb, and there is a rising realization that Peace Must Come from the People. But the idea of positively waging peace—in acts of community-forming, new culture, political reconstruction, economic reconversion—seems not yet to take hold of popular fancy."

The answer many peace people have come up with is that the peace movement must be concerned not just with protesting war but with making peace, and to do so requires both a program and a vision of the end toward which it strives. Those pacifists most concerned with the long range are "radical pacifists" (though, as we have seen, all peace movement pacifists, if not all pacifists, are essentially radical).

A handful of organizations house the radical pacifists: the Fellowship of Reconciliation, organized in 1915, whose thirteen thousand members, among them several thousand clergymen, are required to sign a pledge that they will neither take part in war nor sanction military preparations; the Committee for Non-Violent Action, formed by FOR, WRL and AFSC as an action arm (the AFSC, though it is more concerned with service and peace education, has figured considerably in nonviolent action); the War Resisters League, with 6,000 members, which is the secular branch of FOR. In practice, it is virtually impossible to separate these three programs. And other groups can be mentioned, too—the Catholic Workers, for instance, an indefatigable group of Catholic-Socialist pacifists who carry out nonviolent action, although their primary purpose is to help the poor on New York's Bowery.

For these peace people, survivalists like SANE, as Nathan Glazer puts it, are "too sober, too much concerned with political realities, too responsible, too accepting of the world as it is and of things as they are." "We began as a protest against war, but we find the roots of it in every aspect of the social struggle," says FOR's executive secretary, Alfred Hassler. "We feel that we are doing a more basic job than the survivalists are." Indeed, the tactics used by radical pacifists to win support for their ideas, or at least make the public aware of them, differ markedly from those of the survivalists. The advertisement of the radical pacifist is himself.

He offers himself in a number of ways: picketing, walks (Quebec-Washington-Guantánamo, for example), vigils and fasts (such as the one that lasted for a year and a half at the biological warfare center at Fort Detrick, Maryland), sit-downs (as at missile-launching sites), trespassing at military installations, civil defense disobedience, submarine boarding and so on. It's not as though he hopes to change laws or even convert many people. But he does wish to bear witness against a contemporary evil and, by what has been called "moral jujitsu," to set an example for others to follow later on. The first "freedom ride" to the South, for instance, was the Journey of Reconciliation, sponsored by the FOR, in 1947, and it was almost fifteen years before freedom-riding began in earnest.

One of the men who went on that ride—serving twenty-two days on a chain gang as a result, and whose articles about the ordeal were responsible for changes in the North Carolina penal laws—is a tall, keen-eyed Negro wearing a bushel basket of gray hair who has been called the "Socrates of the civil rights movement." His name is Bayard Rustin. He is former executive secretary of the War Resisters League, from which he is on a protracted leave of absence, a member of the governing council of the International Confederation for Disarmament and Peace (formed in 1963 in opposition to the World Peace Council) and an organizer of marches—on Washington, in 1963, for civil rights; the first Aldermaston March in England, 1955, for peace; the San Francisco-to-Moscow peace walk; and many others. Rustin is a Quake (as peace people call the Quakers). As a sort of free-lance civil rights leader, Rustin has no organizational base, and his support, less than $100 a week, comes from Quaker donations. "I have refused affiliation with any rights group," Rustin says, "so as to be of service to all of them."

Peace and civil rights leaders like Rustin have more training in both the theoretical and practical sides of their profession than many people appear to suspect. Rustin had a brilliant record at American universities. For over a year, he studied Gandhian nonviolence in India, and he understands the tactical side of Gandhi in a way that more academic students do not. (Rustin pointed out to me that everything Gandhi did had a purpose. If he was a vegetarian, it was because beef was short in India; if he practiced celibacy, which Gandhi did in a rather unusual fashion, sharing his mat with young girls but refusing to touch them, that, too, had a function, emphasizing the need in India for birth control.)

Rustin's own voyage of discovery took him first to the Young Communist League because, he says, it stood for both peace and

civil rights, but its support of the "people's war"—World War II—
and its demand that civil rights agitation stop until after the war's
end, in the interests of national unity, were against Rustin's principles. He quit and joined FOR, where he became field and later
race relations secretary and he was also the first field secretary of
the Congress for Racial Equality (CORE). During the war, Rustin
spent two years in the federal penitentiary at Lewisburg, Pennsylvania, as a conscientious objector.

When Rustin looks at peace, he sees not only nonviolence but
race relations and "cybernetics," and he, like Pauling, is part of a
group that plans to fight for "the triple revolution." "I take the
view," he says, "that these problems are tied up with the nature of
our institutions, and to get at them requires a vigorous attack on the
contradictions of our society.

"I'm prepared to lie down in front of a truck to get work for
Negroes but also for white people to get work because if there isn't
work for one there is not work for the other. This is tied to peace
because the billions spent on defense ought to be spent on a war on
poverty—not President Johnson's watered-down war on poverty, but
billions. But those jobs won't be created unless automation is tackled
as well. I am a unilateral disarmer, but in stages—not disarmament a week from next Thursday, because the public isn't pacifist
and wouldn't have it. I don't have a blueprint.

"To get anywhere we shall need a revolution in the attitudes of
men. People will have to have a willingness to expand the public
sector of the economy, to have a planned society. The sort of
planning I have in mind is democratic planning in which people
themselves have a say. I'm for the people owning the means of
production, but not in a dogmatic sense, that is, where capitalism
does not harm people I would leave it." Rustin went on to mention
an old peacenik dream: a new political party fused from labor,
civil rights and peace.

I asked Rustin who his main intellectual influences had been,
and he answered, without hesitation, "Gandhi, and A. J. Muste."

"For many thousands of Americans (including myself)," Paul
Goodman has written, "and especially for many of the best of the

young, A. J. Muste is an authentic Great Man, not a stage hero nor an image of public relations. We in America are very much lacking admirable fathers at present—I cannot think of a single person in high public office whom many intelligent persons regard with deep respect—but A. J. is always regarded with respect."

Abraham Johannes Muste is eighty years old. He is an ordained minister of the Presbyterian Church, but he was a Congregationalist minister as well, until he had to resign as a clergyman because of his pacifism in World War I. He helped form the American Civil Liberties Union, and he was active in the American labor movement, administrating a labor college and assisting those on picket lines. For a brief period he turned his back on pacifism and became a Trotskyite, but then it was religion and pacifism again. He introduced Gandhian nonviolent resistance to the civil rights people; Martin Luther King, for instance, first heard of nonviolence from A. J. Muste. He has washed and trained a whole generation of radical leaders. Reinhold Niebuhr, his alter ego in religious philosophy, thinks he is a soft utopian, as opposed to the hard utopianism of the Communists. Niebuhr calls him a "perfect innocent." Muste thinks he is a Gandhian, but Paul Goodman calls him a "populist." Nat Hentoff, who wrote his biography, calls him "a peace agitator." Many people feel he should be awarded the Nobel Prize for Peace.

There is no reason to suppose that A. J. Muste is a saint. True, he has a saint's contempt for money and material objects of any kind. Deep in his seventies he was to be found, tight-lipped, climbing over the fence at a Nebraska missile base. A. J. is against war and weapons of war, and he was trying to stop the world from killing itself. Two Air Force policemen were waiting to arrest him. The Air Force policemen were enforcing the law. The Air Force policemen probably believed the missiles stood between themselves and war. Just as fervently, Muste thought not. This does not make him saintly; it is merely his side of the case.

Besides, he does not look like a saint. His nose is too long and his mouth too wide. Mostly, he is not emotional—no ringing phrases, exhortations or incantations for peace. Only once in a while does he sound like a preacher, as he did in Nebraska that day. "The great stretch of land which is being used for military purposes at Mead belongs, in the last analysis, to God, as does the entire earth. . . . It was given to [man] for the production of food and clothing and shelter and that he might enjoy its beauty. . . . This is a desecration of God's own gift to mankind which must not be permitted to happen again."

Like many other people in and out of the peace movement, Muste believes that the war of 1914 amounted to a "fall of man."

Technology and economic organization were making the abolition of poverty a realizable and fairly near goal. Man's knowledge of himself and of his history on earth had likewise developed to a point where men were able, certainly in a considerable degree, to shape their future. There were social elements, such as the modern working class and intellectuals whose immediate needs tied them to a movement with revolutionary aims and possibilities. There was a long, deeply ingrained prophetic tradition. There was a belief that men could decisively influence their destinies and there was hope in contrast to the present day apathy and feeling that all problems are so complicated that they have to be left to the "authorities" and the "establishments" to decide. Western men had not experienced the orgies of hate and slaughter which marked subsequent decades.

It might be observed that a similar argument on artistic development is offered by Jacques Barzun, who feels that the new art movement, centering around cubism, was destroyed by World War I.

Muste has written many words about the "war system," the uses and abuses of nonviolence, the need for the peace movement to stop being "good-natured, easygoing optimists," that the world must give up war ("What," he asks many times, "are any of us waiting for?"), but, as I read him, Muste's essential appeal is to hope. The peace movement, and the country, ought to recapture the ideological Eden of pre-1914, to feel that the problems *can* be solved. It is for this reason that, while tempering himself with pessimism, he consistently says that those impossibilities of the radical dream are not impossibilities at all.

Old tactician that he is, Muste has some very clear ideas about
the cadres of young people developed by the radicals for submarine boarding and civil rights. "You can go on for years with
peace education," he says, "but at the moment of decision you find
that nothing has happened. Your support melts away. We seek
to develop a core of people who make a fundamental commitment,
people who have made the break and are capable of fully challenging the existing setup."

"How many are there in this radical core?" I said.

"Perhaps ten thousand who meet all the specifications, who
would stick it out under any conditions."

"And what is the goal?"

"I can only speak for myself," Muste said, lighting a cigarette.
"I haven't really got a blueprint, though I think in terms of de-
centralization of authority and power. I'm a socialist of sorts, and
I do believe that planning in a technological situation is necessary.
I'm not really an anarchist either, though I've a strong libertarian
bent. I'm out of the prophetic tradition rather than the Marxist-
collectivist tradition. The difference between me, say, and Strausz-
Hupé is that between those who say you must operate within the
existing situation and those who feel, looking ahead, that you must
operate outside of it. I would say I am more interested in the means,
too, than Strausz-Hupé is. Somewhere in here comes my answer
to Niebuhr. You start out by saying that as a Christian theologian
you must reject the Bomb but under certain circumstances it might
be justifiable, and you end up by justifying the weapons, even
though you say the moral situation is impossible. What we say is
that this is a compromise, a rejection of morality, a destruction of
the social standard. We start from that point.

"Of course, I recognize that this is a hard choice. Getting rid of
nuclear weapons means new standards in power relationships between nations—deep psychological and moral change. I think it
means rather important changes for the U.S. We will have to find
a new style of life, one that doesn't rely on power. The period of
worry would be that of the transition, but I would rely on non-
violent defense. There is always the possibility that we would be

defeated, of course, but nations have been defeated and recovered before. I feel this whole argument about states that are that hostile to us is abstract. But at the same time it's true that we would no longer be the world's leading power. Neither would the Soviet Union. We ought to accept that the big superpower idea is dead. We must recognize that our day of domination is over."

But since, as Muste says, the peace movement missed its chance in 1914, there was no reason to be certain it would not miss its chances again and again. Muste, I thought, must have been sustained over these years by an enormous faith, and I asked him how he accounted for it, and he quoted to me a line from Albert Camus, " 'But I have always held that, if he who bases his hopes on human nature is a fool, he who gives up in the face of circumstances is a coward.' " Muste paused reflectively. "My own mainspring, when you get right down to it, is my religious faith. I don't believe in God as someone who will do the job for you but rather in God as a moral compulsion. In the end you are confronted with yourself, obeying the command which is the only one ultimately demanded of you: to be yourself."

For Muste, the goal is a classless, warless world, and if he had no blueprint as to what it might be like, I suspected that he at least had a picture of it, and I asked him what it was. He mentioned a book called *News from Nowhere,* which, I happened to know, is a romantic utopia written by the English poet and guild socialist William Morris, in 1891. Morris' idea was to combat what he called the "cockney dream" of the American utopian, Edward Bellamy, who called for, in *Looking Backward,* an industrial army. Morris envisioned an Epoch of Rest, and presented a world of craftsmen who live simple, joyous lives with almost complete sexual freedom. There are no working classes whatever, Parliament has been turned into a dunghouse, education is progressive, and there are no police since there is no crime, except for an occasional *crime passionel,* for which there is no punishment beyond a mild, temporary ostracism, since the murderer's remorse is punishment enough.

I mention this only to point out that the radical pacifists are inspired by more than a vision of ending war, that they dream dreams of a larger end. This is what Muste means when he says, "If war were really to be abolished, its abolition would entail very radical changes in the economic structure, the relations between nations, the standards of values, the types of human beings in . . . all nations. For those who want such changes, the war issue is the handle, therefore, to achieve them, rather than the radical economic revolt being the way to abolish war. But, equally, unless people are concerned with such profound problems as these, they are not really working for peace."

Utopia has always had the attribute of offering goals, and often it has foreseen social change long before society at large. It has, also, always had some marked deficiencies. One of these is that it has failed to solve the problem of leadership, that is, who would lead a utopian society and how he would be prevented from exercising dictatorial power. The radical pacifists have arrived at a new answer to this question, in the shape of nonviolent resistance. They also tend to want to solve the difficulty by doing away with the institutions of power altogether. "Put your finger on a pacifist," Bayard Rustin says, "and you put your finger on some degree of anarchism."

"Anarchists," says Lawrence Scott, director of the Peace Action Center in Washington,

while few in number, have had a disproportionate influence on the peace movement: much religious pacifism has no realistic political content and has only peripherally attempted to deal with the problem of power in this world; pacifist youth, who are rightly in revolt against the kind of society which has got mankind into this mess, readily tend to accept anarchist analysis and solutions, and many pacifists who are not anarchists accept in practice that position because of opposition to the use of police force, the force of courts, and jail and prison restraint.

Scott argues that pacifists themselves could not even ensure law and order in American cities. The only solution for the world, he says, is the power of the world community under law and government.

Anarchism in the peace movement is not officially represented by any major peace organization, perhaps the only avowedly pacifist-anarchist group having been that called World Wide General Strike for Peace, which has carried out several demonstrations. Perhaps the nearest thing to an anarchist in the peace movement is the writer Paul Goodman, on whom I made my last call in the war-peace establishment.

Goodman has written such books as *Drawing the Line, Growing Up Absurd, Communitas* (in collaboration with his brother Percival), and *Utopian Essays and Practical Proposals.* During a World Wide General Strike for Peace, Goodman, having to picket somewhere, picketed his publisher, Bennett Cerf of Random House, who sent out a cup of coffee. (In my opinion, Random House had gotten back at Goodman with their advertising slogan, "Goodman matters," with its hint of "Surprise! Goodman matters!" raising doubts.) Goodman, says George Steiner, "is trying to restore to a society gone violent or indifferent (and the violence is bred of the uncaring) a sense of live, exploring debate. Between the closing walls of technological determinism and political cliché, he is trying to hack out elbow room for the imagination."

In Goodman, the ideas of the radical peace movement reach a kind of a logical climax. Society is an organism, not unlike a human organism, and what happens, say, in Vietnam shows up as social behavior on city streets: "It takes a lot of bad education, a venal economy, and a really insane foreign policy to achieve that hoodlum strut, that junky slouch, that hipster cool, that college attitude." But foreign policy itself is determined entirely by the domestic: "Throughout the world, it is bad domestic politics that create the deadly international politics." The power urge—Goodman refers to the "mesmerism of abstract power"—upon which much of deterrence analysis rests is an illusion and not a natural function of man.

This solidifying of national sovereign bellicosity is at present all the more irrational, and of course all the more necessary if the sovereigns are to maintain themselves, since the cultural, technological, economic and communications relations of the world are now overwhelmingly supra-national. . . . The only possible pacifist conclusion from these facts is the anarchist one, to get rid of the sovereignties and to diminish, among people, the motivations of power and grandiosity. . . . My own bias is to decentralize and localize wherever it is feasible, because this makes for alternatives and more vivid and intimate life. And it is safer.

Goodman wrote these words in the pages of *Liberation,* whose editorial board includes A. J. Muste and Bayard Rustin. Yet while Rustin believes in over-all planning and accepts centralization, and Muste will take some centralization despite his interest in guilds, Goodman goes almost all the way to a rejection of the State itself. His position was characterized by Arthur Schlesinger, Jr., as that of the "utopian left," who said that one difference between the utopians and the practicalists such as himself is that the practicalists were willing to work from the inside and accept its limitations. Apart from civil rights, Schlesinger said, the contribution of the utopian left was practically nil, and he quoted Goodman on his own program: "an occasional fist fight, a better orgasm, friendly games, a job of useful work, initiating enterprises, deciding real issues in manageable meetings, and being moved by things that are beautiful, curious, or wonderful."

I took up some of these issues with Goodman himself, finding him to be a dark-haired man in his early fifties, with a gentle, slightly puzzled expression, seemingly unperturbed by his baby who crawled on the floor. Goodman's New York West Side apartment was anything but opulent. I surveyed the surroundings for a moment and wondered out loud how Goodman was doing these days, now that he mattered.

"My income's jumped a good deal these last five years," Goodman said. "You know, I get five hundred dollars a lecture, which is ridiculous. No lecture is worth that much. It's really cold war money because the value of everything's inflated. I got along for years on practically nothing, and I guess I got used to it because I find my standard of living hasn't changed. What do you do with twenty thousand a year? I really didn't mind being poor because I never got down to the level of drudgery. Poverty is an advantage so long as it doesn't mean a loss of integrity, but it would be spiteful to tell that to the rich."

There was something so unprofligate about that statement that it almost sounded conservative, I said, and Goodman answered, "Why, yes! I'm an intensely conservative person, didn't you know? My only objection to self-styled conservatives like Goldwater is that they are not conservative enough. I go back to neolithic man. Red cheeks, sunshine. I guess cars are okay so long as they don't get in the way of kids. No anarchist is ever a radical. Radicals always have blueprints. I'm decidedly for piecemeal solutions. Goldwater and I are against the same things—only he's not for what I'm for. He's for private power, and I'm against both private power and public power."

But utopians *are* blueprinters by definition, I said. Goodman replied, "I call myself a millennialist. Millennialists agree that paradise *is* lost. No sense crying about that, baby. Millennialists go for more short-range, practical solutions. People think they're *impractical* only because deep down they make sense and so people feel threatened. Really impractical ideas, on the other hand, don't bother people at all."

One of Goodman's millennialist ideas is peace. I wondered how he felt about the Soviet Union. "The Communist position is a power position. I see no difference between Communist nations and other nations with respect to the organization of the good society. What we have today is two mad groups in cages, threatening each other with the Bomb. It's a situation of saturation parity —or parody. But who wants to live in a madhouse? If the power structure of the world is insane, then one must deal with it by psychiatric means, like deterrence.

"But I refuse to accept that people are mad. What we've done, because of our fixation on power, is to allow such a vital thing as war to get abstracted, to have removed it from what should be our total concern with animal feelings, community arrangements and so forth. The Russians aren't the menace; the power structure is. You might even say that our acquiescence to abstract power is a sign of our own frustrations, sexual and otherwise. Our whole notion of self-conquest, of keeping things under control, of will power, is obsessional. It's the same on the national level."

But what did he want to *do?* I said.

"I'm not a unilateralist," Goodman said, "any more than I'm against violence. The reason I'm a pacifist is that I'm against doom. There won't be permanent peace until we get rid of the power structures; therefore you can't solve the problem of war in terms of nation-states. You can't trust them. Unilateral disarmament is a contradiction of principles because the power structure is the price of nation-states. For this reason I'm suspicious of world government, though I might settle for it. But the real solution is to get rid of national boundaries."

"How do we do this?"

"You tell me. I'm inept when it comes to putting proposals into effect. I think of a movement of the American people, but I'm not a leader, and there's no reason I have to be. It's a kind of avoidance to demand that people explain exactly how they propose to accomplish something that is right and just. That's *your* duty. But I am sure that we will never arrive at peace in anything less than the complex way I've suggested. Gimmicks won't work. We've had war for eight thousand years, and it's persistently gotten worse.

"And what is peace? It's important here that you try to understand me. The great values of life are unutterable. You don't have a definition of them. The purpose of social institutions is to make life tolerable, not to make it *happy.* So peace, in this sense, is a negative term, a tolerable term. I'm after something else, a kind of happy society in which there *is* conflict, only not of the organized kind, in which people live organic lives in organic communities, in which we have life's grand quality, adventure."

I said good-bye to Paul Goodman and the thinkers of the war-peace establishment. On the way out, I suddenly remembered that, a hundred or so conversations ago, Dr. Robert Strausz-Hupé, the forward strategist, had said that he and Paul Goodman shared the same vision of the end, an anarchic society organized into small, happy, peaceful communities. And so, oddly enough, the argument has come the full circle, the classic circle of political science.

But how was that possible? Clearly, the two could not really agree on anything that had to do with present policy—the forward strategists advocating carrying the cold war to the enemy, Goodman finding in the cold war the antithesis of everything he believed. Instead of a circle, I decided, the figure that might represent the thinking of the war-peace establishment could be described as a horseshoe, or, even better, a coil. And the judgments that continually separate people in their appraisals of present and future center on the questions of power, probability and time.

PART FOUR

The Search Ends

IX

The Arguments Appraised

FOR THE PEOPLE OF THE UNITED STATES THE TWENTY YEARS SINCE
World War II have been years of international crisis virtually unin-
terrupted. Many of us (the author included) have never lived out
from under the shadow of nuclear war, and in this period we have
all come to know the Bomb in our bones. Despite protestations of
peace emanating from leaders the world over, no one can say we
are markedly nearer disarmament than we were a decade or two
ago. What, if anything, shall we do?

The choices are not simple, and they are even less so when one
has finally come to understand the arguments. When we speak of
war and peace, the avoidance of one and the achievement of the
other, we are dealing with a complicated set of appraisals about the
world, our adversaries and ourselves, and all philosophy bears on
our decisions. Everybody says he wants peace and hates war, and
the differences on this question cannot be accounted for by easy
assertions that this position is bellicose or that simple-minded.

As evidence of the complexities of the war-peace debate, I offer
the following chart—itself tentative and oversimplified—on how the
dominant groups in the U.S. separate in their appraisals of the
three central issues of power, probability and time.

One sympathizes with the lady who announced at a peace meeting, "I'm tired of all these arguments about peace. Let's throw
them into a computer and get the answer." Unfortunately we are
left with the difficult task of sifting out answers for ourselves. The
choices are partly imposed on us by others, but it is also ours to

	POWER	PROBABILITIES	TIME
Deterrers	Power urge inevitable in states and people. Expresses itself as military power. Military power must be deterred by counterpower. Fear controls power. Nations operate in terms of self-interest as defined by power. They cannot take the "long view," or be "reasoned with" except in these terms. Hostility is a normal part of the international order. War arises out of clashes of self-interest. It can't be abolished, therefore must be deterred.	Thermonuclear war: moderate so long as we deter. Aggression by Communist or other states without nuclear deterrence: high. Sweeping changes in state system, states or people: generally, low. Serious disarmament: very low, in foreseeable future.	Enough, under present policies, to find alternatives to thermonuclear war. Buy more through deterrence. Hope for, in the long run, changes in the Communist world. Work, generally, for short-run stability.
Experimentalists	States can be made to see that their self-interest lies in the absence of military power. Thermonuclear weapons are responsible for this. Power urge not inevitable. People and states are modifiable. War arises out of misunderstanding and habitual reliance on military systems. Fear increases tension. Try generosity instead. Nonetheless, habits are deeply ingrained so move with deliberate speed. Can war be abolished? Cautiously, yes.	Thermonuclear war under present policies: high. Aggression by Communists: low, but hedge with minimum deterrence. Sweeping changes in state system: good. Serious disarmament: good.	Not enough under present policies. Buy more through change. Work for drastic change in war system now.
Peace Movement	Return to humanistic values of man. Concept of "natural" power urge is false. Military power not symptom of hostility but cause of it. Do away with military power. War is a habit. Either centralize existing military power in international institution or disperse. War can be abolished.	Thermonuclear war: very high as long as weapons are in national hands. Aggression by Communists: low, but be prepared to deal with through nonviolent means. Sweeping changes in states and people: good.	Very little. Nuclear disarmament the only hope. But in long run go beyond disarmament to the real problem of war, which lies in social organization and/or people.

choose, even if it is the assent indicated by our silence. That choice is particularly significant today, because the world appears to have reached a kind of historical plateau from which the path may be up or down. Should we further arm, in the name of peace? Should we be content, even gratified, with a nuclear standoff, under the name of stabilized deterrence? Or should we seek disarmament, either gradual or precipitate? Which?

What follows is the writer's own attempt to answer these questions.

It must be said at the outset that the arguments of the American theoreticians on war and peace have been made to seem more isolated and abstract than they are in the real world. "Certainly," as Robert Levine says, "the values and analyses on which real policy is dependent can never be sorted out completely neatly or satisfactorily." There is no reason why one cannot be unneatly eclectic in one's approach, as are many of the war-peace intellectuals themselves. It may even be possible, by borrowing from various positions, to reach a satisfactory synthesis.

I, for one, will have to put the forward strategy behind me. Its reliance on force or the threat of force appears excessive—its "model" awards too high a role to the power of unfriendly persuasion. The forward strategist position seems to be based on the superiority of Western values, leading to a parochial self-righteousness that puts those very values in doubt. It appears to me that the forward strategists have exaggerated the malignity of the Communist world and underestimated the probability of nuclear war if the arms race should continue, as they insist it must. I *am* attracted by the forward strategist notion of a stronger tie between the U.S. and Europe, even if it means forgoing elements of national sovereignty, but I am dismayed that so transcendentally important an event should be seen by the forward strategists in military, anti-Communist terms. This view accepts as semipermanent the division of the world into two or more armed camps.

Of course, there is the logical possibility that the forward strategists are right in this and still another idea—that modern technology, at least in the confines of the present international situation, is more or less uncontrollable. But rather than accepting this as given, I would bend every effort to find out if the opposite might not be correct. If we are to be manipulated by a weapons science in a world of implacable hostility, then I would be strongly tempted to vote for the unilateral disarmament of the United States as the slim but sole hope of avoiding catastrophe. But I do not accept the forward strategist evaluation of the world.

Therefore I am compelled to part company with the radicals of the peace movement who advocate unilateral American disarmament. In seeking a correlation between personal and national pacifism, the radicals are guilty of too much consistency. There is nothing to suggest that any nation is going to disarm unilaterally, unless so compelled, and the radicals demand too much of the mass of wills known as a nation. The blunt morality of the radicals leads them to overlook some of the important intangibles as well. What would happen to the self-confidence, and with it the economy, of a unilaterally disarmed United States? Nor is it certain that nonviolence is always an effective way of defending oneself or asserting those interests one holds to be vital. And so I am forced to strike unilateral disarmament from my platform, and I think the radicals would be wise to do the same.

This being said, I would not want to overlook what the radicals have to offer. Because I conclude, painfully, that force is a necessary feature of justice does not mean that nonviolence must be rejected, and I would be pleased if my country resorted to armed violence only when it could bear the strain and risk no longer. It seems to me that the radicals are right in saying that the answer to war, in the long run, can come only in deep changes in our style of governing, even in ourselves, and to me the utopian vision, what Martin Buber calls the "wish picture," is a real power in human affairs, giving us energy and pointing out the goals. I share the radical hope that someday a new world will come to pass.

To turn to my synthesis proper, I begin with the analysts. The peace movement is seriously misguided in talking about the analysts, with their strategies and game theories, as though they favored, or even caused, wars. On the contrary, the analysts deserve high marks for years of careful study and planning. On the whole, they have tried to deal with the facts of the matter and tried not to indulge in long-range speculations or moralistic cries. They raise a difficult question. Suppose, they say, the cause of the present crisis *is* "politics" or "misunderstanding"; the weapons still exist and are not likely to be gotten rid of soon. That being the case, the analysts insist on a careful management of force. Even in deterrence, the analysts declare, nations can cooperate to avoid war.

Where I am forced to doubt analytic thinking is over the question of strategic deterrence itself. As worked out with statistical precision, nuclear deterrence tends to assume that military strategy is itself fearful enough to dominate the logic of the other side. This in turn assumes that fear will keep both sides at nuclear peace at least. There is no doubt that we want to be logical and rational in this situation, but there is a great deal of doubt as to whether we can depend on the mathematics of destruction to keep the peace. Too much of our experience points to illogic and self-destructiveness. The analytic "model" has led it to acquiesce to high levels of nuclear arms as a method of controlling the opponent and managing war. I think these ideas are too narrow, and I wonder if the analysts have fought hard enough for change away from the use of military threats.

When we reach the realists, we are deep in the speculations of philosophy, and here, truly, it is one person's logic against that of another. But one piece of realist thought I must add to my synthesis—that the collective will, though stemming from the sum of individual wills, may have characteristics quite different from those of individual wills. To me, the realists are right in saying that nations cannot help acting in terms of power and self-interest. It follows that nations must seek to protect themselves, that they will change only slowly, and that they will disarm only when they feel utterly safe. One must not expect too much from them. My reservation about realism is one of degree—I think realism is too pessi-

mistic about the possibilities of change. And I'm afraid that the
realist view of man, as afflicted by original sin, the power-urge, and
ignorance, leads too easily to the conclusion that man must be deterred against himself. Before long, realism hardens into the view
that man is controlled only by the fear of force.

Government idealism, as we have identified it, may be described
as the realism of a nation-state overlaid with the country's ideological aspirations. (This observer thought it rather a tribute to the
ability of our public officials that they are able to function, and
apparently effectively, amid the rush and harassment of modern
Washington.) I am suspicious of the present practice of justifying
our international commitments in terms of safeguarding freedom
and democracy around the world, and uncertain as to the necessity
or wisdom of trying to secure a democratic world environment. I,
for one, would remove the ideological labels from our policies, on
the grounds that liberty, democracy, free enterprise, and so on,
have specialized meanings in the U.S. not necessarily applicable
or even helpful elsewhere. To be sure, I am concerned, and I hope
the country is, with the welfare of the peoples of the world, but
rather than justifying our actions with ideology I would have us
try to meet human needs as such, whatever they are.

And I think the peaceful aspirations of our country would be
more convincing were its disarmament objectives better codified.
Crucial to my synthesis is a change away from high-level deterrence, and here I am buttressed by the minimum deterrers' declaration that national security would not be jeopardized, and world
security increased, by reducing the nation's nuclear armory. It is
not that I believe the U.S. will start a nuclear war, or that counterforce strategy is wicked; it's just that I see no long-term stability in
large numbers of these devices, and I believe the U.S. must abandon its notion of nuclear superiority if it is to get arms agreements.
Finally, I am in essential agreement with those we have called experimentalists that in the long stretch deterrence through fear is
no very adequate way of dealing with an opponent.

Some experimentalists believe that international conflict is rooted in misunderstandings and that only strong unilateral initiatives will clear them away. I approach this point of view with caution. For one thing, it may be that instead of misunderstanding each other in this world we understand each other only too well. For another, I sympathize in my imagination with a President who had to explain to the American right wing why a bold and generous series of unilateral initiatives failed. Nonetheless, though I wouldn't put all my faith or face in them, I would support unilateral American initiatives for peace, and to my synthesis I will add the experimentalists' conviction that imagination, along with a spirit of trial and error, is needed. I would have the United States (and the Communist nations, too) be more boldly experimental in searching for peace.

Embedded in war-peace theory in the nuclear age are two questions of enormous difficulty and import, and if one is to take a position at all (as opposed merely to resting one's case on hope or despair), one must try to confront them in full self-honesty. The first, simply stated, is whether one is prepared to employ nuclear weapons even in self-defense. As we have seen, a deterrent doesn't qualify as such if we are not prepared to authorize its actual use. The other is whether, to achieve peace, we must demand the abolition of war. Let us see what answers to these questions are offered by the survivalists of the peace movement.

I must begin my characterization of the peace movement by admitting to a certain bewilderment. Though the survivalists want to be practical, their policies often sound like wish-fulfillment. I am depressed by the peace movement's over-use of fear in some of its propaganda, and its way of considering people who don't agree with it as warmongers. (On the other hand, the peace movement has been quick sometimes to press into service certain arguments of people it might not otherwise accept—its habit, for instance, of quoting President Eisenhower on the dangers of the "military-industrial complex.") Those who struggle for peace in the name of humanism do not always seem to understand the problems imposed by modern science, technology and military strategy. And I find myself unimpressed with moral cries, ethical fulminations, neat nostrums, and so on, against "war" and for "peace"—we've had all this before without a visible shift away from the "war system."

Having entered these caveats, I cannot turn my sympathies away from the peace movement altogether. I find myself agreeing with its argument that the United States, since World War II (perhaps in the course of overcoming its isolationism), has relied too heavily on the seemingly simple and expeditious instrument of military force to solve its international problems. And I am grateful to the peace movement for what I believe to be its fundamental stand, on values, on generosity, charity, purity of purpose. I am thankful that it has raised, again and again, the question of the whole future of the human race. I am glad it has been willing to act.

The peace movement has been no more successful than any other group in solving what I take to be the essential contradiction of the nuclear age—our agreement to hold on to these weapons and what I assume is a near-universal rejection of their use. But its philosophers have at least made the contradiction clear, and helped us to understand that we are balanced uneasily between today and tomorrow, between reality and hope. Our situation contains much of the absurd, and only as we begin to recognize the full measure of the contradiction, as we come to grips with the nuclear absurdity, will we begin to find that many things are possible which seem impossible now.

So I return to the question with which I began my search for peace—what should my banner say? I know now that its legend will offer nothing simple or final, nothing pleasant or easy. It will eschew slogans like "Abolish war" because of my apprehensions about the likelihood of armed conflict, the constant clash of interests between men and nations, the necessity to use force at times, indeed, the immaturity of the human race; it will reject "peace through military strength" for exactly the same reasons. In composing it, I will bear in mind both the deterrers' desire for the management of force and the peace movement's call for morality.

But my banner will say experimentalism. It will accept, for a time at least, the contradictions of the nuclear age as being insoluble. As a first step, it will ask for a minimum deterrent leading from there by stages to genuine universal nuclear disarmament. It will insist that the United States has not been aggressive enough in searching for peace. It will have us conduct that search in a manner both open and optimistic, with strong imagination and bold inquiry, in a spirit of humility about the rightness of our own positions, and it will have us understand more clearly that others, as well as ourselves, suffer from nucleomitophobia, the fear of atomic attack.

Index

Format by Katharine Sitterly
Set in Linotype Fairfield
Composed, printed and bound by American Book–Stratford Press
HARPER & ROW, PUBLISHERS, INCORPORATED

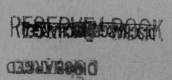